## What Others

Over the years I have watched the growth of Joe Jackson's ministry. The many times he has preached and shared in song have truly inspired thousands. We were blessed that he served as church evangelist at Phoenix First Assembly of God for almost thirty years. I'm excited about *Championship Sunday*. For the believer, there is never an off-season or bye week. I'm so proud of you, Joe, and love you dearly. You are a champion in and out of season!

— **Pastor Tommy Barnett**
Global Pastor of Dream City Church in Phoenix, Arizona, Founder of the LA Dream Center, Chancellor of Southeastern University in Lakeland, Florida

My old friend, Joe Jackson. Glad to hear about *Championship Sunday*. I'm looking forward to reading my autographed copy. I will never forget when we ministered together in Minnesota back in the '80s, then reconnecting in the '90s. I was at a crossroads looking for direction, and your words were confirmation that my boxing career was not over. Thanks, Big Joe, for your encouragement.

— **George Foreman**
Olympic Gold Medalist and two-time Heavyweight Boxing Champion of the World

Championship Sunday takes you on a journey. From a boy born and raised in urban America to a man competing in the NFL, Joe Jackson's story evokes both inspiration and motivation. *Championship Sunday* is a testimony that dreams can still come true. A nobody can become a somebody when they allow God to direct their steps. This message will awaken the champion within you!

— **Dr. G. Craig Lauterbach**
President and Founder of LifeWord Publishing

I first met Joe Jackson at a Minnesota Vikings chapel service in 2010. He has always been my big brother who leads by example. My wife and I believe in Joe Jackson's ministry. We support the call of the evangelist. Joe's love for God is amazing. He understands and realizes that everyone is not at the same level in their walk with Christ. Joe Jackson meets people right where they are and encourages them to become the champions and role models that are so needed in today's culture. I'm buying the first copy of *Championship Sunday*!

— **Jared Allen**
Minnesota Vikings defensive end, Future NFL Hall of Fame Inductee

Joe Jackson was a good athlete whom some would even say is great. However, there's no debate about his commitment to his Savior Jesus Christ. When we were in the NFL we had many battles. We're still in the battle, but this time we're on the same team. Joe is always willing to share the gospel as an evangelist, and he is a role model for me and my family. I know that *Championship Sunday* will be a blessing for all.

**— J.D. Hill**
Buffalo Bills wide receiver, founder of Catch the Vision

Joe was a good football player, but he was a better person on and off the field. I can't wait to read *Championship Sunday*.

**— Bud Grant**
Minnesota Vikings Hall of Fame Head Coach, led the Vikings to four NFC titles and Super Bowls

Joe Jackson is not only a good friend and former teammate, he's family. I remember when I was recovering from a serious accident and Joe visited me in the hospital and prayed for my healing. He also introduced me to AIM. That mission trip to Chile changed my life. Those memories bring tears to my eyes as I reflect on the good times. I often think about how eye-opening the trip was. Joe, we go back; we've been there for each other. I can't wait to read *Championship Sunday!* God bless you, brother.

**— Jim Marshall**
Minnesota Vikings defensive end, All-time Viking Great

I loved you the minute I saw you. Jesus shines out from you. Thank you for blessing our church—especially our young people. If you're ever in this area again, I'll buy you lunch. (If you don't eat too much. Ha!)

**— Adrian Rogers**
Former Pastor, Bellevue Baptist Church

When I think of Proverbs 27:17, "As iron sharpens iron, and one person sharpens another," I think of Big Joe Jackson. Over the years we have ministered together in high school assemblies, churches, and prisons. We even broke into a church one night. We have been there for each other during our darkest moments. I never thought I'd have a close relationship with a defensive end; God still does miracles. Joe, I'm excited about your book, *Championship Sunday*.

**— M.L. Harris**
Cincinnati Bengals tight end, Super Bowl XVI

Joe, I vividly remember your phone call thirty-four years ago back in 1987. Little did I realize that we would become the best of friends, but more importantly see thousands of professional and collegiate athletes and coaches impacted by the AIM conferences. This endorsement, though well deserved, can never tell the complete story of how our relationship has transcended into a brotherhood of love, trust, and vision. Joe, let's go for another thirty-four. Love you, brother!

**— Larry Kerychuk**
Winnipeg Blue Bombers quarterback, Executive Director of Athletes International Ministries

*Championship Sunday* is not a game plan for a football player; it's a game plan for life that can be used by all of us. Joe Jackson has a great ability to explain biblical lessons and show us how to improve our everyday life. I can't wait to read *Championship Sunday*.

**— Doug Martin**
Head Football Coach, New Mexico State University

I have had the insightful benefit of sitting across the table and enjoying many meals with Joe Jackson. It wasn't the NFL football player Joe Jackson, nor was it the evangelist Joe Jackson; it was the man Joe Jackson. When you share a meal, true conversation develops. People often only see the anointed evangelist or the six foot five giant of a man who played professional football, and they get caught up in his amazing accomplishments. I have had the honor of hearing and seeing Joe's character and, more importantly, understanding the journey that got him there. As exciting as game day is, it's the journey that counts in getting there; it's the journey that creates championships; it's the journey that produces anointed preaching. In reading *Championship Sunday*, you will discover the importance of the God-made, Spirit-led journey of a man who is living a championship life for Christ, and it will challenge you to realize that you can be a champion for Christ as well.

**— Tom Rakoczy**
Lead Pastor, Chandler First Assembly of God

Joe's compelling story of transformation is one that speaks to the heart. In this personal and insightful book he gives readers the inspiration to dream big and learn that failure is not final unless you don't learn from it.

— **David Laurell**
Sports and Entertainment Journalist

My husband, Mark Medoff, was Joey's English professor at New Mexico State University some fifty years ago, and while Mark admired Joey's athletic prowess, he also recognized the young man's intelligence and innate goodness—both, he knew, well worth encouraging. Never to be misquoted, Mark referred to Joey as "the real deal," someone who was determined to not allow his failures and mistakes to define his future.

I first met Joey Jackson at a New Mexico State University Aggie football game in 2017. I vividly remember how absolutely delighted Mark was when we ran into him. I was immediately taken by his aura of goodwill and contagious smile—the real deal.

Just before Mark passed in 2019, Joey gave him a copy of his manuscript, *Championship Sunday*. I don't know how much of that manuscript Mark was able to read, but he would have endorsed the champion spirit that gave Joey Jackson the courage and faith to transform him into Joe Jackson—the same kind of faith, Joe lovingly teaches us, that transformed Abram into Abraham.

—**Stephanie Medoff**
Wife of award-winning American playwright, director, actor and college professor Mark Medoff

# Championship
# SUNDAY

## JOE JACKSON

**LWP**
*LIFEWORD PUBLISHING*

Library of Congress Control Number: 2021919580

ISBN:   978-1-7363911-2-9 (Paperback)

         978-1-7363911-6-7 (Hardcover)

         978-1-7363911-3-6 (E-book)

Printed in the United States of America

# Contents

Foreword                                                                                       9

Chapter 1: My Beginnings                                                              11

Chapter 2: Madisonville Memories                                              24

Chapter 3: 1968                                                                            32

Chapter 4: Go West, Young Man                                                 37

Chapter 5: Louisiana Tech                                                            43

Chapter 6: Home for the Summer                                                49

Chapter 7: There's Snot on My Jacket                                         52

Chapter 8: Clergy or Coach?                                                        54

Chapter 9: Show Me the Money                                                   59

Chapter 10: Drafted Again—in the First Round                           62

Chapter 11: Rookie Training Camp                                             65

Chapter 12: Joe Wants Dough, Says He Can Play Better          69

Chapter 13: Bills at Shea                                                              74

Chapter 14: Boy, Do Yo Mama Know Where You Is?               78

Chapter 15: Prepped for Surgery                                                 83

Chapter 16: Pooh Bear                                                                 86

Chapter 17: Juice on the Loose                                                    91

Chapter 18: Mays, Rikers Island, or the Minnesota State Fair   94

Chapter 19: Purple Tales and Kelley Green Tales                      98

Chapter 20: Don't Worry; I'll Let Go of the Contract             105

Chapter 21: From Super Bowls to Saving Souls                      108

Chapter 22: Athletes International Ministries                          116

Chapter 23: Purple Rain and Big Chick                                  123

Chapter 24: I Don't Want a Singer in My Pulpit                     126

Chapter 25: The Man from La Mancha                                   128

Chapter 26: The Briefcase                                                        134

Chapter 27: Be a Doer of the Word                                         137

Chapter 28: Hall of Faith                                                          141

Chapter 29: The Big Dipper, Rosey, and Evander                  143

Chapter 30: Ministry Tales                                                       146

Chapter 31: The Buddy System/Prime Time                           172

Chapter 32: Runaway Bride                                                      176

Chapter 33: Is That Jim Brightbill?                                          179

Chapter 34: T-Jack, My Righteous Fox                                   181

Chapter 35: Guess Who's Coming to Dinner?                         184

Chapter 36: I'm Brett, I'm Jared, I'm Joe 190
Chapter 37: A Small Cloud 194
Chapter 38: United Flight 93 196
Chapter 39: Are You Steve Harvey? 201
Chapter 40: I Know You'll Pray for Me 205
Chapter 41: Who's That Guy? 208
Chapter 42: Singapore 211
Chapter 43: Sydney and the All Blacks 213
Chapter 44: Joe, You'll Have to Fly This Bird 215
Chapter 45: Mr. Universe, Barbecue, and Barnett 217
Chapter 46: The Unit 221
Chapter 47: The Ram in the Thicket 225
Chapter 48: I Don't Believe It 232
Chapter 49: Take This Job and Shove It! 234
Chapter 50: Roommates, the Mover, and the Mack 239
Chapter 51: From Boys to Men 241
Chapter 52: You're Dreaming 244
Chapter 53: I'm a Sheepherder 249
Chapter 54: God's Grace and Mercy 254
Chapter 55: Barriers Broken 260
Chapter 56: The Arizona Bowl 264
Chapter 57: Snoop Dogg 266
Chapter 58: Dan Quayle 269
Chapter 59: I'm a Packer Fan 271
Chapter 60: Superstition Mountains—Majestic and Deadly 276
Chapter 61: New Season 278
Chapter 62: Joe, Say It Ain't So 284
Chapter 63: First the Car Keys, Then the House Keys 285
Chapter 64: Withrow's '68 Class Reunion 287
Chapter 65: Walking among Giants 292
Chapter 66: Intent and Content 294
Chapter 67: Lost at Sea 297
Chapter 68: Along My Path 299
Chapter 69: New Knees, New Miracle 303
Chapter 70: Championship Sunday 306

# Foreword

Forty-eight years ago in the summer of 1972, a slumbering, lumbering rookie named Joe Jackson meandered out onto our New York Jets practice field during training camp. He was one of the most low-key guys I'd ever met. I remember thinking, *Man, this guy can barely walk!* He was *so* slow! With All-Pros Gerry Philbin and John Elliot, along with veterans Mark Lomas and the Big Devil John Little, the Jets were loaded with defensive talent. There were ten defensive linemen in the camp, but the Jets would only keep six. But that big, quiet guy that kept to himself not only surprised us all by making the team, he went on to tie for second in quarterback sacks and was an all-rookie selection for the league.

Joe and I ended up playing three full seasons together before he was traded to the Vikings. But those three seasons were just the start of what has turned into a nearly life-long friendship. He was one of our coaches at the Joe Namath/John Dockery football camp, so we spent many summers together. We've gotten to know each other's families over the years, and I've even been fortunate enough to attend some of Joe's sermons. Talk about surprised; I had no idea he could sing so beautifully!

Reading *Championship Sunday* left me with a lot of those "Man, I had no idea" moments. Moments when I realized we had more in common than I ever knew, starting with the fact we were both "Joey" while growing up. But the adversity and the challenges that Joe faced were fierce, and I commend him for his determination to succeed. Those who believe that achievement is for others, will see and understand how Joe tackled challenges and redefined his life to win victory after victory. It takes a strong person to overcome so many odds and come out on the other side with a positive attitude, let alone to preach and share the joys of life.

I've always been reasonably religious, but while praying in the hospital after my first knee operation in '65, I really learned to connect to a higher power. That was just the first of many necessary spiritual lessons and conversations for me. There are times when we all feel alone, and having a connection to a higher power is sometimes the only strength we can rely on. I still speak with God every night and thank Him for what I have and what I've been given in this life. My teammates (and a few coaches) being some of them. And while Joe and I might've only played on the Jets a few years together, we'll forever be teammates in God's game of life. I stand with Joe Jackson in his effort to remove stereotypes and walls that divide us and embrace his vision to build a bridge that unites us all as equals. *Championship Sunday* is a story of overcoming nearly insurmountable odds, and, hey, who doesn't like a good underdog?

Super Bowl Champion, Super Bowl III MVP, NFL Hall of Fame

# Chapter 1: My Beginnings

My earliest memories are of crying in the front yard of our house located at 5332 Ward Street. I must have been three or four years old. My mom once told me that I cried about everything. I was the second oldest child of a family of seven, with two brothers and two sisters. Even though my older brother, Jerry, was from my mom's previous marriage, I was never allowed to claim rights as the oldest sibling.

What I did claim was a secret dream that I never shared with anyone. Although I received love and affirmation from parents and grandparents, I struggled with a lack of self-esteem. I wanted to be known as somebody great and admired—someone special. In my dream, I would proclaim to friends that I was this superhero. My powers were unrivaled by any force or anyone on earth; I was the best of the best. I told them that if they didn't believe me, they should ask God. He never lies. In the dream, they would ask God, who would reply, "Yes, Joey is the greatest boy in the world!"

Who knows, maybe this narcissistic prophetic vision motivated me to get off the porch. This dream would come and go until I was around six or seven years old. In reality, I struggled with self-esteem. Towering over my peers, I was one hundred and six pounds by the third grade and thought I was not only different but weird, awkward, and clumsy.

We celebrated my fifth birthday in my grandparents' house. They had a full basement—plenty of room, plenty of cake and ice cream, and lots of neighborhood friends. We played Pin the Tail on the Donkey and bobbed for apples. I thought my grandparents' house was the prettiest house in Madisonville, a Cincinnati suburb.

Madisonville was an old neighborhood with most homes constructed from wood and some covered with aluminum siding. My grandparents built a beautiful red brick home in the early '50s with green awnings, a huge picture window, and a large kitchen.

For every election, my grandparents' home was used as a polling station. Voters would come through the garage or the front door to voting booths in the basement, which were monitored by election judges or scrutineers, independent or partisan observers. I didn't understand voting. I just figured it was something adults do and didn't seem to be much fun.

During that era, the republican candidates could always count on the Negro vote. Republicans would place signs in my grandparents' front yard promoting their candidacy. I can remember seeing placards reading "Vote for Charles Collins. He's Our Man." The shift from Republican to Democrat gradually began with FDR's New Deal. By the time John F. Kennedy was elected, the Republican Party could no longer count on the Negro vote. The days of my grandmother's affirmation, "I'm Republican," were no longer the landscape and package in the Negro's forty acres and a mule. I don't think she ever voted for a Democrat. She once told me that Negroes vote Republican.

I said, "Mom, we're called Black now."

She said, "Nope, I'm a Negro." I didn't argue.

Like other minorities, our identity continues to evolve. In the '50s, we were colored; '60s, Negroes; '70s, Blacks; '80s, African Americans. What next? The term *Black* looks good on me, and like my grandmother, I'm staying there.

## Ward Street House

William Joseph Jackson is my full name, but everybody called me Joey. William sounded too stately for me. My childhood memories began at the small five-room house with two bedrooms with a front porch on Ward Street. In the winter, the coal truck would deliver coal to each house in the neighborhood.

I'm not sure how often the coal truck would make a delivery, but it was exciting to see the truck back up to our driveway. We would hear the sound of the air brakes as the truck stopped just short of the basement window. The bed of the truck would rise hydraulically, which we thought was so cool. Once the coal chute was lowered into the open window, the coal came tumbling down into the basement coal room. Many, if not all, of the homes in our neighborhood used coal for heating.

Coal was an excellent way to heat the house as long as the furnace was properly attended. My dad would check it periodically and shovel in coal whenever the fire got low. Between our living room and dining room was a three-by-three-foot grate on the floor. Sometimes this got pretty hot. You couldn't stand on it without wearing shoes. One time I was chasing my brother between rooms. We were barefooted but would carefully jump over the register. On one jump, my foot hit my leg, and I fell on the hot metal grate. The pattern from the hot surface is still etched on my stomach, arm, and thigh. I never did that again!

My younger brother Mike, my older brother Jerry, and I slept in the same bedroom, which led to the only bathroom. My sister Mary slept in my parents' bedroom. With the arrival of my sister Barbie Lynn Jackson on January 16, 1959, we realized we would need a larger home. Our small two-bedroom house would not accommodate a soon-to-be family of seven. So in June of 1958, we moved into a large three-story colonial home on the corner of Chandler and Ravenna. I don't remember much about the Ward Street days. I later found out that Madisonville's first permanent settler was some guy from New Jersey named Joseph Ward. He had two kids with strange names. One kid was named Usual and the other Israel. We learned about Israel in Sunday school, but I never heard of anybody named Usual.

Our Ward Street driveway was shared with the Jones'. They had one child, Willie. He was a couple of years older than me. Willie had some nice toys and a great Lionel train set.

The summers meant barbecue ribs. My dad would barbecue almost every weekend. He built a barbecue pit made from cinder blocks. Mom made the best barbecue sauce in my neighborhood. I remember my dad was barbecuing and went inside to get a mop for the sauce. He wasn't gone more than two minutes, but that's all it took. Two big German shepherds seized the moment, grabbed a rack of ribs, and ran down the driveway. From then on, it was my responsibility to guard the ribs.

Besides the barbecue pit in our backyard, we had a sandbox, a cherry tree, and a pear tree. My older brother, Jerry, had a 1949 black Mercury coupe with whitewall tires. The interior was red with a pair of white dice dangling from the rearview mirror. That car was loud and fast. Either the headers were uncapped, or it had some loud gas-packed mufflers. Before Jerry's cool car was Jerry's cool bike. Jerry had the nicest English bike I had ever seen. You could hear a ticking sound from the rear wheel of his bike. It had lights with a real generator, skinny whitewall tires, a saddlebag, and a horn. My bike had nothing but two tires, a seat, chain, and handle bars. I hoped Jerry's bike would get passed down to me, but it didn't. I wasn't tall enough. It had a twenty-eight-inch frame.

When I started kindergarten, Jerry would walk me to Madison Road before catching the bus to Withrow High School. Madisonville Elementary was only a block further.

## Elementary Memories

Ward Street led you right to the front steps of Madisonville Elementary. It was about a mile walk from my house. Mrs. Villhauer was my kindergarten teacher. Kindergarten was a half day. The only other thing I remember about kindergarten was that on rainy days I would get to wear my yellow raincoat and hat.

I had my tonsils taken out while in the first grade. Just before they put me under, I imagined the doctors sharpening a long knife. I screamed, "Please don't cut me, please don't cut me!" The next thing I recall is counting backward from 100. I think I got to 99. For the next three days, it was a steady diet of cherry Jell-O. Sixty-three years later, I still have the homemade get-well cards that Mrs. Smith, my first-grade teacher, asked my classmates to send me. For second grade, my teacher was Mrs. Norman. I sat next to Rhonda Innix. She was so cute, and I was smitten. I don't remember saying one word to her all year—I was too shy.

# Chapter 1: My Beginnings

In the third grade, Mrs. Illbrook gave us students a spelling test, and Jakey Moody and I were the only ones who scored 100. We were asked to stand in front of the class for getting a perfect score. It was a bit embarrassing, but a great memory. My parents were proud. Another third-grade memory was getting three swats for fighting Oscar Jackson. We were sent to the coat room. Mrs. Illbrook called Mr. Harris, the assistant principal, to hand out the punishment. Mr. Harris spanked Oscar first. He cried like a baby. Next was my turn. Each painful whack stung and burned like the brand of a hot iron. I was determined not to cry, and I didn't. As we walked home from school, Oscar told everyone that I cried. We got into another fight.

Mrs. Webb taught fourth grade. She was mean and seemed to always be a little tipsy. She liked to overload us with homework, even on the weekend. I couldn't wait until the fifth grade. One spring afternoon, I was walking home from school with my friend Tommy Baker. While we walked home, Tommy and I started wrestling in Mr. Chambers's front yard. I weighed 158 pounds. I easily flipped Tommy onto his back, then dove on his stomach with all of my weight. At that moment, he screamed and cursed at me to get off of him. When I landed on his stomach, unbeknownst to me, the pencil he had in his front pants pocket penetrated into his stomach. His cry haunts me to this day. I was scared to death. I thought I killed Tommy. Mr. Chambers called the ambulance, and he rushed Tommy to the hospital. I ran home thinking I was going to jail. Tommy survived the pencil attack and was back at school in a couple of days. What a relief.

In the fifth grade, I could ride my bike to school, provided it passed the safety lane inspection. There was no other place that I could spend hours and hours just looking and dreaming than Atkins Bicycle Shop. It was one of the greatest places on earth. At Atkins, bikes were hung from the ceiling, lined up in rows on the floor, and attached to the wall. They were everywhere! You could find Schwinn, Huffy, Monark, and English bikes waiting for new owners. The smell of rubber and the sight of shiny fenders was all it took to imagine myself peddling down Ward Street on a new bike.

My dream came true on my ninth birthday. My grandfather bought me a bike from Atkins Bicycle Shop. It was my blue and silver dream bike with streamers coming from the hand grips—a deluxe model with all the options you would want on a bike. It even had a fake radio. We would take a clothespin and clip baseball cards to the rear spoke to make ours sound like a motorcycle. For weeks, I was the happiest kid on Ward Street—until I ran over a nail. The nail not only punctured my front tire, but also took some luster from the gleam of my shiny new toy. I discovered that it was only a bike.

The school lunch was only twenty-six cents. It wasn't very good, so my little brother and I would walk to my grandparents' house for lunch. En route was Madison Bakery. Madison Bakery baked the best doughnuts in the world. There was no sweeter aroma than the smell of fresh pastries from Madison Bakery. It's hard for me to say this (and you didn't hear it from me), but Madison Bakery would send my grandmother's blackberry cobbler and sweet potato pie with homemade ice cream to the bench. The best of all was that those cinnamon rolls and jelly doughnuts were only four cents apiece. Just think, you could buy twenty-five doughnuts for a dollar! In those days, we had very little money, so even four cents was hard to find.

## My Mother, Colenia

Colenia Blondean Lyle, my mother, was born on April 15, 1921 in Winder, Georgia. She was the middle child of three children. I don't know exactly when they migrated north to Cincinnati, but my grandmother raised three children during the depression, cleaning floors as a domestic. Mama Rosa, my grandmother, made the best sweet potato pie in America. Mom never talked very much about her father, who was half-white. I know very little about him but would like to know more about my family tree.

My sister Barbie told me that she attended a family reunion on my mom's side. She was surprised to see that many of our *family* on my mother's side were white. My grandfather divorced my grandmother after a short marriage; I don't know much more than that. I also know very little about my mother's first husband. Mom got pregnant at seventeen years old. She married the father, but they got divorced in less than two years. Mom told us that she once tried contacting her father in Washington, D.C. She even moved there to find a good job.

In Cincinnati, good jobs were scarce post-depression. I suppose you could always find work as a domestic like my grandmother, Mama Rosa, but she wanted more. In another time and era, my mother easily could have modeled or been an actress. She couldn't sing but was very pretty with beautiful black hair and Lena Horne features. However, in the 1940s, there were hardly any professional opportunities for people of color. Plus, she only had a high school education. She found a job as a secretary. There's so much unwritten history of what could have been.

Mom eventually located her father. She hoped to reconnect with him and build a relationship. When she knocked on his apartment door, he barely opened it and rudely said, "Get out of here, I don't want anything to do with you." That was the last time she ever saw him.

There are certain things that punctuate your life, like a quotation mark in an autobiography. It was 1959 when I heard Marty Robbins' song "El Paso." I had no idea what the word meant. So I wouldn't forget the song, I phonetically wrote "L Pas So" on a piece of paper. Robbins' voice was soothing and warm. I was especially captured with the story of Feleena, the Mexican maiden whose eyes were blacker than the night. I was certain Marty was saying Colenia, my mother's name.

I said, "Mom, you're in a song called 'L Pas So.'"

She listened but was not impressed. She asked, "Are you sure he's saying Colenia?"

I said, "Yeah, Mom, he's saying your name."

At nine years old, I bought my first 45 rpm record. The more I listened to that record, the more I doubted the name of the Mexican maiden. After I slowed the record to 33 rpm speed, I figured maybe he could be singing "Feleena" and not "Colenia." Whenever I hear that song played, I still sing "Colenia."

During that era, westerns ruled the TV Guide. My favorite cowboy was Cheyenne Bodie, played by Clint Walker. He was my favorite because of his size. He stood six feet six inches and weighed around 240 pounds. I could relate to someone who was different. Who could have imagined that ten years later, that West Texas town of El Paso and the Badlands of New Mexico would essentially become my homeland?

It was a warm spring day in the late 1950s. I was around eight years old and up for any challenge. As we walked past Madison Bakery and Millers Paint and Supply Store, several older boys jumped over the chain that separated the two stores. They dared me to make a jump. They said, "I bet fat Joey can't do it." I said, "I bet I can." I was ready for any challenge.

As I jumped, my lead foot caught on the top of the chain. Unaware of how to control my body for a fall, I fell facedown. I broke my front tooth in half. Not only did I have a chipped tooth but also a huge gap, which would prove to be a major contributor to my lack of self-esteem. I would make a mold from chewing gum to form the bottom half of my tooth. Of course, this didn't work, especially during meals—but I was desperate.

My mom later worked as a dental assistant, but she never encouraged me to get a crown until my senior year in high school. Guess they couldn't afford the price of a crown. Can you imagine going through elementary, junior high, and high school with half of a front tooth?

## The House on Chandler Street

Before we settled on the three-story colonial house on Chandler Street, we looked at homes on Anderson Place. Anderson Place was where many of the Black professionals lived—the school teachers, doctors, and lawyers. It was one of the nicest streets in Madisonville.

I remember we looked at a fancy red-brick home with an arch and courtyard. I was hoping dad would pick that one, but $15,000 was out of his price range.

Mr. Thone owned the Chandler property. It was located on the corner of Chandler and Ravenna. He was one of the last white homeowners in the neighborhood. I didn't understand the term "white flight," but I guess the neighborhood was changing too quickly for him.

Mr. Thone was a nice man. The Chandler house had a chicken coop and a lot of cool tools. Also, the house was heated with gas and priced at $12,000, which was more affordable. To this day, we still own the house on Ward Street and my grandmother's red brick house on Kenwood Road.

The neighborhood was an upgrade from Ward Street. It was also closer to Stewart Park. The house had a full attic, which could have been easily converted into an apartment. It had no bathroom on the first floor, only on the second floor, and an unfinished bathroom in the basement. But we didn't care about that when there was plenty of yard space to play, trees to climb, and a large lot that my dad converted into a garden. It even had a small shed and a grape vine.

## Little League Jackson

Stewart Park was a tremendous outdoor classroom where I learned to swim, play basketball, football, baseball, and dream. It had a football field, tennis courts, two basketball courts, three baseball diamonds, a horseshoe pit, and a swimming pool. It was also the home of the Madisonville Eagles, my first little league baseball uniform. I was too big to play Pop Warner football.

There was no weight restriction in baseball. Early on, I realized that I was a natural athlete. All sports came easy to me. I loved baseball and did well on the softball team. But fast pitch, hard ball was another story. I could run the bases, catch, and throw, but lacked the skill set and confidence to hit the fast pitch. The first little league game we played was an away game against the All Saints Warriors. Although Mike, my little brother, was a better baseball player and athlete than me, we played whatever sport was in season. Sometimes we'd play all day or until my dad would whistle, which meant it's time for dinner, the game's over. My father could really whistle loud. It didn't matter what side of the park we were playing; I could always hear his whistle!

Buddy Jones, our new neighbor, was one of the baseball coaches. After our first game, my dad asked me how I did. I told him, "I hit a home run, double, single, and we won 7-4." My dad was a great athlete, and I wanted to make him proud of me. A couple of days later, he ran into Buddy Jones at Carl's Grocery Store. He congratulated Mr. Jones for the team's first win and was pleased with my success. Mr. Jones said, "If Joey keeps trying, he'll get his opportunity to play."

My dad was surprised by that comment because I told him I knocked the cover off the ball. Mr. Jones said, "Joey didn't even play." When my dad got home, he was furious. I was punished for lying. I can hear my dad's descriptive voice saying, "Get upstairs, you good for nothing, low down, trifling dog!" My dad was disappointed with me. I think his words were a little harsh, but that was Big Jack.

I don't know why I was such a deviant. There was something in me—given the choice of right and wrong, I'd probably choose wrong. Stealing, fighting, lying, and doing stupid things were the choices that I made while growing up in Madisonville. It's a miracle I made it to the NFL. Before my eighteenth birthday, I was shot in the shoulder, expelled from school, sliced with a razor, busted twice for car theft, and on my way to reform school. Many of my friends didn't make it to the minor leagues of life—and I could have easily been right with them. It's possible that someone else could be writing this story about how I ended up dead on some street corner.

Stewart Park was also the home field for the Madisonville Panthers. They were a semi-pro football team. I was around ten years old when first I saw and heard the Panthers play. The sound of shoulder pads and helmets crashing into each other was something I'll never forget. It was so exciting to watch Ruben Belew take a kick-off ninety yards to the house. From that moment on, I knew that I wanted to be a football player. The Panthers were the closest thing to the NFL, and they played right in my backyard.

## Reverend Mosley

In 1961 Reverend Harris retired, and Trinity Baptist Church welcomed its new pastor, the Reverend William D. Mosley. Their family was hosted by my grandparents. The Reverend Mosley was a great preacher and singer. He was educated at Morehouse College and served as Trinity's senior pastor for twenty years. Even though I didn't care too much about church, I loved his message on the valley of dry bones from Ezekiel 37. Reverend Mosley would begin his sermons in almost a whisper. When he finished, his voice could be heard throughout the neighborhood. He was tall, thin, and a lot younger than Reverend Harris.

Reverend Mosley was from West Virginia. He sort of had a southern accent but was a great orator and classmate of Dr. Martin Luther King, Jr. At Trinity Baptist Church, services were like an event. It wasn't a circus, but you could probably sell tickets for admission. Every time the offering plate was passed, people would make change. They would put in a ten-dollar bill and take seven back! That was a part of life. It's inconceivable today.

There was always Shoutin' Miss Jones. At about one o'clock on Sunday afternoon, she would feel the Spirit move or "get happy." Sister Jones would jump to her feet, screaming, "Thank You, Jesus, thank You, Jesus!" Then associate pastor Reverend Clay would scream, "Thank Him; thank Him, church!"

I remember one Sunday morning. Reverend Mosely started preaching. In the Black church, they call it hooping. As he backed up against the choir loft, Sister Lewis was seated in the first row. She was overcome with emotion. She then stood to her feet and wrapped her arms around Reverend Mosely's chest, screaming, "Oh, God, oh, my God." Sister Lewis had a full Nelson on Reverend Mosely while he still preached his sermon in her grasp. My grandfather and the other deacons rushed to the pulpit and intervened, and she finally let go of the pastor. The reverend didn't miss a beat. He stepped forward as if nothing happened. It was a great service!

My grandfather was an entrepreneur. He worked at the post office for thirty-three years and owned property in Cincinnati and Newport,

Kentucky. Grandad always drove a Cadillac. I thought they were so rich—nice house, nice car. No, they weren't rich, just worked hard. He was the Sunday school superintendent and church treasurer. Every Monday, he would count the offering from the two Sunday services. Grandad would spread the offering out on the dining room table. I never saw so many shiny dimes, nickels, quarters, and fifty-cent pieces. The paper money didn't mean very much to me. At that age, my world was pennies, nickels, dimes, quarters, and fifty-cent pieces. Not that silent money.

On Sundays at church, my grandfather and grandmother never sat together. He sat on the front row with the other deacons. We *had* to go to Sunday school and church. My grandmother, Mom Jackson, would tell me, "Joey, if you sit next to grand mommy and be really good and keep quiet, grand mommy gonna give you a little piece of money." Back in the day, a little piece of money would last you for about a month. I tried to be good, but what kid could be quiet for three hours of church? Church was *too* long.

## Joining the Church

One Sunday morning, Reverend Mosley asked if there were any present who wanted to join the church. I was probably around twelve years old. Although I attended Trinity Baptist Church, I was not an official member. I raised my hand and came forward, much to the shock of my parents.

Reverend Mosley asked me the question, "Son, how do you come? Do you come by letter or your Christian experience?"

I said to myself, *I...I don't have any kind of letter.* I reasoned, *My grandfather's a deacon, my great grandfather was one of the founding pastors of the church, this is a Christian country, and therefore I come by my Christian experience.*

Two things happened next: my name was added to the church directory, and I was baptized in water. For the next six years, I was the same person I always had been. Nothing happened on the inside. I brought my street tactics, street attitude, and carnality into Trinity Baptist Church every Sunday. The only thing that I had was a superficial, razor-thin veneer of Christianity applied to the surface of my life. I was lost as a ball in high weeds—and didn't care.

When church was finally over each Sunday, we'd usually have lunch at my grandparents' house. The menu served all my favorites: corn pudding, fried chicken, string beans, collards, yams, and blackberry cobbler with homemade ice cream.

Everybody called my grandmother Mom or Mom Jackson. Sometimes a white family who attended Trinity would also come for lunch. My grandfather told me they were related to us, but I can't remember how. They had a cute daughter with a pointed nose and red hair who looked just like her mother. Her father was a tall, striking gentleman with a Caucasian appearance. After some research, I learned of the identity of their father. He was First Lieutenant Eugene D. Smith, a distant cousin who flew with the Tuskegee Airmen during World War II. Upon his return from the war, he was notably unaccepted by both sides (Black and white) of a nation filled with racial tensions. He earned a law degree from Franklin College in Columbus, Ohio. Attorney Smith practiced law in Cincinnati for fifty years. He once argued a First Amendment case before the Supreme Court of the United States.

# Chapter 2:
# Madisonville Memories

Madisonville was once a thriving community. There were no malls or shopping centers, only downtown. When the Kenwood Plaza was built, it featured some of the same department stores that you'd find downtown. Now, instead of driving all the way downtown, fighting traffic, and finding a parking garage, a five-minute drive was all it took to shop at Cincinnati's first major department store, Shillito's, located at the new Kenwood shopping center. You can't blame progress, but over time this destroyed Madisonville's economy.

Most of the businesses were white-owned. Black or white, they couldn't compete with the new Kenwood Plaza and the 1968 riots, so they gradually closed. Gone were Madison Furniture (my first real job) and forty other small businesses. Everything was gone. It's sad to drive down Madison Road and see empty stores, boarded-up buildings, graffiti, drug dealers, and young brothers walking the streets with no place to go and no vision to get there. Even Dairy Queen and Art's Chili Kitchen are long gone. The only business left is the post office where my daddy worked. Recently, my brother informed me that it's gone too.

To earn a living to support a family of seven, Dad worked as a mailman, and Mom was a secretary and dental assistant at Madisonville Elementary. It was fun to walk the route with my dad. Every house had its own mailbox. Some of the steps leading to the boxes were very steep. Cincinnati is known for its seven hills. Dad would say, "Joey, take this mail to this box for me." Sometimes he'd even let me ride in the mail truck. I don't think that was legal even back then, but it was fun just being with my dad.

My dad had a second job cleaning stores in the new Kenwood Plaza. He hired a team of men who needed some extra cash and didn't mind hard work. Mike and I would sometimes get to tag along. He would put us to work scraping chewing gum from the floors or whatever he needed to be done. It was kind of cool being in these stores after hours. It was like we owned the place.

Everyone called my dad Jack or Big Jack. His first name was William, but I can't remember anyone referring to him as William or Bill. This is the same with me; I don't answer to William either. I'm not sure why I was given a name that no one calls me. The only place the name *William* can be found is on my birth certificate and social security card.

My mom's job as a secretary at Madisonville Elementary School was good and bad. It gave me a good feeling when other kids would ask if she was my mother, but if I got in trouble in school I'd be in trouble at home. I can remember getting five swats with a paddle at school for fighting. When my dad came home, he gave me another whipping. He would probably be arrested today for child abuse for the beatings he gave out when we got in trouble. Big Jack didn't spare the rod. We got spanked with a belt, and I probably deserved every spanking I received.

My mother didn't give us a lot of discipline. We didn't mind a spanking from her. She was left-handed and didn't have spanking action down as well as Dad. My dad was ambidextrous. He defined the true meaning of a switch-hitter. That's how parents and teachers handed out discipline in those days.

## Times Changing

I remember my first year of teaching at John F. Kennedy High School in Bloomington. I put my hand on a student's shoulder to get his attention. His response was, "Let go of me, or I'll call my lawyer." Maybe I should have snapped that remark back at my sixth-grade teacher, Mr. Jones, when he dragged me into the coatroom and paddled my behind.

Times were different then. Some of the old ways were good ways. Some of the old ways were not so good. There was a church next to Madisonville Elementary School where you could go and learn about the Bible. They called it "release time." I can remember having release time to go to church school. I signed up for church school to get out of class. I didn't care anything about the Bible. After three weeks, I was kicked out of church school for cussing and fighting—another spanking when my dad came home.

Even though I was a young rascal, I loved and respected my dad. I was always eager and proud to hear stories of my father's greatness as an athlete. Dad's friends would tell stories of his gridiron glory, which inspired me to reach higher. He is the single reason why my brother and I made it to the NFL. My dad never missed a high school game and always encouraged my brother and me to be the best students we could be. He never encouraged us to be great athletes; he didn't have to. One of Big Jack's favorite sayings was, "Get your grades, get your grades." He also warned us to stay away from certain neighborhood kids. I can remember him telling me, "Stay away from black Betty Johnson's boy." His name was Tony. Tony Johnson had a dark complexion and stayed in trouble. His complexion had nothing to do with his troubles. He was raised by a single mom who did her best. Somehow Tony always found himself looking for a fight. Today he's a drug addict, walking the streets of Cincinnati looking for a handout.

By the time I was in the seventh grade, I was almost six feet tall and weighed over two hundred pounds. My pant size was never slim or regular. It was always husky. The name *husky* even sounds fat. I was teased about being overgrown and clumsy, but I yearned to be accepted by my peers. I wanted to fit in and belong. Being wanted and admired meant everything. Consequently, this led me down a road of poor choices. I was a thief, stealing everything—my dad's 1961 Mercury Comet, my older brother's twenty-dollar bill, a beautiful watch, down to a bag of Oreo cookies. I was almost willing to pay any price for my peers' acceptance. My problem was that I was hanging out with the wrong peers.

In our home, there was always conversation about treating all people with respect regardless of color. My parents knew that was the right thing to do, and we were raised that way.

In Ohio, integration of the public school system happened in the early 20th century. My grandfather graduated from Higgenport High School in Ohio. His class had Black and white students. This was the same with my dad when he graduated in 1934 from Withrow High School. There were ignorant pockets of racism like Mr. Siegel, who lived next door to us on Ward Street. Mr. Seigel was the last white homeowner living on our street. When Blacks began to move into the neighborhood in the 1940s, the whites slowly started moving out. In Madisonville, all the businesses were white-owned. There were a handful of Black businesses in the neighborhood, like Thomas Barbershop, Chambers Upholstery, The Brown Pelican bar, The Soul Lounge bar, and the Pony Keg. The whites owned the banks, grocery store, pharmacy, clothing store, restaurants, and even the library.

One day, we played baseball in the street, and I hit a foul ball that rolled into Mr. Seigel's yard. Yes, maybe I should have knocked on his door and asked permission to retrieve the ball, but instead I ran into his yard and picked it up. Old man Seigel came off of his porch screaming and calling me names, saying, "Get out of my yard; I'm calling the cops." He called the police just because I knocked a ball into his backyard.

My father arrived at the same time as the cops, and my dad was furious. I can't remember ever seeing my dad so mad! This was the first and only time I heard my father swear, saying if the cops weren't there he'd break my neck.

## Sunlite Pool

We moved to Chandler Street a year later, thank God. There was an amusement park called Coney Island in Cincinnati's Anderson Township. Coney Island boasted America's largest outdoor recreational, recirculating swimming pool named the Sunlite Pool. There was even a little song on the radio that said, "Ride, swim, sing, and dance at Coney Island." The pool that we had swum in at Stewart Park had no diving board, deep end, or blue water. The water was sort of brown-looking. The water at the Sunlite Pool seemed to be bright blue.

After an afternoon of riding roller coasters, go-carts, and swings, a refreshing plunge would cap a perfect day. We'd change into our swimming trunks, grab our towels, and put our thirty-five cents on the counter, but every time we tried to enter the pool, the little white girl would tell us, "Sorry, we can't admit Negroes." I didn't understand this and would say to myself, *I don't take 'em either, I just want to swim!* It wasn't her fault. It was a Jim Crow system that needed to be replaced, not repaired.

Once a year, Trinity Baptist Church would sponsor a picnic in Middletown, Ohio at Dunkers Pool. For years, I called it Duncan's Pool until I ran into NFL Hall of Famer Chris Carter at a Viking alumni event. Chris was born and raised in Middletown. He told me the correct name is Dunkers Pool. Even though Cincinnati was a northern industrial city, certainly north of Selma, it had its share of bigots and racists. There were certain places we couldn't live.

My father told me that when he attended Withrow High School, colored students were only allowed to swim in the high school pool during the last hour of school on Friday. The pool would be drained and cleaned the next day. A few decades later, my brother Mike was a member of the varsity swim team.

Integration into the Sunlite Pool didn't occur until May 29, 1961, six years after the amusement park opened its gates to *Negroes.* They had their pool and we had ours, except ours was not much larger than a backyard play pool. With the arrival of Kings Island, Coney Island was torn down in 1971.

## Bad Decisions

The movie *Hercules,* starring Steve Reeves, was playing at the 20th Century movie theater in Hyde Park. Greg Williams' parents dropped us off to watch the action thriller. Reeves had a body like a gladiator. That's what I wanted. It was a matinee, and we thought it was so neat to be in an air-conditioned theater in the afternoon. Madisonville is about ten miles from Hyde Park. Greg's parents gave us money to call for a ride when the movie ended. However, we spent all of our money on popcorn and candy. Even though it was only ten cents to use a payphone, we didn't even have a penny, so we decided to hitchhike.

As we walked down Madison Road we passed some white guys leaning against their car. This didn't feel good.

We hadn't passed the group when one of them shouted racial slurs at us, asking, "What are you doing in Hyde Park?"

I asked who he was calling that name, and he said it was me, throwing in another racial jab while he was at it. That's all it took. A riot broke out on Madison Road. Punches were thrown, clothes were torn, and blood was spilled. After several minutes they summoned other recruits. We had no choice but to run for our lives. They chased us down Madison Road until we heard sirens from police cars. This was one of the few times I was glad to see the cops. I don't remember much beyond that, but it was the last time I ran from a fight—outnumbered or not.

I told my older brother what happened. He was furious. He called his friends and went back to Hyde Park, looking for trouble. To this day, he never told me what happened, and I never asked.

A few years later, we were in Kennedy Heights looking for trouble. We walked by several white guys who said hello. Then we asked, "What are you looking at?"

They said, "Nothing. We're just hanging out."

Someone shouted, "You calling me nothing, honky?"

"No," they protested, "we don't have anything against Black guys."

"Who you calling Black?" I asked.

He answered, "I have many Black friends." (In the '50s and '60s, the term *Black* was like a racial slur.)

Another riot erupted on the streets in Kennedy Heights. This time we finished the fight, we didn't run home. Both fights were stupid and senseless and should never have happened.

When I think back to what happened in Kennedy Heights, I shake my head in shame. What was my mindset? When we were fighting, nobody carried a gun. A fight was settled with our hands, not a handgun. Today you don't know who's packing. It's better to walk away and live for another day than to make a decision that will cost you greatly in the end. I'm so sorry for what I did. If it wasn't for the Lord's grace and mercy, I'd be living with enormous guilt and remorse.

## Football Beginnings

My sophomore year at Withrow High School was my first year of high school football. Even though I stood about six feet four inches and weighed around 250 pounds, I wasn't the biggest player on the team. There were two larger boys. Big Beau Heard and Terry Moffet were six feet five inches, and both weighed over 300 pounds.

This was my dream—to play high school football at the school where my dad had starred thirty-one years earlier. I had a great summer football camp. When the season began, I was the only sophomore in the starting lineup—Jackson at right defensive tackle.

We had just finished morning practice. Between the morning and afternoon practice, we broke for lunch. Whoever had transportation could go home to eat. Most of the players stayed on campus.

On one hot August afternoon, several players walked into a small grocery store. We were stupid kids. We stole everything from hotdogs to cigarettes. On our way back to campus, we bragged about our take.

Someone asked, "What you get, Joey?"

I shouted, "I got a bag of cookies."

They all laughed and gave me the nickname "Cookie." Whenever I go and visit old high school friends and teammates, some still call me Cookie. My mother thought it was because of her chocolate chip cookies with walnuts.

Stewart Park was more than a place to run, jump, and swim. It gave me a dream. I saw the big boys who came before me, like Pete Pearson, who played with the Madisonville Panthers and Philadelphia Eagles, and Dickie Gordon, who played with the University of Michigan State the Chicago Bears. They made it. Maybe I can too.

These were some of my heroes and role models. In spite of the craziness of my choices, I knew there was another path that could potentially lead to greatness. When I entered my senior year at Withrow High School, I somehow became smarter and more serious about my present and my future. I needed to narrow my circle and become more selective of whom I allowed to speak into my life. It was like a light finally turned on in my brain, and I started to *get it*. My study habits improved. My social life changed. The things my parents warned me about made sense. When my father would tell me to stay away from a certain kid in the neighborhood, this time I would listen. Those kids are now dead or in jail.

# Chapter 3: 1968

History records 1968 as one of the most historic years in modern history. It was historic for me too. I finally had my front tooth capped. No more chewing gum to mold a fake tooth. Now I could enjoy a dinner date without the worry of eating a Frisch's big boy burger and fries only on the right side of my mouth.

The Withrow Tigers were city champions. For some reason, the city high schools didn't participate in the state playoffs in football. That year, Withrow won championships in football, basketball, and baseball. I'm not sure that's ever been accomplished again. I was named to every all-star team in Cincinnati and Southern Ohio.

When I graduated from high school, Reverend Mosley presented all the seniors who attended Trinity with a red-letter edition of the King James Bible with my name inscribed on the cover. Up until that point, the only time I ever opened the Bible was to put four-leaf clovers inside. We were told that if you were lucky enough to find a four-leaf clover and put it in the Bible, you'd have good luck. Every Saturday in the summer, my friends would come to the house. We'd search our garden, looking for our ticket to riches. Sometimes we would even find five-leaf clovers, which meant that we'd inherit a fortune.

For some strange reason, I opened the Bible—not to find a resting place for a four-leaf clover, but to read it. I remember reading the Bible once and hearing footsteps climbing up the stairs. I put it down quickly because I was ashamed to let anyone know was I reading the Bible. I started taking Reverend Mosely's sermons to heart. Either his messages were better, or I started listening better. I wondered if I was getting religious or something.

Unbeknownst to me, the Lord was doing a work in my heart, even before my encounter with Ken Johnson. God was preparing me.

Senior prom and graduation would spell the end of high school. The year 1968 was flying by. It was now track season. To keep in shape for football, I threw the shot and disc and I did the high jump. I wasn't very good at any of those, however, because my main sports were football and basketball. I loved basketball. I could dunk the ball in the ninth grade. Coach Bryant, the assistant basketball coach, asked me to try out for basketball. I played basketball and football in elementary and junior high but I refused to even try out in high school. The only reason was because I was embarrassed to be seen in shorts because I thought I was too fat. I've always regretted the decision. Instead of playing with my high school team, I played for the Cincinnati recreation league throughout high school.

## Senior Prom

I finally got the courage up to ask Pat for a date. She was tall with pretty green eyes. What senior boy didn't have a girlfriend? If you were a senior and weren't hooked up, people would call you a jive turkey. Pat and I began to date and planned to go to the senior prom together. There was a furniture store in Cincinnati that advertised their furniture with the jingle, "Save your dough at Pat and Joe's." Because of that, I thought we were meant to be together forever. I was really looking forward to the prom and being with Pat.

Two weeks before the big dance came another disappointment. Her freshman orientation at Kent State was the same weekend as the prom. She called and said that she would have to miss the big dance. I was disappointed but committed to going. I reached out to Mary Beth because we went to her senior prom the previous year. Both of our families were close, but now she was in college. I wasn't sure she would be interested in going to a high school dance, but surprisingly, she said yes! We had a great time and then went to my grandmother's house for an after-prom dinner.

## Losing Our Moral Compass

On April 4, 1968 I was standing at my locker when someone said that Martin Luther King, Jr. had been assassinated in Memphis. My heart sank—another Black civil rights leader killed, but this time it was the leader of the movement. After Dr. King was assassinated there was rioting and looting in Cincinnati. At Withrow High School, we protested by marching for equality.

Five years earlier, I was in Mr. Butt's science class when an announcement came over the PA system that President John F. Kennedy had been assassinated in Dallas. They dismissed us early. Now it was Martin Luther King, Jr. Where's the Elisha who would pick up the mantle? Who would continue our fight for equality? Who would be our voice? I believe Dr. King was God's gift to the world. His oratorical skills were matchless. There was a believable tone in his voice. It was powerful, commanding, and strong, yet peaceful—and resonated across racial, political, and even religious boundaries.

America needs a Dr. King today. Today's leaders have their own agenda. It's about building their own footprint and kingdom. No one wants to serve. Jesus said that He came not to be served, but to serve and give His life as a ransom for many (Mark 10:45). Nobody has come close to picking up Dr. King's mantle in the struggle for civil rights.

America has come a long way in turning the corner on civil rights, but there's still much work to do. Laws are sufficient in changing how people are governed, but this can be a very slow process. The love of God can bring a change of heart in the twinkling of an eye.

In April of 2007 I was preaching in the Amish community of Shipshewana near Angola, Indiana. When we were kids, my family would vacation in Angola at a campground called Fox Lake. I hadn't been to Fox Lake in probably fifty years. I asked Pastor Harold Gingerich if he could take me to the hotel where we vacationed. He knew right where it was located, but neither one of us knew the history.

We got out of the car and walked around the property. It had been sold several times and was in need of repair. There was a carpenter fixing a window who immediately walked toward us. I told him that our family came here on vacation in the early '60s. Without hesitation he said, "I want to apologize to you." I had no idea what he was apologizing to me for.

He told me that the lake that we were looking at was called Black Lake. I still didn't catch on. He said, "This was the only lake where colored people could swim." I was shocked. For all the times we came to Fox Lake, it never entered my mind that not only our choices for accommodations were segregated, but even swimming in an outdoor lake was segregated. When I think about that, it sickens me. Not just the racism, but how the Christian church could be so ineffective and lukewarm.

We know what Jesus says about a lukewarm church (Rev. 3:16). On one hand, we campaign and march against abortion and homosexuality, but some of these same people will not join you in the fight against racism and bigotry. They say, "We shouldn't get involved with social issues; let our elected officials deal with that." I disagree. We should get involved in social issues—there's nothing more social than the sinful nature of man that needs redemption.

You can't do anything about the past; you can only learn from it. When people say, "Let's go back to the good old days when prayer and Bible study were allowed in the public schools," I know what they mean, but from my perspective the good old days weren't all that good for everyone.

I do believe that our moral values have deteriorated because prayer and the Bible have been expelled from the public schools. Our generation has no moral compass. Where do we go for truth? For the sake of inclusion, we've lost biblical reason and common sense. Today, it's secular humanism. Yesterday, it was "separate but equal." In any era, I will not allow society to define morality.

When I was a kid, I once I said, *"Heck* no, Mom."

My father rolled his eyes and said, "Get upstairs to your room."

I said, "Dad, Dennis the Menace says 'heck' on television."

He said, "I don't care what Dennis the Menace says, you're not saying it in this house."

Wow!

## Another Assassination

My high school graduation was Saturday, June 8, 1968, two days after Senator Bobby Kennedy was assassinated, and sixty-three days after the assassination of Dr. Martin Luther King, Jr. What should have been a joyful time of celebration for accomplishment and achievement proved to be just short of a memorial service. How could this happen again? Where are we headed as a people?

The graduates were supposed to march around the track then onto the football field. Because of the threat of rioting, we marched from the administration building then directly across the fifty-yard line.

After Martin Luther King, Jr. was killed, neighborhoods of Cincinnati were ablaze with rioting and anger. There was much debate as to whether we would even have a graduation ceremony. The police officers were stationed around the first curve of the track and in the stands. It was a picture of martial law.

The city was on high alert. I don't remember anything about the speeches, only walking across the stage to receive my diploma and throwing my cap into the sky. Another chapter was closed. I never played another game at Stewart Park or Withrow High School.

# Chapter 4: Go
# West, Young Man

My parents dropped me off at the Greater Cincinnati, Northern Kentucky airport. They were sending junior off to college. Saying goodbye to parents wasn't easy for an eighteen-year-old leaving home for the first time. This was the only time I saw my dad tear up and tell me he loved me. Even though I knew that he loved me, he'd never told me until then.

The stewardess instructed us to fasten our seatbelts and extinguish cigarettes to prepare for takeoff. After three and a half hours, the Eastern Airlines Boeing 707 landed in El Paso, Texas. From my window seat I could tell that this wasn't Kansas anymore. On my recruiting visit in April, I didn't notice all the cacti, tumbleweeds, and brown everywhere. New Mexico State football training camp opened the next day. A new chapter of the Joey Jackson story had begun.

It was 1968. I was a seventeen-year-old freshman on the campus of New Mexico State University. My roots were deeply planted in the Midwest—born and raised in Cincinnati, Ohio. Las Cruces, New Mexico was never on the radar as a potential landing spot to play college football. I had never heard much about New Mexico—and nothing about Las Cruces! My only reference to New Mexico was in the Marty Robbins classic *El Paso*, where he quoted the *badlands of New Mexico*. It was bad alright. What was I doing here?

I was recruited by the University of Michigan, University of Illinois, University of Cincinnati, and a few other schools. However, because I hadn't taken the ACT test, my options were limited. At the top of my list was Ohio State University, but I never heard from the Buckeyes. My transition to Las Cruces, New Mexico was not seamless. It was a slow, stubborn, and painful adjustment. From my perspective, everything about this place was negative. I remember complaining about everything— there was no snow in November, no this or that, tacos smell like underarms. The gas was so cheap—only twenty-two cents a gallon? I'm out of here!

I reached out to Coach Jenkins from the University of Illinois. They recruited me, so I figured that maybe he could help. Coach Jenkins called New Mexico State and told them that I wanted to leave. Our head coach, Jim Wood, said I was tampering and couldn't transfer. I was stuck in the desert for the next four years.

My high school football coach, Marv Merritt, wanted me to attend the University of Cincinnati, but the University of Cincinnati wasn't good enough. Plus, it meant I would be staying home, and I want to go away to college. So away I went—1,523 miles from home. I was homesick and lonely. The University of Cincinnati sure sounded good now. I thought that maybe Coach Merritt could help me get home, so I wrote a letter to Coach Merritt and told him, "Coach, I made a mistake. I'd like to transfer to UC."

Coach Merritt played college football at UC. He accompanied me on my recruiting trip to UC. I knew that he would be excited to hear that I wanted to come home. Finally his letter came, and he said:

> Joey,
>
> Good to hear from you. It's too late to transfer. Stay where you are and make the best of it!
>
> Sincerely,
>
> Coach Merritt

*Make the best of it? Are you kidding me?* I didn't like anything about Las Cruces, New Mexico. I Didn't like Mexican food, the desert, or country music. Having been born and raised on that sweet soul music, good soul food, and cool soul brothers, I wanted out.

## ACT Test and College Recruiting

Jim Eddy was a backfield coach at New Mexico State. He had recruited me during my senior year at Withrow High School. Withrow was one of the larger high schools in Cincinnati. With an enrollment of over 3,600 students, the Tigers were always a contender for the public high school football championship.

Thirty-two years earlier, my dad broke the color line to play at Withrow High. The media referred to my dad as Jackson, the Negro half-back. He was a gridiron great, certainly a serious prospect for the next level. My dad was six feet two inches tall and weighed 210 pounds with speed like Jesse Owens, yet he never received one offer from a college scout. Many times my dad would lament, "Joe, I was born too soon." Looking at today's NFL salaries, I can relate.

Coach Jim Eddy was a smooth talker and a great recruiter. He convinced me to come to Las Cruces, take the ACT test, and to take a look at NMSU. It sounded great. They promised that I would be playing in a brand new state-of-the-art stadium my senior year. My plan was, they would fly me in, I'd visit a college campus, take the ACT test, come back home, and sign with Michigan State.

The night before we took the ACT test, the coaches gave us a copy of the exact test to study. I never had much of a problem with grades because I had a good memory. I figured it would be a piece of cake.

The next morning I was ready. There were about six football recruits among the thirty students who would be taking the test. There was to be no talking and we had to finish in an hour. A professor would walk down each row to monitor us. I couldn't believe what happened next.

Several times during the test, the professor would stop next to my desk and look at my answer. If I had a wrong answer, he would tap my foot and whisper the correct answer to me. I couldn't believe it. I thought, *Wow, this is great!*

After the tests were graded, the coaches told us the results. They looked me in the eye and told me that I scored a 14—a very low score for that test—and that nobody scored higher than a 14 that day. Because

NMSU was independent with no conference affiliation, they told us this was the only school where we could earn an athletic scholarship with such *low scores*. I was too embarrassed to call my dad and ask for advice.

We all signed the letter of intent. They told us to never tell anyone about it. Two weeks later, the university sent the actual scores home to the parents. My score was 28. The coaches lied to us! I could have gone to Michigan or anywhere else, but it was too late now.

## Traditional or Transitional?

In the mid-'70s, I attended a Fellowship of Christian Athletes summer conference in Estes Park, Colorado. To my surprise, Bobby Gill, one of my college coaches, was there. Coach Gill had given his life to Christ and was eager to share his faith. Coach Gill confessed to me that he was sorry for what happened at New Mexico State. I told Coach that I loved him and was glad he received Christ. I had moved on and had absolutely no regrets. I wouldn't trade my college experiences for any other university; NMSU was where God wanted me, regardless of the circumstances that led to my enrollment. In Genesis 25, Jacob received a birthright—not because he was a crafty schemer, but because of God's divine and sovereign appointment.

The Bible says that all things work together for good for those who love God, who called according to His purpose (Rom. 8:28). Old things are passed away; behold the glorious new has come (2 Cor. 5:17). God has done a tremendous work in my life. Guess what? *I love Mexican food and country music, and I live in the desert.* Can you believe it?

Transition is not always seamless. Many times God will ask if you are traditional or transitional. In other words, are you flexible? Can you adapt? Can you transition?

For the first eighteen years of my life, it was my way or the highway. My plan was to go college, earn a degree, and sign an NFL contract. This dream was born at Stewart Park when I saw the Panthers and reinforced later when I watched the Cleveland Browns' fullback, Jim Brown, break tackles and outrun smaller defenders for touchdowns.

Jim Brown was a man among boys. In a sense, I was also a man among boys simply because I towered over most of my friends and I could run. At Stewart Park, I once scored nine touchdowns in a pick-up game. Like Jim Brown, I could outrun smaller defenders, including my little brother—at least until he entered college.

My first year of organized football came at Lyons Junior High School in the seventh grade. As kids, whenever we played at Stewart Park, we took our shoes off and played tackle football without equipment—no pads or helmet. We could always run faster without shoes. Junior high school football was very different. We were issued real equipment and a playbook, and we practiced.

When coach asked each player what position they wanted to play, without hesitation I said, "Fullback."

Coach Barrett took one look at me, standing six feet tall and weighing well over two hundred pounds, and said, "I don't think so, son. You're going to be playing on the line; as a matter of fact, as big as you are, you might be the entire right side."

I said, "Coach, I want to play fullback like Jim Brown."

He said, "Okay—you can be a third string fullback or first team right tackle."

I choose fullback and didn't play one down that season. The next year I changed my position to right tackle. For the next twenty years of my football experience, I only scored one touchdown in an official game.

Team sports is a metaphor for unity and teaches many life lessons. I fell on a fumble in the end zone once. I learned that playing defensive end is just as important and fulfilling as rushing for 1,863 yards in an NFL season.

For personal and team success, sacking a quarterback is just as meaningful as a touchdown. Today in the NFL, edge rushers are paid more than fullbacks and even some running backs. They're said to be the rock stars of the NFL.

41

One of the positives about New Mexico State was that you could play on the varsity team in your freshman year. At that time, very few conferences allowed freshmen to play varsity. Because of the non-conference status of NMSU, you didn't have to wait for your sophomore year to play. If you were good enough, then "Put me in, Coach, I'm ready to play *today*."

We started the 1968 campaign in a hole, losing the first two games to Utah State and North Texas State University. North Texas State's roster was full of future NFL players, including four-time Super Bowl champion and Hall of Famer Mean Joe Green. That night, Green couldn't be blocked.

Mean Joe Green dominated our offensive line. We even moved our all-American defensive tackle—six-foot, five-inch, 300-pound Ruby Jackson—to offense to help slow down Mean Joe. We were blown out by North Texas State, 47-20. There's no classroom course that can prepare you for real-life experiences more than winning and losing in athletic competitions. The Lord taught me valuable lessons on my journey of faith.

# Chapter 5: Louisiana Tech

A fter the first five games of the season, I was itching for action with the varsity. The freshman season was over. We finished with a 4-0 record. By now, I was six feet five inches and 245 pounds, and I voiced my desire to play. I guess Coach Wood got the message, because I started at quick side defensive end on the varsity team for the remainder of the season. We finished the season with a 5-5 record.

I recorded five sacks that year, including sacking all-American quarterback Terry Bradshaw. What a thrill for an 18-year-old freshman! Terry played for Louisiana Tech, which was our last game of the 1968 season. Bradshaw would later join the Pittsburgh Steelers, leading them to four Super Bowl championships and MVP honors.

After we landed in Shreveport, Louisiana, we boarded two Trailways motor coaches for the 69-mile trip to Ruston, Louisiana. It had been a long day of travel, starting in Las Cruces with a 45-minute bus ride to the El Paso International Airport, then flying to Dallas, and finally connecting to Shreveport. We arrived at the hotel around 7 p.m. I couldn't wait to check in, but the coaches ordered us back on the bus. Was this the wrong hotel; were they overbooked?

No, it was Jim Crow's last stand—Negroes weren't allowed on the property except as maids and dishwashers. The New Mexico State University athletic department wasn't aware that Jim Crow was alive and well in Ruston, Louisiana, nor were they aware of *The Green Book*, an annual guide book for Negro road trippers.

*The Green Book* was published by a Black mailman from New York City named Victor Hugo Green. Because of the hardships faced by Black

Americans—such as white-owned businesses refusing accommodations, restaurants denying access into their establishments, and the threat of violence—Green founded and published *The Green Book* to avoid such problems and make the trip more enjoyable.

On that Friday night, where would we find *The Green Book* or a hotel that would have at least forty available rooms to accommodate Black and white players? The first hotel we stopped at directed us to a motel that would accept Negroes. We checked into the Sleep Right Inn.

This was an important game that would make or break our season. If we could win impressively, Coach Wood said we'd have a chance at a bowl invitation. We were leading Louisiana Tech at half time, but they came back and won 42 to 24. This was the first and only time I remember being called racial names by my opponent, and that was the only motivation I needed. I wanted to put that person on the ground. Years later, I talked with Terry Bradshaw about that game and experience, and he apologized for what happened that night. We've come a long way since 1968. Yet there's still more to do. A champion is never satisfied with a victory trophy because perfection is rarely attained through sports.

## My Conversion

In the spring of 1969, I was walking home from spring football practice when a student named Ken Johnson intercepted me on my path to Milton Student Union. He said, "Hey, big man, have you got five minutes?"

I said, "No, man, I'm hungry. I'm headed to the training table. We had a long scrimmage today."

He said, "This won't take long."

Ken looked harmless so I obliged. He opened a pamphlet called "The four spiritual laws." Ken told me that God loved me and had a plan for my life.

I said, "Man, that smells like religion. Aren't there Ten Commandments, and you're going to teach me? I'm out—not interested."

He said, "No, brother, hold on a minute; it's not religion, but relationship."

I told him, "I tried that religion thing when I was kid. It didn't work out."

Ken explained that because of sin there was something called a chasm between man and God. I knew I was a sinner but I had never heard the word *chasm* before. Surely he meant to say *cash*. I said, "Man, I got some cash in my pocket."

He said, "I'm not talking about money." He proceeded to explain that Jesus was the bridge to bring me into a relationship with God. I didn't know too much about a chasm, but I did have a praying grandmother who was believing God for my salvation. The Bible says the effectual, fervent prayer of a righteous person (grandmother) has much power (James 5:16).

I said, "I believe in God. I'm a Christian. I don't do drugs or alcohol. I'm not perfect, but I've never killed anyone. I go to church sometimes."

He said, "Great!" Then he showed a diagram with two circles. One circle had ego on the throne and the other has Christ on the throne. Then he asked, "What circle best represents your life right now?"

I muddled that, "It's the one with ego on the throne." I still didn't think this was going anywhere. I figured I would just hear the brother out, make him feel good.

He said, "Well, that can change right now," and asked if he could pray with me.

Before then, nobody had ever asked if they could do that. I said to myself, *Is he going to pray right here on the street? This will be embarrassing. Let's at least go to the dorm or around the corner. I don't want my teammates to think I'm weird or something.*

Before I could say no, Ken Johnson clasped my hand in his and wouldn't let it go while passersby stared. He asked me to repeat a prayer after him.

I prayed the prayer with him but didn't close my eyes. After the prayer, I walked away feeling no different; I didn't see a bright light, hear a voice, or get knocked off my donkey onto my hindquarters. It wasn't a Damascus-road transformation like Saul of Tarsus, but I believed Christ came into my heart and I've never been the same!

Gradually my life began to change. I experienced the new birth and began to grow in Christ. It was hard to explain, but for the first time in my life I understood that I could have a relationship with God. I grasped the concept of relationship. I had relationships with family, friends, and teammates.

As a defensive player, I've never been intercepted—that's my job. My job is to make plays and create turnovers. Turnovers can decide the outcome of a game. An interception can kill a drive and momentum. Ken Johnson intercepted me, and the Lord took it to *the House* for a pick-six all the way to glory.

## Protests and Movements

During the late '60s and early '70s, the college campus was a fire keg for young radicals. There were marches and protests for anything and everything. You could always count on the hippies, Jesus freaks, nonconformists, free lovers, acid trippers, flower people, and the streakers. If you wanted to protest something as insignificant as walking on a sidewalk crack, you could always find someone to march with you.

It seemed everyone was shouting the same words: "Peace and love, baby!" Everyone was carrying a sign. I remember after the Kent State shooting there were moratoriums on every major campus in America.

A group of students on the NMSU campus decided that we would join the rally. We made signs, Christian banners, and t-shirts that read "Jesus is the answer, another student for Christ." We were able to witness to many students that real peace and love only comes through a relationship with Jesus Christ, the Prince of Peace. The Jesus Movement was a radical dispensation that changed the lives of tens of thousands of college students in America. It gave me the boldness I needed to stand and fearlessly make the gospel known to others.

During my freshman year, we lived on campus in Garcia Hall, a brand new residence hall. My roommate was a six-foot-eight-inch sophomore basketball star named Jeff Smith from Camden, New Jersey. Jeff played on NMSU's Aggie basketball team that finished third in the nation in the final four. That was a great team that included future NBA stars Jimmy Collins, Sam Lacy, Jeff Smith, and Charlie Criss.

One day I asked Jeff if he wanted to go to church and he said yes. We didn't have a car, so we started walking. There was a small Black Baptist church on the other side of Las Cruces, but that was too far to go. Across from Garcia Hall was a small A-frame church within walking distance, so we started our journey. When we approached the long driveway, the church sign read "University Reformed Presbyterian Church."

Neither one of us knew what that meant, but we decided to go anyway, so we started up the long driveway. We came to the front door and pulled it opened. Man, that church was quiet! We quickly scanned the congregation and, of course, we were the only two chocolate drops in the box. I thought about leaving, but an elder waved us forward so we found a seat *up front*. The worship service was completely different from any church that I ever attended. There was no hooping, no Shouting Miss Jones, no hand fans advertising Johnson Funeral Home, and the service didn't last three hours like Trinity Baptist. The style was completely different. It was only 28 minutes. *I think I found a church*, I thought.

This was my first experience in an all-white church, not to mention in a Reformed Presbyterian church. The pastor's delivery was much like the style of a lecture from one of my college professors—not much emotion. But during that 28-minute sermon, I learned more about a relationship with God, the providence of God, and the grace of God than in the first eighteen years of my life.

In his message, Reverend Ted Martin would reference people like C.S. Lewis, Francis Schaffer, and Martin Lloyd Jones. I had never heard of them before. Reverend Mosely would only reference Martin Luther King, Jr.

As we made our exit, Wayne and Sue Kellogg extended a lunch invitation to us for the following Sunday afternoon. I don't think I would have come back, but I was tired of cafeteria food and the thought of a home cooked meal was hard to pass up. It was genius.

Every Sunday after church, some family would invite me to their home. The next week, Oscar and Harriett Black did the same thing. The following week, the invitation came from Dana and Sandy McQuinn, the Mieners, the Bales, the Lines, or John and Susan Pickett. This happened every Sunday for the next ten years. The church members were very friendly and kind. Some of my dearest friends in the world are from the University Presbyterian family.

It's amazing how the Lord used a lunch invitation from Wayne and Sue Kellogg in 1969 to open a door I would have never entered. I grew up in the Black Baptist church—and there was nothing Baptist, and certainly nothing Black, about University Presbyterian Church! The preaching and music were good, but the style wasn't mine. One of the song leaders played an acoustic guitar, which was unthinkable at Second Trinity Baptist Church.

Sometimes I would hear a rumor that "Mr. So-and-so is from Texas and he's real prejudiced. He doesn't like Black people at all." I would say to myself, *I never saw that in him, and I've been in their home many times.* I think the Lord was breaking down barriers on both sides.

I finished spring football as number one on the depth chart as quick side defensive end. After the spring game, I was awarded "most valuable defensive player." My defensive line coach, Don Kloppenburg, took me to lunch at my favorite buffet, The Mission Inn. All you could eat for $1.75. I remember that they had the best fried chicken in Las Cruces.

# Chapter 6: Home for the Summer

When my freshman year at NMSU was completed, I couldn't wait to get home. As we traveled to the El Paso airport in the spring of 1969, there was a song on the radio by The Archies called "Sugar, Sugar." I didn't know who The Archies were, but I loved that song. It was something about that melody that put a smile on my face. In the wake of the Vietnam conflict and unrest on campus, that song was the medicine for the soul and heart. It made you feel good. It sold well over a million copies, and even soul man Wilson Pickett recorded that tune. I love Pickett's take on the song, but I like The Archies' version better.

My dad found me a summer job at Dorman Products. Dorman Products was on his mail route, and he recommended me for a summer job. At one time, you could find Dorman Products' nuts and bolts in every auto parts store in America. At Dorman, most college students worked as stock boys or order fillers. If you were an order filler, you made thirty cents more an hour. Once I asked if I could be an order filler. Mr. Van Cleef advised against it, so I never asked again.

There were no Black students who were order fillers. Many of the employees didn't even have a high school degree. Some had been working there for twenty-five years only to earn fifty-seven cents an hour more than me. I would ask myself how I could do this kind of work for only $2.90 an hour. I suppose it was honest work, and people earned a living doing it, but I wanted something more.

During my first week at Dorman, I discovered that stock *boys* fifty and sixty years old were making the same hourly wage as me—an eighteen-year-old just out of high school. This was a reality check for me! I determined that if the NFL didn't work out, at least I would have a degree.

Old man Dorman would park his green 1967 Cadillac Coupe de Ville convertible in a special spot near the entrance. During lunch, I would go to the parking lot and dream about owning a car like that one day. That was all the motivation I needed. For four summers, I worked as a stock boy putting boxes of nuts and bolts on shelves.

There were two shifts at Dorman's. The early shift started at 8:00 a.m., and the afternoon shift was from 4:30 p.m. to midnight. I worked the first shift my first two summers, and I had a hard time punching in on time. I had no excuses; I used my grandmother's car and was only fifteen minutes from the plant; I was just lazy and not very motivated. In my last two years, they switched me to the afternoon shift. This was fine with me because I made thirty-five cents more per hour. I could visit friends and train in the morning. Even though I worked the second shift, I still had a hard time getting to work on time.

I remember being reprimanded by the plant manager, Joe Wegezer, for too many tardies. He told me, "Joey, if you're late one more time, we're going to have to let you go."

I was determined not to be fired, so on the last day of work, I added some water to the radiator of my car, which I would soon drive to Las Cruces. The only problem was the Corvair doesn't have a radiator. It's air-cooled. Consequently, I poured water into the oil spout and down into the crank shaft. On my way to work, the car began to backfire and sputtered along, spewing black smoke. The car died just short of the Dorman parking lot. I ended up pushing the car into the lot five minutes tardy. Because this was my last day before I went back to college, I didn't get fired. Even though there was not a bright future at Dorman's, the experience taught me responsibility.

During the summer, it was hard to find a place to train. My only options were the YMCA and my high school. The fitness center era was at least a decade ahead. My college coaches didn't give us an off-season workout program. I guess training was optional or on the honor system. Like the NFL, many players would use training camps to get in shape.

I was always into lifting weights, even in junior high school. When I was fourteen, my dad bought me a 110-pound weight set, and we didn't know anything about weight training. I started lifting weights so I could look like Charles Atlas, have more definition, and get more girls to like me.

# Chapter 7: There's Snot
# on My Jacket

Summer break ended, and I was back to NMSU for my sophomore year. Like many students, I was unsure of a major. To be honest, I really didn't care too much about a college degree. My real concern was signing an NFL contract. That was why I came to New Mexico State University, *I thought*. The football coaches at New Mexico State wanted me to major in physical education, which was fine with me. I figured I would be a gym teacher after my NFL career. I didn't care; I was going pro anyway.

My education curriculum included a creative writing course. Our sophomore English professor was Mark Medoff. Yes, the famous Mark Medoff, writer of the screenplay and movie *Children of a Lessor God*, *Everest*, *Clara's Heart*, *Good Guys Wear Black*, and his latest, *Walking with Herb*. Mark Medoff was a brilliant teacher and communicator. He knew how to motivate his students.

The class had just begun. Mark was at the podium when someone burst into the room, cursing and shouting, "You got snot on my jacket, I'm going to kick your butt!" We were stunned with silence.

I thought about intervening. *Maybe I'll give this idiot a forearm shiver or tackle him to the ground.* I thought that surely one of the other professors would come in before the first punch was thrown. Just as I began to stand up to make my move, Mark said, "This is acting; I want you to write what you just saw." What an object lesson for a classroom of eighteen- and nineteen-year-old students. I never forgot that.

After grading my paper, Mark told me that I did a good job of expressing my thoughts and said I should consider English as a major. No one ever encouraged me to consider English as a major. Yet when I look back over my life and the road that I've traveled, I see the hand print of a sovereign God leading along each step. The Lord will use different individuals to help us reach our destiny and fulfill God's purpose for our lives. I majored in English literature.

In 2017 I attended a New Mexico State football game. It was the alumni weekend. I was running late and didn't want to miss the kickoff. As I walked toward the gate, I passed someone I recognized but couldn't remember who it was. Before I took another step, I thought, *Could that be Mark Medoff?* It was! He was there with his wife. We had a great visit. I told him that he was the reason I majored in English and never forgot the object lesson about the snot.

He laughed and said, "Joey, you have a great memory." He told his wife, "This is Joey Jackson; he was the real deal."

I'm not sure what he meant by that, but I assume it was a compliment. We remained friends on social media until he passed in 2019. I wish he could have read my manuscript!

# Chapter 8: Clergy or Coach?

I n 1969 the University Reformed Presbyterian church voted in a new pastor, Leonard T. Van Horn. Pastor Van was our summer youth camp speaker. He preached a series of messages called the beatitudes of Christ. Pastor Van reminded me of my high school coach Marv Merritt. He wore a military buzz cut, stood about six feet three inches, and weighed about 235 pounds.

Mr. Van was a former football player and coach. His no-nonsense approach caught some people off guard. His style was all Van Horn. He didn't fit my definition of a minister, but I liked that type of leader and preacher. We bonded immediately.

During his football days, he had been an offensive lineman at Kings College. His mentor was Coach Vince Lombardi. Van knew football as well as he knew the Word. He could have easily been a great coach. His season at University Presbyterian was only four years. During his pastorate, the church grew as it reached out to more University students and faculty. His vision was to teach the Word and evangelism. There was not much on-campus evangelism coming from University Presbyterian compared to Campus Crusade for Christ or the Baptist Student Union.

I don't remember too many sermons from 1969, but his impact on my life resonates today. We closed out the season with a Thanksgiving home game against Colorado State University on November 27, 1969. They had a good team that featured all-American running back and future Los Angeles Ram Lawrence McCutcheon. Also playing with CSU was Earlie Thomas, my future New York Jets roommate.

By our final game of the year, both teams had identical records of 4-5. We needed a win to finish the season at 500. For my sophomore season, the coaches moved me inside to right defensive tackle. My natural position is defensive end. Defensive tackle wasn't where I wanted to play, so I had to adjust.

Colorado State jumped off to an early lead. In the second quarter, our defense knocked out their starting quarterback. From that point onward, we shut down their offense. Their backup quarterback was extremely quick, but he lacked experience. I sacked him twice. We won the game 21-20.

## Christmas Gifts and Heartbreak

The fall semester ended, and I flew home to Cincinnati for Christmas break. If you were a student, you could fly student stand-by from El Paso, Texas to Cincinnati for only $40.40. It was stand-by, and seats were limited, but stand-by was part of the adventure for a college student. I remember when I flew home for Christmas, we got rerouted to Nashville, Knoxville, and Lexington before arriving in Cincinnati, which is actually in Northern Kentucky. I was so excited to be home for Christmas that I took a taxi cab from the Greater Cincinnati Airport to Madisonville. The cab fare nearly broke me. It was $6.50 for a twenty-mile cab ride.

When I arrived home, my father told me that someone stole his car. I was upset because I thought I knew who it was. We found the car about a block away. My friend Greg Williams told me he thought some of my so-called friends had stolen it. If the Lord hadn't changed my life, I would have chased those "friends" all the way to Kentucky to get revenge.

My grandmother surprised me with a Christmas gift that would change my life. She said, "Joey, I want you to have my car." I was shocked. It meant so much for an underclassman to have a car on campus. No, it wasn't a fancy sports car, but it was wheels, a 1964 rear engine Chevy Corvair. I couldn't wait to get back to campus. No more borrowing a friend's car to take my girl to the movies or walking all the way to Breland Hall for a math class.

I had my own ride now. I knew my girlfriend, Yolanda, would be excited that I had my own transportation. Before that, we walked or biked everywhere. My brother and I loaded up the car with Christmas gifts for Yolanda. Mom Jackson, my grandmother, bought her a beautiful coat and purse along with the many presents I had picked out. Our trip was all mapped out by AAA. It would be a two-and-a-half-day drive to Las Cruces. I assured my parents that Mike and I would observe all the speed limits and that I would pull over when tired. It was a great road trip. We spent the night in Missouri and Tucumcari, New Mexico. A few motels said they had vacancies, yet when we tried to check in they said they were full. It was the same old song, and I knew all the lyrics. Other than that, the trip to Las Cruces was safe and without incident.

We arrived in Las Cruces on Saturday afternoon. I couldn't wait to show Yolanda my car and for her to open her Christmas presents. We met that evening. I was looking for a hug and kiss. Instead, she wanted to end our relationship so she could date other guys. My heart sank. I asked why but she never gave me a clear explanation. She said, "I'm very sorry, Joey. It's over." I was so hurt, sad, and embarrassed. I had told my brother all about her, and he was anxious to meet her.

It took me several months to get up from that knockdown. I was in bad shape. I felt like a stupid fool—all those Christmas presents and my grandmother's Corvair. I went ahead and let her keep the gifts.

What made it worse was that I had introduced my roommate, Jeff Smith, to Yolanda's sister, and he was dating her. They got married just before the spring semester ended. I was the best man at his wedding, and her sister Yolanda was the maid of honor. Yolanda was my first girlfriend and true love. But life goes on. I couldn't see it then, but the Lord was protecting me and saving me for Terill. The rest of my sophomore year was a blur. I went home for the summer and back to Dorman Products.

## A Bad Game

My junior season started with a bang. I was preseason all-American, and I was on track to the NFL. My parents flew in for the University of Texas at El Paso Mieners (UTEP) homecoming game. This was their first visit to Las Cruces. We shopped in Jaurez, visited White Sands National Monument, and, of course, we had Mexican food at La Posta. We also went to dinner with Pastor Van Horn and his wife.

Our team had several future NFL players, and the pro scouts were watching. I knew they'd be at the game because I received letters from NFL teams stating that I was a serious prospect. It was all in front of me. I was ready for a great game but didn't play one. I have no excuses either. I should have played better. That loss haunts me today. I wish I could go back! We lost to the Miners, and I probably lost respect in the eyes of the NFL scouts.

Life lessons are learned and taught every day. Even though we can't undo the past, we can undo some of the decisions and habits that cause us to be ineffective. We changed defensive line coaches. Don Kloppenburg, my defensive line coach, took a head coaching job at a junior college in California. Coach Klopp was like Mr. Van—they didn't want us to make excuses, just do the job. They both reminded me of my dad. I understand coaching opportunities, but I wish Coach Kloppenburg would have coached me for my entire football career, including the NFL.

After the game, I was more disappointed in my poor performance than our homecoming loss. My parents traveled from Cincinnati to see me play, and I stunk up the joint! We went to church Sunday, and Pastor Van introduced my family to the congregation. Then we had lunch with the Kelloggs. They flew home Tuesday.

Pastor Van called me into his office on Wednesday. When I arrived, his secretary told me he was waiting for me. I needed a shoulder to lean on and a sympathetic ear, but I got neither.

He closed the door and said, "Joey, sit down."

I didn't get a shoulder to lean on. Instead, I got a foot in the rear.

His first words were, "I don't know what those coaches are telling you, but if I were the coach, I would have benched you; you did nothing the whole game."

I lowered my head in agreement and nodded. I listened to every word. He started with my lack of hustle and ended with my four missed tackles, one penalty, and seeming lack of effort. That was his main concern and criticism.

I can't explain why I played so badly. I certainly didn't plan for this outcome, but it happened. Pastor Van knew the right buttons to push. I was embarrassed and determined to play better for the rest of the season.

He said, "Joey, if I didn't think you were one of the finest defensive ends in college football, I wouldn't be so tough on you." Then he added, "You know I love you, don't you?"

I said, "Yes, Pastor Van, I know that."

I never had another bad game in college football.

The next week against the University of Texas at Arlington (UTA), I battled all-American six-foot, eight-inches, 270-pound Steve Sullivan. I received the skull and crossbones for top defensive player of the game. I made two quarterback sacks in twelve seconds, which is still some kind of Aggie record.

The Lord put Pastor Van along my path to enrich my life with God's character, determination, and boldness. He sends the right people to impact change at the right time. In John 10:10, Jesus says that the thief comes to steal, kill, and destroy, but He comes so we might have life abundantly.

I reached out to Pastor Van several years later and thanked him for being in my life. I told him that I was in full-time ministry as an evangelist, and I was grateful for the impact he made in my life.

He said, "That's great, Joey. I'm so proud of you."

I never saw or spoke to him again. Pastor Van died three years later.

# Chapter 9: Show Me the Money

T he NCAA doesn't allow someone to enter the NFL draft until their class graduates or four years from their senior year of high school. Had that not been the case, I would have declared for the NFL draft after my junior year in college. We were warned not to sign with an agent until the season ended. It would be a violation that could bring sanctions against New Mexico State University.

I received several letters and phone calls from agents who wanted me to sign before the season. Remembering what our coaches told us, I declined. One particular agent asked to meet with me on the NMSU campus. Just talking with the agent wasn't a violation, so we met. I picked him up in my grandmother's 1964 Chevy Corvair. He took a look at my Corvair and said, "Man, I can put you into something sweeter than this thing today." The Corvair wasn't exactly a chick magnet, but at least I had some wheels on campus.

The agent asked if I would drive to the desert and talk. When we were outside of the city, he told me to pull off the road, which I did. Then he looked around before opening a briefcase filled with one hundred dollar bills. He said, "These are yours; no one will ever find out. All you need to do is to sign a contract to be represented by my agency. Your name will be in code." He showed me a list of coded names, all numbers and symbols. He continued, "Brother, you better take this money." It was tempting. Even though I had a full athletic scholarship, I had very little spending money. I was given a stipend of only fifteen dollars a month; besides, no one would ever find out.

For some reason, I began to share my testimony. I told the agent that in the past, I would have easily taken the money without hesitation, but Jesus Christ had changed my life, so I couldn't take it.

He said, "Well, that's great, I love Jesus too, but you'd be a fool to turn this down."

I guess I was a fool. We met several years later when I was playing with Jacksonville. The Lord had done a work of redemption in his life. Neither one of us brought up the money incident.

The 1971 season would be my last year of college football. We opened the season at home with a loss to Utah State and ended the season with a loss to Colorado State. We had losses to Southern Methodist University, UTEP, and North Texas State. It wasn't much to brag about, as we ended up at 500 again. I was looking forward to bigger and brighter days ahead.

Draft day came on February 2, 1972. Back then, there were seventeen rounds for the draft. My agent assured me that I would be selected in the first or second round. There was no Indianapolis combine, no pro day, no NFL two-day draft event in New York City or another NFL city like there is now. The NFL scouts would come to your college campus, time you in the forty-yard dash, then take you to La Posta for some good Mexican food. That was it. The day before the NFL draft, I received a package from the Dallas Cowboys. The letter read that I should be near a phone on draft day. They also told me that I didn't need an agent.

I told my parents that I expected to be drafted by the Cowboys. The first round came and went quickly. Then the second, third, fourth. Nothing—no call from any team. I decided that I needed some air, so I went for a drive to Mesilla Park.

When I returned to campus, a student shouted at me with the news. He said, "Joey, you were drafted in the fifth round by New York!"

I asked, "New York? Jets or Giants?"

He said, "The New York Jets!"

I couldn't believe it. The Jets never sent me a questionnaire, letter, or called. I was very excited. *Wow, I'm going to play with Broadway Joe Namath,* I thought to myself.

The Jets signed me to a two-year contract for a whopping $53,000. This included a $7,500 signing bonus. If I were playing today, I'd be a multi-millionaire. My agent said that head coach and GM Weeb Ewbank wanted to keep me hungry. I didn't care about my contract; I was just happy for the opportunity to play defensive end in the NFL, to live a dream. Several weeks later, I flew to New York City, signed my contract, and met the other rookies.

There were few guaranteed contracts. Each player had to make the team. The contract only protected the team, not the player. The player could be cut anytime and given only an apple and a road map and sent on their way. I immediately gave my parents some money and tithed to my church. I also opened a checking account. Everything was looking good. I was the big man on campus, in the NFL, and I was a long way from Madisonville.

# Chapter 10: Drafted Again—in the First Round

I received a registered letter in the mail. The letter read that I was drafted again—this time, to the military. *Wow, everybody wants Big Joe, including Uncle Sam.* I called the Jets and informed them of my situation. I had already spent some of my signing bonus, so I wondered if I would have to repay the money I spent. I couldn't believe it. Could my NFL career be over before I ever suited up in a New York Jets uniform?

In college, I had two years of Air Force ROTC, which certainly doesn't qualify to prepare someone for Vietnam, but I knew the possibility loomed that I could be drafted into the military. In April of 1972, I received orders to report to Fort Bliss Army base in El Paso, Texas for induction. I had been drafted into the US Army.

Although my dream to play pro football could be put on hold or not happen at all, there was no way I would go to Canada to avoid the military draft. If it was my time to serve, I would proudly fight for my country. My grandfather did in World War I, and my father served as a Marine sergeant in World War II. Yet, to be honest, I prayed that God would make a way, but how would that happen? My military draft number was 35 out of 364. The lower your number, the greater chance you had to get drafted. Although the war was winding down, I wasn't excited about going to Vietnam. But it was out of my hands.

We caught the bus at 7:30 in the morning for Fort Bliss. No one said much during the 40-minute bus ride. We all knew what this trip meant. The young recruits went through a battery of testing. Military doctors examined the results of the X-rays of my knees. During the entire process at Fort Bliss, I kept thinking about the five close friends who never came back from Vietnam—Clarence Hall, Paul Green, James Sonny Carroll, Kenny Allen, and Clarence Mitchell. They paid the ultimate sacrifice, and I am so thankful for their service.

Several others came back different. Junie Rice was three years older than me. His real name was Paul Rice Jr., but everyone called him Junie Rice. He was someone I respected and admired.

Junie was a terrific long-distance runner. He lettered in track at Withrow and later ran in college. We lived on the same street. Junie was drafted into the army and went to Vietnam. Mr. and Mrs. Rice were very active at Trinity Baptist Church. Mr. Paul Rice Sr. was a deacon, and Mrs. Rice was my Sunday school teacher. You didn't mess with Louella Rice. She would tap you on the head with the handle of a church fan if you were disruptive.

I was probably in the tenth grade when Junie came home on leave from Vietnam. We were sitting on my front porch when he began to tell me what it was like to be in combat in Vietnam. He saw death and destruction on both sides. He said you could buy a Vietnamese girl for a can of K-rations. I had never heard of the term *K-ration* before. With soldiers dying around him, he was determined to kill as many of the Viet Cong as he could. These words were so strange from someone who never cursed and was an academic. As he shared each experience, he became more emotional, reliving every battle. He started swearing loudly. I tried to quiet him. Certainly my father would burst through the front door any minute for using bad language. I know Dad must have heard the entire conversation because the living room window was open. Still, there was no response from him.

Maybe my dad recognized the effects of combat on an 18-year-old kid who was fighting for his country. Junie later returned home, graduated from the University of Cincinnati, and took a job on Wall Street. We connected a few times when I played with the Jets.

My grandmother told me that my father never drank anything harder than lemonade and Pepsi Cola. When World War II ended, my dad's sobriety ended. Big Jack came home a different man. He soon divorced his first wife and started drinking alcohol. I know very little about his first wife. I wish I knew more.

At Fort Bliss, I held my breath and whispered a prayer. Just then, they called my name. "William Joseph Jackson, step forward." The military doctors determined that although I was motivated and capable of playing professional football, my knees would not sustain the rigors of being a soldier in the US Army.

"You flunked your physical to be drafted into the army, and you're reclassified from 1A to 4F."

For me, that moment was just like winning the lottery. I informed the Jets, and they flew me into New York City, where I passed their physical. I was shocked. It was only the hand of the Lord guiding my steps. Sometimes a championship is decided by a walkover you never saw coming.

# Chapter 11: Rookie Training Camp

I n the summer of 1972, I was a rookie in the New York Jets' training camp. That's when an NFL training camp was a training camp. Six preseason games, eight weeks of boot camp, with scrimmages twice a day. Over one hundred players fought for a spot on a 40-man roster with the unwritten quota of only 19 Black players.

When I think of training camp, oddly enough I think of my childhood friend Greg Williams. Greg could do it all. He had the looks, personality, and he was a great singer and athlete. We were blood brothers, lived on the same street. We both dreamed of playing professional football. He had all the natural talent in the world. If anyone was going pro, it would be Greg. I thought about the times we sang doo-wop on the street corner, the dumb fight we had in the sixth grade, and the time we stole Mr. Peaks' 1954 Chevrolet.

## Joy Ride Gone Bad

We were in ninth grade and knew where we could pick up a car. Old man Peaks lost his car key and kept the ignition in the "on" position. One night we took his car on a joyride. It was a three-speed standard shift on the column. Greg couldn't drive a stick but wanted to drive anyway. I refused to let him but changed my mind when the alcohol began to take effect.

Greg took the wheel. As he shifted the stick from first to second, he made a right turn that went wide, sideswiping an oncoming car. But it wasn't just any oncoming car and any driver. It was Crazy McCoy that he hit. McCoy had just been released from the Cincinnati Work House.

Somehow Greg was able to get the car in gear, and we sped away then jumped out of the car while it was still running. We sprinted down the railroad tracks that led to the highway. Once it was clear, we walked toward the road. Six miles from home, we started thumbing for a ride. No one stopped.

After a few miles of walking, a car finally slowed down. *Oh no, God, please no.* It was Crazy McCoy. He was nobody to mess with! What would we do? If we ran, he would come looking for us. We jumped in the back seat and kept it cool. McCoy told us what happened to him, and we held our breath as he brandished a .38 special. He swore and said that if he had gotten to his weapon fast enough, he would have blown their heads off. We made some kind of lie up that we were at a party and someone started drinking alcohol. Our parents warned us to leave if alcohol was served at a party, so we were going home. McCoy dropped us off at my house. Before we said goodnight, Greg and I high-fived each other and bragged and laughed. We fooled this chump. I immediately went inside my house and upstairs to bed, said goodnight to my parents, said my prayers, hit the sack, and fell asleep.

A knock on my bedroom door awakened my sleep. It was my sister Mary. She told me a cop was downstairs looking for me.

Someone saw us steal the car and called the police. They took Greg and me to the station, where the cops separated us. Greg told the truth and was released; I lied and was arrested and taken to jail, busted again for car theft. They warned me that if I ever stole another car, I was headed to the Boys Industrial School in Lancaster, Ohio, or BIS for short.

I had good intentions of doing better, but sadly, the threat of reform school and the shame and embarrassment I caused my family weren't enough to keep me from poor choices. It's a miracle I didn't end up in reform school, prison, or worse.

The phone rang after the evening practice in my Hofstra University dormitory room, the New York Jets' training site. The operator said it was a long-distance call for me. It was my dad. I could hear the hesitation and regret in his voice.

He said, "Joey, I…I have some bad news for you."

Immediately I thought of my grandmother.

Dad said, "No, Mom Jackson's fine. Greg Williams was shot and killed last night in Atlanta."

Dad told me how Greg was involved in an armed robbery. I couldn't believe it. Not Greg! I sat on my dorm bed numb and frozen. How could this happen? We were both kids on Ravenna Street with big dreams. Here I am, living the dream we both had, yet Greg's dream was shot down because of a poor choice. I couldn't even attend his funeral. I quickly learned that potential and talent are overrated. It always comes back to good decisions.

## Consequences and Memories

In March of 2018, I went home to Cincinnati. I was driving in my old neighborhood and pulled into Greg's driveway. Ninety-five-year-old Bud Williams, Greg's father, had just parked his car and was walking across the yard.

I said, "Mr. Williams, how are you doing?"

He said, "I'm doing fine, and you, sir?"

I asked, "Do you know who you're talking to?"

He said, "No, I don't have any idea."

I said, "It's me, Joey Jackson." At 95 years, he's a little hard of hearing. I repeated myself.

He said, "Joey, I can't believe it!" We hadn't seen each other in over 55 years.

We went inside his house, and he immediately opened up a photo album. The house looked the same but smaller than I remember. Bud had nine children. Four have passed away. We talked about Greg and what actually happened the night he was killed.

Bud told me that Greg moved to Atlanta and was trying to rob a bank or Brink's truck when he was shot and killed by an undercover cop. No other details were given. After 46 years, I could tell Bud didn't have closure. He wasn't exactly sure how Greg was killed. He told me that after the shooting, Greg's widow came to visit him. When Bud asked what happened, she bolted from the room without saying a word. He never saw her or his grandchildren ever again.

The Jesus Movement was a great era for evangelism, revival, and boldness. Greg and I were born again under this great dispensation when young people's lives dynamically transformed. Students were ripe for something real. Many rebelled against the establishment, the system. They saw Jesus as a nonconformist with a beard and sandals; He was relatable. They discovered that there was no greater high than being high on Jesus. Man, those were some good times. Some of my best friends today were birthed out of the Jesus Movement. But some didn't finish the race. One of the keys to a championship is finishing strong.

# Chapter 12: Joe Wants Dough, Says He Can Play Better

My dream was finally coming true—my opportunity to play in the NFL. I was excited to get to the training camp. I couldn't wait to get started! I was so excited I asked the Jets if I could come in early. That was the first and only time I ever did that. I thought about driving my grandmother's Corvair to camp, but that might be a college move. Anyway, I assumed NFL players didn't drive Chevy Corvairs; they drove Chevy Corvette Stingrays.

Joe Namath was in a contract dispute with the owners and general manager, Weeb Ewbank, who also happened to be our head coach. The two were at an impasse. Joe felt he could play better with a better salary, and Weeb wasn't sure. Weeb knew the value of having Joe in camp and needed to get him signed. He also knew the value of a dollar. Somehow the two sides came together, and Joe's one-week holdout ended.

My defensive line coach, Buddy Ryan, and I were standing in the dormitory lobby when Joe finally reported to training camp. I couldn't wait to meet him. He wore a pair of shades and had a nice tan. Buddy introduced us, and I shook his hand with a big smile on my face. The media followed Joe everywhere. At the very moment that we reached out to shake hands, some photographer snapped a picture that appeared in every major newspaper in North America and even Australia. I was in the right place at the right time!

My father saw my picture and the headline that read, "Joe wants more dough," and immediately thought that I was the one who wanted more money. I told my dad to read the article; it wasn't me.

Coach Buddy Ryan was a results-only type of coach. Excuses had no place with Buddy. His twin sons, Rex and Robb, were skinny kids who would sometimes carry my helmet.

Everyone loved Buddy Ryan who got to know him. Buddy Ryan was the defensive guru of the 46 defense. This helped the '85 Bears become Super Bowl champions. Along with his wit and his no-nonsense attitude, Buddy also was known for something else—ups and downs. For cardio, we didn't run stadium stairs, do wind sprints, or gassers. We did something called ups and downs.

After a two-and-a-half-hour practice, the defensive line would gather around Coach Ryan for final thoughts. Buddy would then line us by twos for cardio. Then he would blow his whistle, and we would run in place. He would yell, "Up, down, back, up, down!" until we did a least a hundred or until someone passed out. How many we did was determined by his mood, our practice, and whoever was our upcoming opponent.

Buddy had a great way to motivate us—through intimidation and fear. I loved Buddy Ryan, but I hated ups and downs. When Buddy took the Vikings defensive line job, I was relieved. I was going to miss a great defensive line coach, but not those ups and downs! But that was short-lived because Buddy had the nerve to take me with him to Minnesota.

When you're a rookie, you're at the mercy of the veterans. You listen to every word they tell you. The only problem with that is they won't talk to you because you're essentially trying to get them traded, released, or waived. You want their job.

The second week of two-a-days, I learned that just because someone calls your name doesn't mean they're talking to you. We just finished a hot afternoon practice. I had one stop before my body collapsed on my bed—the cafeteria. As I was walking along the fence where the fans were standing, Buddy Ryan said, "Big Joe, I think they're calling for you."

He told me the girls like the young rookies because they're single and think you've signed a big contract. The closer I got to the fans, I realized that they were still calling my name.

One cute blonde said, "Joe, we love you. Here's my phone number."

I thought, *Man, this is great!*

As I reached for her number, I introduced myself. "I'm Joe Jackson, rookie from New Mexico State."

She said, "Who are you? We want Joe Namath!"

I looked over, and Buddy and some of the other veterans were doubled over, busting a gut with laughter. Another lesson learned.

## One Win, One Time

One hot July afternoon, the defensive line was working on pass rush. The big offensive lineman was holding me. Coach Ryan yelled, "Joe Jackson, you're getting beat; you're not going to make this team. We're going to send you back to Mexico or wherever you're from because you can't play at this level."

I said, "Coach, he's holding me!"

He said, "This is the NFL; what do you think they do here?"

For pass rush, Buddy would usually match me against Winston Hill (who finally was inducted into the Hall of Fame in 2020). Winston was always my toughest blocker. He had great footwork and technique, and he didn't have to hold you. I never had much success against him. Buddy Ryan was on my case, and none of my college moves worked on Winston. I don't think Buddy liked rookies. Desperation morphed into fear—the fear of getting cut. They were cutting players every day. Louis, my roommate, was cut one morning. I needed a new move and quickly.

The Baltimore Colts were playing the Pittsburgh Steelers in a preseason game. Six-foot, eight-inch, 285-pound defensive end Bubba Smith was playing with the Colts. Smith used a move called the head slap on a Steeler offensive right tackle. It worked. He easily beat his opponent for a sack. I thought maybe I should try that on Winston. But then I thought maybe he would hit me back. At this point, I had nothing to lose. So I tried it on Winston.

Namath started the cadence: "Green 38, Green 38, hut, hut." I sprang off the line like a cobra. I did a quick inside fake, and all-pro tackle

Winston moved to his left to cut me off. I quickly stepped to my left and slapped the right side of his helmet as hard as I could. He looked stunned. I maneuvered past him and wrapped my arms around Namath for a sack but didn't bring him down. No way. A sure way to get cut from the roster was to sack Joe Namath in practice. You don't tackle Joe Namath.

For the first time, I beat Winston Hill. I couldn't wait for the evening meeting to look at the practice film. When that play came up, Buddy Ryan yelled, "Stop that projector!" He said, "Joe Jackson, look at yourself. You beat Winston Hill; Winston Hill's an all-pro. What do you think that makes you?"

I fumbled, "Gee, Coach, I don't really know."

Coach Ryan shouted, "That makes you an all-pro—today."

In my eight-year career, I never made all-pro, but in my rookie year I finished second in quarterback sacks and was featured in Super Star Sports as a most promising rookie. Sometimes it only takes one win one time to eradicate a history of defeat and failure.

The Old Testament book of Ruth tells the story of Naomi and Ruth. Naomi experienced a series of defeats when her husband and two sons died. Because of her losses, Naomi, which means "my joy," said, "Don't call me 'my joy' anymore. Look around me—I don't have a husband, both of my sons have died; call me Mara." That name means "very bitter." She said she went out full but came back empty. She had some losses, some defeats, and they caused her to change her name.

History has taught me never to allow your circumstances in life to cause you to change your name. Little by little, Naomi regained her joy. She directed her daughter-in-law Ruth to a field where Boaz was standing with the reapers. Boaz and Ruth eventually married and produced a son named Obed. Naomi didn't give up and quit. She found purpose.

One win, one time. The Bible tells us that Boaz begot Obed, Obed begot Jesse, and Jesse begot David in the lineage of Jesus. There's a dream that God wants to birth in you. Don't give up; keep looking for that one win one time.

Later I learned that some things in life are taught while others are caught. At first, I didn't understand the value of Buddy Ryan's ups and downs; much later, I caught on to their importance.

Ups and downs were not only great cardio but also a terrific way to maintain your upper body strength during the long NFL season. It was like doing one hundred push-ups. But more than that, we have ups and downs in life. We get cut down, cut off, and cut up as if we're going through a shredder. If you lay there and start feeling sorry for yourself, you'll get run over.

Sometimes we'll find ourselves on the Jericho road, beaten, robbed, and left for dead. Everyone passes by, but no one helps—not even the priest or Levite. Yet help came from an unlikely source—a Samaritan, a *good* Samaritan. A valuable lesson I learned from football is that you never know where help will come from. Also, the scoreboard only tells you who's got the most points. It doesn't always tell you who the winner is. You can recover from a fall, just like ups and downs. You hit the ground, and you get back up.

# Chapter 13: Bills at Shea

Because the game was pretty much decided, Buddy Ryan pulled the starters. This was my opportunity. Technically, Buffalo was still in the game, and Bills quarterback Dennis Shaw had no intention of running out the clock. I was familiar with Dennis Shaw. He played his college ball at San Diego State. Shaw was a brilliant passer who once lit us up; they beat us 70-21. We played them my sophomore year at Jack Murphy Stadium. I never forgot that embarrassing butt whipping—the worst loss I've experienced on any level.

The Bills had a formidable offensive line to open holes for O.J. Simpson. Playing right tackle was the Ohio State all-American and first-round draft choice tackle Dave Foley. Dave was a first-round draft choice of the New York Jets. The Jets traded Foley to Buffalo for future considerations. During training camp, we battled hard in pass rush protection drills. Dave was a good player, and it wouldn't be easy to pressure the quarterback.

We beat the Buffalo Bills 41-3. I sacked Dennis Shaw three times. Was this college revenge? No way. I never even thought about the trouncing that happened in college. That Sunday, I was in a zone. I was unstoppable. I was determined not to fail, not to be denied. Experience, passion, desire, and talent are keys to victory as an athlete. As a believer, my confidence rests in who I am in Christ—knowing that I can overcome all things and that it's not my fight.

That's the struggle I must work out with fear and trembling every hour and day of my life (Phil. 2:12). Victory is determined by yielding to the Holy Spirit. Faith is confidence in what we hope for and assurance about what we do not see (Heb. 11:1). In my flesh, I can't do very much. In Christ, I can do all things through Him who strengthens me (Phil. 4:13).

Buddy Ryan would talk about defensive tackle Steve Thompson. Steve Thompson was on the New York Jets 1969 Super Bowl team and played college football at the University of Washington. He was the New York Jets' second-round draft choice in 1968. Steve had the call of God on his life.

After the 1970 season, Steve felt that God called him to step away from football at the prime of his career. So he walked away from the NFL. Buddy Ryan and many others couldn't understand why Steve would leave the NFL. Buddy would say, "It doesn't make any sense why he would join a bunch of hippies." He thought Steve was involved with some cult of flower children. No, Steve heard the voice of God and was led along a new path.

Winston Hill and my roommate Earlie Thomas would talk about Steve as a man of strong Christian character and faith. After a couple of seasons away from football, Steve felt a release to come back to the Jets. I was excited for the opportunity to meet Steve but wondered how the Jets would keep seven defensive linemen. Back then there were only forty players on an NFL roster. Would I be cut? I wasn't sure what was going to happen, but they added Steve to the roster and kept seven defensive linemen.

Steve played himself into shape but wasn't in football shape. We played the Miami Dolphins in the Orange Bowl. That would be the same Dolphin team to go undefeated. Buddy put Steve into the game. He lasted for only a couple of plays before Larry Little broke his leg. Steve hobbled off the field and never played another game that season. Although his leg was broken in two places, his spirit was intact and strong as ever. That really spoke to me. I'm sure others had their opinions about what happened, but I never forgot how Steve continued to stand for God in the midst of a trial.

In that same game, my faith was put to the test. The Jets had a great opportunity to defeat the 7-0 Dolphins. Namath was hot. The defense held the Dolphins to three and out. They were in punt formation. I was playing on the punt return team. Buddy Ryan told me to go in there and block a punt.

I broke through the line with a clear path to Larry Seiple, the punter. Just as he booted the football, my momentum carried me into him. I received a fifteen-yard penalty for roughing the kicker, number 86. I wanted to go somewhere and hide; I lost the game. We had a chance, and I blew it. I knew when we got back to New York I'd be cut from the team. Maybe they wouldn't even bring me back to New York. Perhaps they would leave me in Miami. I didn't handle my disappointment very well. I was full of fear and doubt.

Steve Thompson broke his leg in two places and was never the same player. Yet he always seemed to look at the big picture. I made a rookie mistake that I could learn from. I thank the Lord for bringing Steve Thompson back to the New York Jets.

We had a great team of believers on the Jets to teach me how to be a Christian in the NFL. If it wasn't for Steve Thompson, Winston Hill, Earlie Thomas, Paul Crane, and others, my faith would have been compromised. Steve ended up pastoring a Foursquare church in Washington State. I've preached for him a couple of times. He and his wife, Starla, attended our athletes' conference.

## "Hey Whitey"

During my rookie year, businessman and friend Joe Defalco asked if I would attend a gala for a charity. Joe is the type of person to whom everybody owes a favor. He helped me purchase my first Cadillac El Dorado from Atherton Cadillac, made sure I got a great deal, and helped to secure my down payment with the least out-of-pocket expense, not including ten game tickets.

Outside of my brother and Junie Rice, I knew very few people in New York, so I was glad to put the tickets to good use. There were several other New York Jets players—Steve Thompson, Roy Kirksey, and John Mooring—who attended the gala event. There were also a few New York

Yankee baseball players. We were introduced, signed some pictures, and squeezed some palms. It was so boring that I don't remember anything else about the evening. I could hardly wait to get back to my apartment and watch a good movie.

I couldn't help but notice that one of the New York Yankee players had twice as many autograph seekers in his line than mine. Who was that gentleman sitting next to my chair? I didn't find out until later. It was Yankee great and Hall of Famer Whitey Ford. Had I known that, I would have lined up for an autograph too. I could have had Whitey Ford's autograph! Sometimes people come into our lives, and we either miss or make contact. God has a purpose for everything we do. Make your connections count.

# Chapter 14: Boy, Do Yo Mama Know Where You Is?

I n December 1972, ABC's Frank Reynolds interrupted the normally scheduled broadcast of Monday Night Football with a special report. The lunar module has just landed on the surface of the moon. I remember him saying, "We have a special report from Jules Berdman: 'The astronauts are fine, the landing was picture perfect.'"

Now back to Monday Night Football. Just before the game started, Glen Campbell began to sing the National Anthem. After Glen started singing, the camera slowly panned both sidelines. It came to a rest for several seconds on a young New York Jets player. The player was Joey Jackson, who sang on key with Glen Campbell. Was this the sign of greater things come? Who knows? All I know is that I sang the National Anthem with Glen Campbell—along with 60,000 other people.

Years later, I met Glen in Branson, Missouri, and I reminded him of how privileged he was to sing the National Anthem with me all that time ago. We laughed and talked about his visits to Minneapolis and hanging out with several players who will remain nameless. One was a quarterback, but not number 10.

The stage was set—Monday Night Football, Cosell, Grifford, and Dandy Don, and I was starting at strong side defensive end. We needed a win against the Oakland Raiders for a playoff berth. Beat the Raiders, and we control our own destiny; lose, and we go home. Even though we had one more remaining game against Cleveland, if the Raiders beat us our season would be over. The Raiders had a very formidable offensive line that featured four future NFL Hall of Famers.

That was my rookie year, and I was starting for the New York Jets on Monday Night Football. Does it get any better? If anyone's interested, you can find that game on YouTube: Jets/Raiders, 1972.

All week I studied game film and prepared for the Monday night matchup. I knew my dad had spread the word to the boys at the post office, "Joey's going to be on Monday Night Football; he's number 86." We didn't have DVR or recording capabilities back then, so if you missed it live then you missed it!

I would be matched up against either Art Shell or Big Bad Bob Brown. The tight end Raymond Chester would determine who I would go up against. If Chester's on the right side, it's Art Shell. It's like pick your poison—who do you want to kill you?

I remember one particular play when I was lined up on the left side in front of Bob Brown. Bob was an intimidating force of power, grit, and meanness who played offensive tackle with a defensive mentality. He wore forearm pads, elbow pads, bicep pads on top of pads. He looked like Goliath in a Raider uniform.

The Raiders broke the huddle, and Goliath was heading my way. As a defensive lineman, you ignore the cadence of the quarterback. You focus on movement. Never allow the voice inflection of the quarterback to draw you offsides. This had been ingrained into my DNA since I was a seventh grader at Lyons Junior High School.

I was down in my three-point stance, and Stabler started the cadence: "Red 42, red 42." Somewhere between hut 1 and hut 2, I lost my focus. A booming voice bellowed from across the line of scrimmage asking this question: "Boy, do yo' mama know where you is?" For a second, I thought, *Wow, that sure is considerate*. Then all of sudden, boom! I was knocked backward several feet; the ball carrier ran through my hole for an eight- or nine-yard gain.

What happened? The offense knew the play; they had the cadence. My opponent outweighed me by thirty pounds; he was a veteran, I was only a rookie, and he was an all-pro future Hall of Famer. But that's not why I got beat. I got beat because I listened to the wrong voice.

In 1 Kings 13, Jeroboam was the new king of Bethel. Bethel was the place where Jacob found a smooth stone, laid his head upon it, and slept. God appeared to him in a dream. He saw a stairway resting on earth and reaching heaven. God told Jacob that He would give him and his descendants the ground that he was lying on. When Jacob awoke, he said, "This place is awesome! Surely the Lord is in this place." He named the place *Bethel*, which means "house of God" or "place of God."

Almost a thousand years passed, and Bethel was full of apostasy, idolatry, and the worshiping of the golden calf. This had to grieve the heart of God. But God is rich in grace and mercy.

As Jeroboam was standing by the altar to make an offering, the man of God came from Judah to Bethel. The man of God cried out against the altar. He gave two prophecies. He said, "O altar, altar, the bones of the high priest will be sacrificed on you." Three hundred years later, this prophecy was fulfilled in every detail when Josiah killed the pagan priest.

The second prophecy was given later that same day. When Jeroboam heard this, he stretched out his hand and cried out, "Seize that man." But the hand he stretched out shriveled up, and he could not pull it back. The king cried to the man of God.

Although the king was worshiping the pagan gods of Baal, he cried out to the one and true living God and asked the man of God to intercede with God to restore his hand. The man of God interceded, and God graciously restored the king's hand.

The king invited the man of God to come home and eat and receive a gift. The man of God answered, "Even if you were to give me half of your kingdom, I won't go with you." He added, "The Lord told me not to eat bread or drink water or return by the way we came to Bethel," and he left another way.

There was an old prophet living in Bethel whose sons came and told him all that happened. The old prophet asked to find out which way the younger prophet went. The old prophet *was* once God's voice of prophetic utterance, but those days were history. He was living in an apostate condition. The father told the sons to saddle the donkey because he had to find the younger prophet. So they rode after the man of God.

Sometimes I'll pull out an old video of one of my games or see myself on *ESPN Classic* making plays. I'll think, *Maybe I can play again. Somebody saddle the donkey.* But quickly, reality steps in and saves me from certain death.

They found the man of God sitting under an oak tree. The old prophet asked, "Are you the man my sons told me about who came from Judah?"

"I am," he replied.

The old prophet said, "Why don't you come back to Bethel with me have something to eat? After all, when is the last time you've had a bed to sleep on, a warm bath, and a hot meal?"

The man of God said, "I've had this offer and conversation with a king, and I'm going tell you what I told him—I'm not going back with you."

Then the old prophet said something like, "Hey, Brother, we're from the same hood. God told me, 'Go get the brother and take him home with you.'" But the Bible says that he was lying.

The man of God who defied the courting of a king listened to the voice of the old prophet and went home with him. I'm sure he was well fed and slept like a baby. The next morning he left Bethel, and he was greeted by someone else. This time there was no invitation to come for a hot meal, take a bath, or receive a gift. He *was* a hot meal for a lion who devoured him and threw his rusty, dusty carcass on the side of the road.

This is what can happen when you listen to the wrong voice, the voice of the old prophet. No, you probably won't be devoured by a lion, but your dreams, future, vision, and destiny can be devoured.

Remember John 10:10—the thief comes to always steal, kill, and destroy. Discerning between the voice of the old prophet and the voice of the Holy Spirit is not always easy.

We know that Satan disguises himself as an angel of light. Only knowing and obeying the Word of God can keep us from making the wrong choice. We do this as we study to show ourselves approved unto God. In 2 Timothy 2:15, we are instructed to take every thought captive to the obedience of Christ (see also 2 Cor. 10:5). Oh, incidentally, we lost to the Raiders, and our season was over.

# Chapter 15: Prepped for Surgery

My first off-season started with a trip to the Lenox Hill Hospital in New York City for knee surgery. I just enrolled in classes at NMSU when one day I noticed my knee was locked. I couldn't straighten it out until I manipulated something called a loose body. Loose bodies are fragments that move freely around the knee in joint fluid or synovium.

The Jets orthopedic surgeon Dr. James Nicholas scheduled me for surgery on February 20, 1973. He would open the knee and remove the loose body. After I checked into the hospital, I called my brother, who was living in the Bronx. I wasn't sure if he would be home because he was always on the road traveling with his R&B vocal group, The Persuaders. They charted big with "Thin Line Between Love and Hate," "Some Guys Have All the Luck" (also recorded by Rod Steward), and "Peace in the Valley of Love."

He was in town and came to visit. It was great to see him. The next morning they prepped me for surgery. After they shaved my knee, next came the anesthesia, but just before I went under Dr. James Nicholas said, "I don't think we're going to do the surgery now."

Why the change in plans? To this day, I can't remember why he didn't operate. He gave me the names of two surgeons, one in Cincinnati and the other in El Paso, Texas—Dr. Morton Leonard. I was very familiar with Dr. Leonard. He was one of our team doctors at NMSU. Whenever the knee locked, I would find the loose body and move it until my knee had full range of motion. I never knew when it was going to lock up.

## Great Memories

Many have asked what my greatest memory is from the football field—not counting choosing up sides and playing with my friends at Stewart Park. I suppose it was April 14, 1973. New Mexico State varsity football team was completing twenty-one days of spring football. They had actually started weight training in January. Spring practice usually ended with the annual red and white game.

However, in 1973 the New Mexico State Aggies challenged the alumni to a game. Aggie alumni came in from all over. Most of these ex-Aggie footballers hadn't been in a uniform in years, and it showed. There were some recent graduates who were in decent shape. But still, how in the world could they compete against the college varsity football team? No way!

The entire coaching staff that recruited and coached me was fired after the 1972 season. The new coach was Aggies Hall of Famer Jim Bradley. Coach Bradley was a New Mexico State legend. He coached at Roswell and Mayfield High School and amassed a record of over 300 wins, the second-winningest coach in New Mexico history.

Surely he would welcome these alumni to the real world—the real world of the Jim Bradley era. I had nothing to lose, so I decided to play. We assembled an offense and defense, drew our equipment, and practiced for *one hour*, period. Clem Mancini, who coached at Mayfield High School, was the alumni coach.

The alumni roster had several pros, including Pittsburgh Steeler Roy Gerela, Buffalo Bill Al Andrews, former Oakland Raider Ruby Jackson, Cleveland Brown Andy Dorris, and San Francisco 49er Hayward Finley.

To no one's surprise, the varsity came out smoking; they had two quick scores in about three minutes. It was a battle of turnovers. Aggie quarterback and future New York Giant quarterback Joe Pisarcik and Doug Baker each had two interceptions. But the alumni soon found their stride. Quarterback Sal Olivas threw for 327 yards and three touchdowns. The alumni beat the varsity 38-28.

After the game, there were more pro scouts in our locker room than the varsity. If there were another Aggie vs. alumni game today, I would play.

Winston Churchill once said something to this effect: This was my finest hour. My most memorable game too.

## Aftermath

My left knee continued to lock. The following Thursday, April 19, 1973, I checked into the Hotel Dieu Hospital in El Paso, Texas. Dr. Morton Leonard performed major surgery on my left knee.

The New York Jets' training camp opened in less than two and a half months. My rehab was right on schedule. I was determined to be ready on the first day of training camp, so I pushed my workout pretty hard. In the NFL, there are no guarantees. You've got to be ready to go, or you're gone. The season started. Our first game was against the Houston Oilers. Their quarterback was Dan Pastorini. I sacked him twice. The rest of the season was downhill. Namath got hurt, and we finished last in our division. I hate to admit this, but after the surgery I lost half a step. I was never the same player. I'll never admit my surgery was the result of the spring game. I don't remember ever being touched.

Maybe it's old age or old injuries or both, but until I have my knees replaced, they are a constant reminder of the abuse I received as an NFL player. Some mornings, I just can't move. I'm trying to keep what God gave me, but eventually both knees will need to be replaced. I'm not complaining; it's just the path of an NFL defensive end. If given the opportunity, I'd do it again in a heartbeat.

Many of my NFL alumni brothers are living on social security check to check. Some have injuries that disable them from finding a good job. Others have addiction problems. Some don't even know their names. Sadly, there are those who feel that the NFL is just waiting for them to die.

This is a heartbreaking reality and one of the main reasons Athletes International Ministries (AIM) extends a hand to the retired NFL player. If you know a current or former NFL player or college athlete who may want to attend our athletes' conference, please contact AIM.

# Chapter 16: Pooh Bear

I f you've never crossed paths with Winston Hill, you missed something special. He was not only one of the best offensive tackles in the history of the NFL, he was a leader and role model you'd want your kids to emulate. His heart was as big as the state he was from—Texas. Winston was affectionately called "Winnie" or "Pooh Bear." He loved his family, life, people, and his Lord and Savior, Jesus Christ.

There's not another player in the NFL who impacted my life like Winston. I loved Winston Hill. Everyone loved Winston, except defensive ends. He was the undeniable leader on that team. Yes, Joe, being a quarterback, was the leader in the football sense, but in a spiritual sense it was Winston. If you had a problem, you'd go to Winston. He had so much wisdom and was respected both in and out of the locker room.

He encouraged me not to give up when he was beating me like a drum. He even gave me pointers on how to beat him. If it wasn't for that, I don't think I would have made the team my rookie year.

Winston and Carolyn Hill had a great marriage. They produced two beautiful daughters, Holly and Heather Hill. Heather became a star on Broadway in the long-running play *Phantom of the Opera*.

Winston played fifteen years in the NFL and was finally inducted into the Pro Football Hall of Fame in 2020. I've said it before and I'll say it again—Winston was the best offensive tackle I ever played against. Winston ended his illustrious career with the LA Rams in 1978. Like seeing Joe in a Ram uniform, it's odd to see Winston as a Ram. Winston retired and opened Winston Hill's Barbecue in Denver, Colorado.

## Earlie and Kathy Thomas

Whenever I was in Denver, I'd visit Winston, my friend and brother. I don't think I ever once paid for a meal at his restaurant. Several years ago, I was preaching in Denver and invited Winston to the service. He came and gave a word of testimony. Winston always seemed to know the right thing to say at the right time. After lunch, we drove to Fort Collins to visit our Jets teammate Earlie and Kathy Thomas.

Earlie earned a PhD in entomology, a branch of zoology that deals with insects. It had been nearly 35 years since our last visit in the early '80s. I don't remember the circumstances, but I ended up at a Denny's in Fort Collins, Colorado one morning, looking tired and worn. Someone approached and asked if he could buy me a cup of coffee. Maybe he thought I was homeless.

We started talking, and I told him I played with the Jets and was there to visit a friend's church. He asked who, and I said Earlie Thomas. He said that Earlie was a good friend of his and that he knew Earlie and his wife well. In just a few minutes, he called Earlie and Kathy, and they gave me directions to their home. I showered, went to church, and sang that morning. That was in 1982.

When Winston and I arrived, they greeted us with warm hugs and big smiles. It was a great family reunion—Winston, Earlie, Kathy, and myself. We talked about the Jets and tried to remember every great play we ever made. I even reminded Earlie of the Thanksgiving game we played in 1969. I reminded him of our win and my three sacks on their quarterback. He said he couldn't remember!

Winnie and I would always see one another at the Joe Namath football camp. In 2014 I brought Terill to Joe's camp to meet the team. Winston had his knees replaced and was using a cane. But he still had the fire and heart as he communicated with the campers. When he spoke, everyone listened. The next year at camp Winnie wasn't there. We heard that he had a heart issue and was advised not travel.

In forty years of Joe's camp, this was the first one that Winston missed.

In April of 2016, Winston called me about information regarding the NFL workmen's compensation lawsuit. I gave him the information he wanted and asked how he was doing. He said, "Joe, I'm in the hospital; I've been in here for a month." I couldn't believe it. His playful and strong voice sounded weak. I prayed for my friend and told him to call me if he needed anything. After hanging up, I called his daughter Heather and asked how Winston was doing. She carefully told me that it didn't look good. I couldn't believe it. I called Joe Namath and Earl Christy, asking them to call Winston as soon as possible.

Three days later, Winston was called to glory. He left this world on April 26, 2016, and was reunited with his wife, Carolyn, who preceded him on October 16, 2014. His legacy lives on in the lives of so many he touched with a kind word, a hug, a plate of barbecue, and that smile. You can still find his barbecue at the Red Rocks Café at Denver International Airport. Winnie, we miss you, brother. I know he's with the Lord, but his passing hit me harder than he ever did during a pass-rush drill.

## New Hometown Memories

The Jets were playing the Cincinnati Bengals in my hometown, Cincinnati. This would be the first time I would play a football game in my hometown since high school. It would be pretty special. Two days earlier, I called and warned my grandmother that I would be bringing four or five of my New York Jets teammates home for lunch. She said, "Great, what do you want me to cook?" I gave her a list of my favorites, including blackberry cobbler, corn pudding, collard greens, fried chicken, turkey, and roast beef. My mother made homemade rolls and sweet potato pie.

Mom should have known better. She drove my Corvair to the team hotel in downtown Cincinnati to pick us up. There was no way that myself, Steve Thompson, Earlie Thomas, John Little, and Eddie Bell could squeeze into my Corvair. I called my dad, and he brought his Impala to the rescue.

It was so special to have my New York Jets teammates come to my grandmother's home for lunch. Who would have thought that the same house that hosted and served lunch for pastors, relatives, and friends would feed a team of hungry NFL football players? After lunch we took pictures, and the players signed some autographs.

On our way back to the hotel, we stopped at two Cincy landmarks—Skyline Chili and United Dairy Farmers. Some will argue that Gold Star Chili and Graeter's Ice Cream are the Cincinnati staples. Don't count on my vote. It's no debate—Skyline and UDF.

That evening at the team buffet, I brought a large contingent of Jackson family members. They all wanted pictures with Joe Namath. Joe kindly obliged and endured the attack. Earlier that morning, we had a special team practice at Riverfront Stadium. The Saturday morning special teams practice is light with no pads. It's also the only practice when you can bring family onto the field.

My dad has always been a big Joe Namath fan. He asked if Joe wouldn't mind taking a picture with him. I asked Joe if he'd take a picture with my dad. Joe said, "Of course, where's he at?" We took several pictures with family members and Joe Willy.

Cincinnati was enjoying a deepening love affair with the Bengals. Coach Paul Brown returned to football five years earlier and fulfilled his promise to make this expansion team a playoff contender. It wasn't a catch-22 or standing between a rock and a hard place for me. Even though I was born and raised in Cincinnati, my loyalties were with the New York Jets. The new handsome stadium was sold out. Riverfront was also the home field for the Big Red Machine. Now, if only the Bengals could enjoy the same success.

The game got underway on a bone-chilling overcast. We trailed at halftime 17-7. Namath hadn't played in a couple of weeks, and we could tell his game was off. In the first half, I hadn't played one down, not even special teams. Surely Coach Weeb would put me in this game. He knew I was from Cincinnati, and my family was all here. Third-quarter ended, and I still had no action in the game. It was embarrassing.

I kept my sideline cape on to avoid being seen by friends and family. Some of the other players noticed that I hadn't played yet. They tried to make small talk to cheer me up. Only three minutes left in the fourth quarter.

The game ended, and I wasn't in there for even one stinking play. I felt terrible. I didn't even care that we lost. I couldn't believe that the coaches didn't put me in the game. I carried a grudge against the Jets for years because of that.

I came out of the locker room and was greeted by parents and family. My dad never said anything about my absence during the game. Maybe he thought that my knee wasn't completely healed from my April surgery. I said goodbye to my family and boarded the bus for the airport. I told my dad that I would see him at Christmas. That was November 18, 1973.

Several years later, I came back to Riverfront Stadium and was starting as right defensive tackle for the Minnesota Vikings. I sacked the Bengals' quarterback John Reeves, but dad was already *gone*.

# Chapter 17: Juice on the Loose

O ur last game was with the Buffalo Bills on December 16, 1973. O.J. Simpson came into the game with 1,803 yards. He needed to rush for 197 yards for 2,000. Jim Brown's record of 1863 had held for ten years. No player had ever rushed for 2,000 yards. If O.J. was able to pull this off, it would be well deserved.

The grass field was white from a weekend snowstorm. It was sloppy and torn up. Conditions weren't ideal for Jim Brown's record to be broken. Even if Brown's record was broken, O.J. would not rush for nearly 200 yards on my watch. And O.J. didn't rush for 200 yards on my watch and home field. He rushed for 203. Our fans who stayed to the end cheered "the Juice" as he ran. I guess you can say that I'm partly responsible for O.J. breaking Jim Brown's record and hitting the 2,000 mark. I didn't make one tackle.

Four years later, I helped Walter Payton set the single-game rushing record on November 20, 1977. I made only three tackles. Payton rushed for 275 yards, a record that lasted until Corey Dillon broke it on October 22, 2000.

## Hard News

After our game with Buffalo, I turned in my equipment and playbook and headed to Long Island. I shared a house with Howie, the cop. My phone woke me up around one o'clock in the morning. It was Mike, my brother. He told me that Dad had a heart attack. I asked how he was doing and what hospital I should call.

Mike said, "Sorry, Joey, Dad's dead."

No way! I just saw him less than a month ago. He was only 57 years old, and I had not even gotten the pictures developed yet. But most concerning, my dad was not right with God. He grew up in a good Christian home, but something happened when he returned from World War II. My father was not ready to die.

The Bible says that it is appointed for all men to die, and after that, the judgment comes (Heb. 9:27). It doesn't matter if you're ready or not; when your appointment time comes, it can't be rescheduled.

The next morning I flew home. My first stop was my grandmother's. My dad was her only child. Mom Jackson looked at me and saw the deep anguish on my face as I tried to reason for clarity. My father struggled with alcohol. When we were at a liquor store, he would go into the liquor store and come back with a bottle of whiskey. Mike and I would laugh at the face he made because of the bitter taste. He was never in a good mood when he drank. There was an expression on his face whenever he was high. We could always tell when he'd been drinking. We were too young to realize the danger of drinking and driving.

For 27 years, my father worked for the US Postal Service as a mailman. Despite his struggle with alcohol, my dad never missed a high school football game and always encouraged us to get good grades. He had five children who earned college degrees.

What my grandmother told me next was simply amazing. She said, "Junior, look at me. The day before your father died, he went to church as usual. This time, when Reverend Molsey gave the altar call, your daddy responded. He asked Christ into his life and made his peace with his Lord." The next morning he went to work, returned home, made it as far as the back porch, and fell over dead.

For 57 years, my grandmother prayed that my father would come to a saving relationship with Jesus Christ. During that time, she saw no change in my dad's heart. But, like that widow in Luke 18:1-8, she kept on praying. The widow had every reason to quit. Her only solution was an unjust judge who didn't care about God or man. He was her only hope. The Bible says that for some time the judge refused, but he eventually relented—not because the judge had a change of heart or recognized the merit of her case. He got tired of her asking over and over. Jesus then asks a question: "And will not God bring justice to His chosen ones who cry out to Him day and night? Will He keep putting them off? He will see that they get justice and quickly."

My grandmother needed her breakthrough quickly. When I last saw my father, he was down to the two-minute warning; he had less than four weeks to live. If something was going to happen in his life, it had to happen quickly. My father didn't have 57 years or 57 weeks. He didn't even have 57 days.

I know that my grandmother was a woman of deep prayer and faith. Did God answer her prayer because of that? I'd want to say yes, He did. I also know that the second half of verse 8 asks, "When the son of man comes, will he find faith on earth?"

Don't look at the scoreboard; keep walking in faith!

# Chapter 18: Mays, Rikers Island, or the Minnesota State Fair

I n the bygone era of multi-purpose stadiums, NFL teams and Major League Baseball teams would share the same facility. The football team usually couldn't get on the natural grass field to practice until the Mets season ended. We were allowed to play our home games at Shea, but we couldn't practice there. We'd arrive at the stadium for practice and then board the prison bus for Rikers Island.

It was the same way with the Vikings. We come to the old Met Stadium, change into our practice gear, then get bused to the Minnesota State Fairgrounds for practice. I wonder if anyone has ever researched teams' success/failure rate who have to make this kind of transition.

One September morning, I hurried through the players-only entrance to the New York Jets locker room at Shea Stadium. I had gotten caught in traffic on the Long Island Expressway and didn't want to pay a heavy fine of $50 for being late to practice or miss the prison bus to Rikers Island, so I hurried. Looming toward me was a familiar figure with a noticeable gait whom I admired as a kid but never rooted for.

My goodness! It was the Say Hey Kid, Willie Mays. Growing up in Cincinnati, I was and still am a big Cincinnati Red Legs fan. Mays, McCovey, Cepeda, Jaun Marichal, and others were just as threatening to Reds fans as the six batters of the New Yankees' Murderers Row of Combs, Koenig, Ruth, Gehrig, Meusel, and Lazzeri.

To some, it's no small argument that Willie Mays was probably the greatest all-around baseball player of all time. They will get no objection or argument from me; he gets my vote.

I extended my hand for a warm handshake and said, "Willie, I'm Joe Jackson. I play with New York Jets. I'm honored to meet you."

He said, "Thank you, young man, I know who you are. Glad to meet you too."

I'm not sure that Willie Mays knew who I was, but that introduction sure meant a lot to me, and I've never forgotten it.

The players went on strike in 1974. We held out for about three weeks. I was getting pressured by head coach Weeb Ewbank and other coaches threatening to waive me if I did not report.

I wished that I had my dad around for counsel. I finally crossed the picket lines and went to camp. There's nothing much I remember about the '74 season. It's a blur. I started against the Giants and the Raiders. We had a new head coach, Charlie Winter, and I had Dick Voris as a defensive line coach.

It was a relief when the season ended. I remember playing the St. Louis Cardinals at Shea, and someone kicked me in the head. For a brief moment, I couldn't figure out where I was or who I was. Concussion protocol is vastly different today; however, the trainers treated me and made an evaluation.

Buddy asked, "Big Joe, you're ready to go back in the game, aren't you?" I didn't know if that was a question or an order.

Whether I was ready or not, I said, "Yes, sir. I'm ready." I was back in the game making plays.

## Stars and Misunderstandings

My years with the Jets were not very rewarding in terms of wins and losses. In four years, I don't think we ever finished above 500. Whatever the Jets had in the Super Bowl III victory against the Baltimore Colts was gone.

We had several coaching changes, including the hiring and firing of Charlie Winner, Coach Weeb's son-in-law, and Lou Holtz. In 1974 the World Football League (WFL) was birthed. They were comprised of sixteen teams, including the New York Stars. The Stars were coached by former New York Jets quarterback Babe Parilli. After six games, the Jets released me.

The Stars had my rights. The World Football League was throwing around numbers to attract NFL players to jumpstart this new league. The Stars offered me a contract that was twice the amount I had signed with the New York Jets. To me, it was a no-brainer.

The Jets cut me, and I wasn't going to wait around to be claimed by an NFL team when I could make $40,000. The WFL had signed many NFL stars to large contracts. Give me the pen! It was great to join my New York Jets teammates John Elliott, Gerry Philbin, John Dockery, George Sauer, and Mike Taylor, who were already playing with the Stars. We played the Detroit Wheels in New York. On the Wheels sidelines was Marvin Gaye.

I thought, *Wow, this league must be for real if Marvin Gaye is here!* Marvin was considering giving up singing and playing professional football even though he never even played high school football. He dropped out of school at seventeen to pursue music. After about a week, I realized this league was not the NFL and I had made an enormous mistake.

The New York Stars were sold to Charlotte. We became the Charlotte Hornets. I finished out the season in Charlotte, then drove to Las Cruces for the off-season. The Hornets promised me a nice signing bonus. I'm still waiting for the check. I felt my contract was breached, so I reached out to the NFL. My agent negotiated a two-year contract with the LA Rams. I felt no loyalty to the Hornets, so I informed the Hornets I wasn't coming back. After all, they didn't fulfill their commitment in regard to my signing bonus. Why should I honor a contract I felt was void? The Hornets sent me a letter threatening a lawsuit. I told them to go ahead and that I would be reporting to the Rams' training camp.

I was in camp for about a week when my agent called and said, "You better get to Charlotte; they have you under contract."

I said, "There's no way I'm going to Charlotte; I've got a chance to make this team."

The Hornets threatened to sue the Rams too. I didn't feel the Rams had my back, so I left camp and went back to Charlotte to avoid a lawsuit. The media reported that I *walked out of camp*, but that wasn't true—I was forced out.

When I arrived in North Carolina, the Hornets quickly traded my rights to the Jacksonville Express, which are now the Jaguars. While I was there, I loved playing in the Gator Bowl with the Express. I love Florida. We had a pretty good defensive line that included Carlton Oakes from the Raiders and ten-year veteran Don Brumm, who played with the Cardinals and Eagles. Had that league survived, I would have never come back to the NFL. It was a lot of fun playing in Jacksonville, my town.

On a Tuesday morning in late October of 1975, I arrived at the Gator Bowl for practice. On Tuesdays, we watched a game film and had a slight walkthrough. This time something was odd. None of the players were dressed in their uniforms. Everyone was standing around waiting for the big announcement.

Our head coach, Charlie Tate, lowered his head as he walked into the locker room and said, "Boys, the league has voted to fold."

After the shock of that statement sank in, we embarrassingly looked at each other and cleaned out our lockers. For some, it was a relief. The rumor mill had reported that the league was in trouble but would most likely survive the season. I don't think anyone saw this punch coming.

It was a sad day in professional football. I immediately reached out to the Rams. They never responded. Several players in the WFL were picked up. Eventually, I returned to Las Cruces and took a coaching job at New Mexico State.

# Chapter 19: Purple Tales and Kelley Green Tales

B uddy Ryan took the job as defensive line coach with the Minnesota Vikings, and I like to say he took me with him. I signed a contract with the Dallas Cowboys, but I flunked the physical. I was then picked up by the Redskins and was waived. Discouraged, I began to think my football career was over.

I planned to go back to New Mexico State and coach the defensive line for the Aggies. The Redskins were to fly me back to El Paso with a stop-off in Cincinnati.

I was in my grandmother's living room when the phone rang. She answered and said it was for me. "It's Bobby Ryan."

I said, "Bobby Ryan?" I wondered who that was.

I said hello; it was Buddy. He said, "Big Joe, how fast can you get to Minnesota?"

I said, "Coach, I can be there in the morning."

He said, "No. I want you here tonight! We'll you send an airline ticket." Buddy explained that the roster was expanded to 45 players, so I had an opportunity to land a spot.

The Vikings were loaded with defensive linemen, including two first-round picks—Mark Mullaney and Duck White. They had never kept seven defensive linemen before. How would I make the team? I had a great preseason camp and an especially good game on Monday night against the Miami Dolphins. It was a nationally televised game with the Monday night crew of Don Meredith, Howard Cosell, and Frank Gifford.

In that game, I sacked Bob Griese and tackled Norm Bulaich for an eight-yard loss. I figured that even if I didn't make the Vikings, other teams would be watching and offer me a contract. The week before, I recorded another sack against the Browns. I was pretty sure I had made the team. Buddy Ryan called me aside just before the last preseason game and told me I made the team but could be cut from the roster any time. I don't know if he said that to keep me hungry or he meant it; either way, I was never completely comfortable that season simply because seven defensive linemen wasn't the norm on an NFL roster. Teams usually keep only six defensive linemen. However, God had a plan, and making that 45-man roster was a big part.

## Comebacks and Facts

The Minnesota Vikings were playing the San Francisco 49ers on December 4, 1977; we were at a disadvantage. Our future Hall of Fame quarterback Fran Tarkenton was injured with a broken leg. We needed a win for a playoff berth. When I played with the Vikings, we played outdoors.

Head coach Bud Grant didn't believe in sissy heaters or gloves. We were the Minnesota Vikings who played at the old Met Stadium where men were men. For some reason, the teams had to share the same sideline. Both benches were on the same side of the field, which is unheard of today. Did I mention it was cold? Just five degrees above zero. At halftime, we were trailing behind 24-3.

Enter our young rookie quarterback from Rice University named Tommy Kramer. Kramer led the Vikings to a 27-28 comeback win, which, even to this day, is the greatest deficit a Viking team ever overcame. I've learned not ever to allow circumstances to circumvent my dream, my goals, or God's plan for my life. Don't give up!

How many times have you been told this: "Look at the facts; facts don't lie"? I beg to differ. There is a marked difference between *fact* and *truth*. Facts are based on knowledge and experience, while truth is derived, birthed, and conceived in "thus saith the Lord." In John 14:6, Jesus never said He is the way, the facts, and the life—He said He is the way, the truth, and the life. Facts can be amended. Remember, it was a fact that I was not good enough to swim at the Sunlite Pool because Negroes were barred.

I realize that I spend too much time looking at the past, thinking about what could have happened. In my rookie year, I started at strong-side defensive end for the New York Jets. We played the Cleveland Browns at Shea. The Browns called sweep right, 38 toss. I read the play perfectly, and I was in hot pursuit. The left side of the defensive line did their job. They closed down the corner. The ball carrier was trapped; he had nowhere to go. I was going to make a tackle for a five-yard loss. He planted and ran almost into my arms, then put a juke step on me. Instead of making a tackle for a five-yard loss, I was grabbing air.

What I thought was going to be a great play on my highlight reel turned into an exciting play on Hall of Famer Leroy Kelly's highlight reel. I must've made some plays in that game, but that missed tackle is like a scratch on an old 45-rpm record. I relive it over and over and over.

And how about this—what if we would have beaten Dallas in the NFC Championship game in 1978? We could have gone to back-to-back Super Bowls. I really believe that we would have beaten the Denver Broncos in Super Bowl XII. We'll never know.

## A Surprise in My Suitcase

When we landed in Minneapolis after playing the Oakland Raiders, I walked to the baggage area and waited for the carousel to start moving. Finally, the bags started sliding down. I was looking for my sky-blue Samsonite suitcase. The old-school Samsonite suitcase had the texture of a golf ball. Once locked, you could open it with a fingernail file. There were no wheels or strap, only a handle.

All the bags were delivered—where was mine? I went to the Northwest Airlines baggage office and filed a claim. They checked the computer and determined my bag never left Oakland. They said, "No problem, Mr. Jackson, your suitcase is scheduled for delivery tomorrow by five p.m."

When I returned from practice the next day, it was at my door. I had a couple of nice suits in that suitcase, so I opened it up and hung my suits in the closet. As I unpacked, I notice something that I can't ever remember seeing in my lifetime. It looked like a bag of coffee, but I don't drink coffee.

On further examination, I discovered what it was. Someone placed a one-pound bag of marijuana in my suitcase. I couldn't believe it. Were they trying to make up for the delay of my bags and thought a bag of pot would make the world a lot better place to live? I don't know how or why. I opened the baggy and flushed it down the toilet, then threw the baggy away. At Wednesday's practice, I told some teammates my story. When I told them that I flushed it down the toilet, one of my teammates shouted a racial slur at me and said, "Are you crazy?" No. I'm not into drugs. Buddy Ryan said I did the right thing.

## Heading to the Super Bowl

Buddy helped the Viking win an NFC Championship and a berth in Super Bowl XI. Surely this trip to the Super Bowl would produce our first win. There's absolutely no way we're going to lose to the Raiders. Early in the big game, Minnesota Viking outside linebacker Matt Blair blocked and recovered a punt. We had the ball inside the Raiders' ten-yard line.

With Fred Cox, our field goal kicker, at least we'd score three points and have an early lead. We never got the opportunity because the offense fumbled the ball inside the Raider five-yard line. It was all downhill after that. *We'll get 'em next year*, I thought.

The next year was 1977. Joe Namath and Winston Hill left New York for the California coastline and South Beach in Miami. Joe Willy signed with the LA Rams and Winston with the Dolphins. In mid-season, the Dolphins traded Winnie to the Rams. Something wasn't right seeing Namath and Winston in anything but New York Jets Kelley green and white.

That year we played the Rams three times, losing twice, including a Monday night thriller. The third time we played the Rams was in a divisional playoff game. Usually, the Vikings would have home-field advantage, but we were the wild card because of the Rams' better record.

The Rams hated coming to cold Minnesota in December and January. We beat the Rams in the NFC game in Minnesota in 1976, and now they would host the second round of the NFC playoffs in sunny Southern California. The Vikings were always a bad-weather outdoor team, and our coach, Bud Grant, was old school. He wouldn't allow heaters on the sidelines or gloves. We were Vikings. That weekend it rained for three solid days, and the Los Angeles Coliseum turned into a perfect field for mud wrestling. There wasn't a lot of offense; it was a defensive struggle and a matter of survival. After the dust—or mud—settled, we won 14-7 and were headed to Dallas to play for a berth in Super Bowl XII.

Before I boarded the team bus for LAX, I went to the Rams' locker room to say hello to former teammates Joe Willy Namath and Winston Hill. It was so good to see them. When I played for the Jets, Joe's locker would always be a parking lot for media and the press. I was hoping to at least say hello.

To my shock and amazement, Joe was sitting alone at his locker. We had a brief visit, reminisced about our days in New York, and wished each other well. Winston gave me a high five and a hug. I wouldn't connect again with Joe and Winston for twenty-five years.

## Off-Season Basketball

After the 1978 loss to the Dallas Cowboys in the NFC Championship game, I headed to my off-season paradise—Las Cruces, New Mexico. Because we went pretty deep into the playoffs and I had a commitment to the Minnesota Vikings off-season basketball team, my journey didn't begin until mid-February.

The Vikings' basketball team was like the Harlem Globe Trotters. They weren't as talented by any stretch, but we played all of our games on the road too. It was a good revenue stream and also a good way to stay in decent shape. We played most of our games around the Twin Cities of Minnesota, Iowa, and Wisconsin. These games would be played against the police leagues, firefighters, high school teachers, or church leagues. I think we made about $150 per game.

One night we drove to Iowa for a game. The roads were slick because of a Minnesota winter snowstorm. The conditions slowed traffic north and southbound on Interstate 35 to around 45 miles per hour. There was a white van just ahead of us that began to fishtail out of control. It must have hit some black ice.

The driver skidded off of the road. The van flipped over twice before landing on its side. We stopped and rushed over to help. Gratefully, everyone was okay. We stayed there until the emergency vehicles arrived, then continued on to our game.

When we finally arrived at Mason City High School, we could see the gym parking lot full of cars. We were twenty minutes late and, of course, there were no cell phones in those days. We explained why we were late and quickly changed into our uniforms. They were thankful that we weren't a no-show because they had sold 650 tickets.

The game started, and we quickly jumped on them and never looked back. Paul Krause, Bobby Bryant, and Matt Blair controlled the offense. I'm usually a defender, but that night I scored a double-double, twenty-one points, and ten rebounds. This was my last game. When Bobby gave me my check, he asked me if I could finish out the season. But I was determined to leave the cold and become a snowbird in Southern New Mexico. My car was already packed, and there was no changing my mind. If I had to do it again, I would have stayed in Minnesota that entire off-season.

## Eating a Seventy-Two-Ounce Monster

Foolishly, I owned three cars, including a 1976 Corvette, a 1977 Cadillac El Dorado, and a 1973 Cadillac Fleetwood Deville. This would be my third trip to Las Cruces transporting cars. Once I settled in Las Cruces,

I sold the 'Vette and the Deville. Again, with hindsight being 20/20, I would have never purchased more than one car.

On the way to my off-season paradise, I'd drive through Amarillo, Texas, the home of the Big Texan Steak Ranch. You'd see billboards as far east as Oklahoma City advertising a free 72-ounce steak—absolutely free if you could eat it in an hour. I didn't think this would be much of a challenge for me.

When I was in grade school, my mom would pack my lunch box with four cheese-and-bologna sandwiches. I knew I could eat the big steak and was determined to get my picture on the wall with others who scarfed down the 72-ounce monster.

If you couldn't eat the steak in an hour, it would cost you $18. Today the price is around $75. Well, I was ready. Bring it on! I ate the steak in around 38 minutes. I was stuffed! Where do I go for my picture? I failed to read the small print, which stated that I had to also eat the baked potato, salad, and dessert. I couldn't do it. There would be no hall of fame picture on the wall for me—only a receipt for $21, which included a drink and tax. That was 1974. I never tried that again when I traveled through Amarillo.

Recently I saw a video about a lady who weighed around 118 pounds who ate two of the 72-ounce steaks in less than an hour. Yes—two! I couldn't believe it. How is that possible? Maybe I should go back to the Big Texan and ask for a redo. Maybe it's the championship spirit that's willing to pay the price for another bite at the T-bone, or it's a bruised ego shamed by a 118-pound female who engulfed 144 ounces of red meat plus the trimmings in 37 minutes.

# Chapter 20: Don't Worry; I'll Let Go of the Contract

T he 1978 season would be my last year in the NFL. The Vikings were always the last team to start training camp. We had drafted defensive end Randy Holloway in the first round. I knew the Vikings couldn't keep eight defensive linemen. Plus, the only defensive line coach I ever knew was now the Chicago Bears defensive coordinator.

Neil Armstrong, who was our defensive coordinator, was now the new head coach of the Chicago Bears. He took Buddy to be his defensive coordinator. That season, I lasted six games. The Vikings released me, and I was naked and afraid. I reached out to Buddy, but the Bears were interested in Alan Page.

I waited for an NFL team to call and pick me up but got nothing. Vikings defensive coordinator Bob Holloway called me a couple of times to check if I was still around. I guess they were looking for insurance in case something happened to one of their defensive linemen. The only real interest I received was from the Canadian Football League. Nothing against the CFL, but I wanted to finish my eight-year career in the NFL. After several weeks passed and I still had no word from the NFL, I decided to sign with the Edmonton Eskimos.

I went to Edmonton, Alberta, Canada, took my physical, and checked into the Edmonton Inn. With quarterback Warren Moon from the University of Washington and Jim Germany from New Mexico State University, the Eskimos were poised to make a run for a Grey Cup championship.

In 1978 Warren Moon led the Washington Huskies to a Rose Bowl win against Michigan, being named the Rose Bowl player of the game. NFL scouts were not impressed. He was undrafted by the NFL, yet won five Grey Cup championships in Canada. During that era there were no starting Black quarterbacks in the NFL. I met with the Edmonton Eskimo GM Norm Kimball and head coach Hugh Campbell and told them of my desire to play in the NFL. They said, "We understand if any NFL team contacts you with a contract offer, we will release you from our contract." I didn't sign anything about this; I only had their word. Like an idiot, I agreed and signed a contract with the Eskimos.

The next day Bobby Beathard, general manager of the Washington Redskins, called and wanted to sign me. They contacted the Vikings and tracked me down in Edmonton. They had me in camp a few years ago and knew I could play. I rushed down with excitement to the Eskimos' office. I told the general manager about the offer I received from the Redskins.

Their reply was, "Joe, you know we can't let you out of the contract."

I said, "You promised you would!"

They said, "We can't do it." Another lie from a coach. I finished up the season with the Eskimos.

We won the Grey Cup, but I never received my championship ring. After the season, I returned to Minneapolis. It was the first off-season I didn't spend in Las Cruces. My off-season job was as a light bulb salesman for Jewell Electronics. No, I didn't do very well at that either!

The next year I went to the Eskimo training camp to begin the 1979 season. I was in camp for three weeks before the Eskimos cut me. They said that my negative attitude was a distraction to the team. They were probably right. My heart wasn't in playing for the Eskimos, especially since they lied to me.

Again, there were no do-overs, but I should have had a better attitude. Make them cut you, don't cut yourself. I flew back to Minneapolis. The NFL season had not started, so I contacted several teams. The Kansas City Chiefs and the Tampa Bay Buccaneers responded. They both were interested in signing me to a one-year deal provided I could pass the physical.

My old coach Dick Vorris was coaching the defensive line in Tampa, so I selected the Bucs. Looking back, I should've picked the Chiefs.

There was a stupid rule that wouldn't allow players from the CFL to come to the NFL in the same year, even though you can go to Canada from the NFL anytime. I knew the rule but didn't care. I didn't think anyone knew that I was in Canada. Besides, they weren't honest with me. But there was an NFL scout who saw me in Canada. I saw him at the Buccaneers training camp and held my breath. *Maybe he won't recognize me.* Wrong! The following day I was told to pack my bags. It just wasn't the Lord's will.

# Chapter 21: From Super Bowls
# to Saving Souls

I n 1980 I signed a two-year contract with the Toronto Argos. Something strange was happening. For the first time in my life, I didn't have the fire to compete. This was weird. I always had a fire and passion for football. Something was wrong.

Camp started, and I was off to Toronto. The first day of training camp is when you meet some new players or coaches, receive your playbook, and take your physical. I had passed almost every physical I'd ever taken, except with the Dallas Cowboys and the military in 1972. Surely this physical wouldn't be a challenge. I was in pretty decent shape. After my physical, the orthopedic surgeon summoned me to his office.

He said, "Son, sit down." Then he raised some x-rays to light and said, "Son, these x-rays look like they are from someone much, much older than you. Your left knee has gross degenerative arthritic change. I'm so sorry; your football career is over."

I couldn't believe it. Over! My eyes began to burn as though something bright was shining on my face. I went to Coach Tommy Hudspeth's office and turned in my playbook for the last time. My football career was over.

I decided to stay in Minneapolis. The Twin Cities is a great place to live and raise a family. Minnesota is very diverse with a multi-ethnic culture, both rural and urban. Minneapolis is one of the healthiest cities in America. Believe it or not, some of the best barbecue I ever tasted was from Rudolph's and Moma Lou's in Bloomington, Minnesota. I still had a lot of teammates on the Vikings. Maybe I could get a job at one of the twenty-five Fortune 500 companies in Minnesota. I don't know why, but for some reason, I just felt that Minnesota would be my new home.

## Public Speaking Fears

When my window closed to be a professional athlete, I had to make a transition. Football was not only my career; it was my passion, identity, and, in a sense, my calling. Could I find something that would bring the same kind of fulfillment and fire? Sonny Carlson, whom I met at Hope Presbyterian, asked if I wanted to coach and teach. He coached and taught at Kennedy High School. Coach Carlson said, "I think I can get you a job at Kennedy High School." I told him that sounded great.

I had such a fear of public speaking that the thought of standing in front of a group of high school juniors and seniors would be dreadful. I couldn't do it. God said, "Trust Me, you're going to see My glory." I was totally out of my comfort zone. I had to call the roll, give a lesson plan, then read from Shakespeare.

This was torture. However, I didn't have very many options.

I wanted to quit every day during my first year of teaching. I even filled out applications in the corporate world, but nothing opened. The only voice I heard was the one inside saying, *Don't quit; don't do it! There's something great coming for you.*

Why would the Lord dropkick me into an environment I loathed, where I felt like a failure and completely unprepared? Usually, when you graduate from college, you go into your field of study. When I graduated, my field of study was not teaching a high school English class. It was a 100-yard *football field*. In spite of my fear of public speaking, I've always loved pretending that I was a DJ on some R&B radio station. I even enrolled at Columbia School of Broadcasting. Teaching at Bloomington, John F. Kennedy, and Thomas Jefferson helped pave the way for what would be my life's work. For five years, I taught and coached in Bloomington and Burnsville school districts 271 and 191.

It wasn't easy. I knew the material but didn't have much confidence conveying that. I was reminded of an opportunity I had in the fifth grade when my science teacher, Mr. Minning, asked the question, "For ten As, who can tell me the meaning of the word *zephyr*?" I knew it meant a soft, gentle breeze, but I never raised my hand. I sat on what I knew.

On another occasion, Dr. Andrew Wall was teaching African-American studies as a graduate course at New Mexico State. Dr. Wall was a good friend of mine, so I signed up for the class, thinking it would be an easy A. In the curriculum, he announced that an oral book report would be required. I was so scared of doing an oral report that I dropped out of the class the next day. Fear is a monster.

## An Open Door

One event in the spring of 1980 would change my life. The Minnesota Vikings Bible study met each Thursday at offensive tackle Steve Ervin's house for prayer and study. This particular Thursday we decided to attend a gospel concert featuring gospel powerhouse singer Evie Tornquist. The term *ticketed gospel concert* was foreign. Most of the gospel concerts that I attended were in churches on a free-will offering basis. At that time, I hadn't heard of Evie Tornquist.

She had a powerful voice. I thought, *How does all of that volume come pouring out of such a small person?* After the concert, Wally Hilgenberg introduced me to the promoter Marilyn Shandorf. She owned Rainbow Productions. They were one of if not the largest concert promoters in the Midwest.

Wally said to Marilyn, "You should hear Joe Jackson sing."

I tried to get Wally to be quiet, but the more I tried to shush him, the more dramatic he became. He told Marilyn about the time we were in training camp at Mankato, and Fred McNeil and I were singing in the stairwell.

In response to the story, Marilyn said, "If you ever want to do something in gospel music, give us a call."

We exchanged contact information, and I thought nothing more about it. However, I was impressed that 14,000 people would buy a ticket for a gospel concert. At that time, I was still under contract with the Toronto Argos. Of course, that ended a few weeks later when I flunked my physical.

The Lord did a work of grace in the heart of Wally Hilgenberg. Wally played outside linebacker with the Minnesota Vikings for almost fifteen years. He was a ferocious hitter, a tremendous player, and a great personality. Everyone loved Wally. His smile was infectious. He was a great communicator, provider, and leader.

The only thing missing in Wally's life was a relationship with the Lord. For years, his wife, Mary, prayed that he would accept Christ as his Savior. God answered that prayer in 1978. Wally Hilgenberg prayed the sinner's prayer and was born again.

Because of Wally's encouragement, I reached out to Marilyn Shandorf and Rainbow Productions. I loved music and would sing on the street corners in Cincinnati and in the showers after practice. I didn't know hardly any gospel songs except for the old standards sung at Trinity Baptist. Outside of the Clara Ward Singers, Five Blind Boys of Alabama, James Cleveland, and The Mighty Voices of Thunder, I hardly knew any gospel music.

The Voices of Thunder would annually come to Second Trinity Baptist Church for a concert. That was about the only time that I ever wanted to go to church. I loved to hear The Voices of Thunder. Those brothers could really sing!

Marilyn told me that she was bringing Bill Gaither to the Twin Cities for a ticketed gospel concert at the St. Paul Civic Center. I had heard of Bill Gaither on the Christian radio station but wasn't familiar with his music catalog. Marilyn said, "I can get you an audition with Bill; he's a great guy and likes football." I agreed to the audition.

Late in the summer of 1980, I drove to Anderson, Indiana, where I met Bill and Gloria Gaither. They were so gracious and kind. We sat around his nine-foot grand piano while I auditioned several songs. I was a little intimidated and very nervous. Bill said, "Just relax, and we'll find something." Finally, he played "The Blood Will Never Lose Its Power" by Andre Crouch. Bill said, "When I come to St. Paul for the concert, I want you to sing that song."

I couldn't believe it—I was going to sing at the St. Paul Center Civic Center with Bill Gaither! For three exciting months, I worked to promote the concert by doing radio and TV commercials, buying advertising, and putting up posters in different churches. Could this be my new calling? I never imagined there would be anything to replace the void after my NFL career ended. Combined with teaching high school English and coaching all sports at John F. Kennedy High School, my plate was full.

The Lord didn't tell me to become the church evangelist of one of the largest churches in America, to preach the gospel in every state, to hold a revival in the largest Assemblies of God church in Singapore, or to become pro director of Athletes International Ministries. I didn't hear any of that. He impressed me to coach football and teach English. He said, "I want to see if you can get excited about something in seed form; then I'll gradually unveil the greatness I have for you."

Sometimes God hides the orchard in the seed. He said, "I want you to serve at Rainbow Productions and learn; you won't get paid. I want you to teach English and coach football. You won't make very much money there either, but I'm preparing you for something great."

No, I couldn't see the end. I couldn't see that the Lord was calling me, preparing me to lift the light in a dark world as an evangelist. And when I say *great*, I'm not defining material terms, but being able to share my thoughts audibly with confidence was something I was never *great* at doing.

## Singing with Bill Gaither

Here we are, September 28, 1980. The Bill Gaither Trio was to be in concert that night at the St. Paul Civic Center. Tickets were sold out. For three months, I'd practice singing in Doug Delin's garage. Doug and Marilyn managed the Charleswood apartment complex where I lived. Several Vikings lived at that apartment complex. I couldn't afford a garage, so Doug gave me the keys to his garage, and it became my studio.

Doug was an awesome friend. He had a great sense of humor and was a natural comedian. He loved the Lord, his family, and the Vikings. Every day he wore the same big smile and blue sweater. Doug told me he played high school football in Tacoma, Washington. He was around six feet two inches and weighed 325 pounds. He once said he needed to get in shape, so I encouraged him to start working out, and we started running together every morning for about a week.

Doug and I arrived at the venue early for my soundcheck. My stomach was in knots and my knees quivered, but somehow I got through the soundcheck. I played in championship games and the Super Bowl in front of millions of people, but this was totally out of my comfort zone. I was extremely nervous.

We ate a light dinner and Bill said he would most likely call me up to sing during the first half of the concert. The stage was round and spun slowly. The first half came and went. It was the same feeling I had on draft day eight years earlier, wondering when he would call me on stage.

Then the moment came and Bill said, "There's a guy here who some of you know as a Minnesota Viking, but I bet you didn't know he can sing. Joe Jackson, come up here. He's scared to death."

Thanks Bill—that sure didn't give me any confidence. Bill started playing the piano, and I started to sing. The sound system was incredible. I said to myself, *This really sounds good*, and began to sing more soulful. It was just great. He even called me back for an encore. Unbelievable!

What started in my friend Doug Delin's garage became the vehicle to transport me to open for Andre Crouch, The Imperials, Leon Patillo, Amy Grant, The Archers, Gaither Vocal Band, Russ Taft, my favorites Andrus and Blackwood, Barry McGuire, The Cruise Family, Dallas Holm and Praise, and many others. All thanks to Doug.

Eventually, I formed a band with good friend Murray Adam. We called ourselves the Jackson Adam Band. Murray is a great singer and worked full-time with the Billy Graham Association. At that time, the Billy Graham world headquarters was located in Minneapolis. I recorded an album in Nashville produced by the Imperials. Over the next eight years we played in churches, coffee houses, prisons, the Minnesota State Fair, and bars. One of our special concerts for me was to sing at the Minnesota Vikings chapel service. That was awesome!

## Unexpected Turn of Events

In the summer of 1981, I was asked to perform music at a crusade in Wisconsin. The speaker was a charismatic and anointed man of God, Mark Evers. He pastored a large church in Joplin, Missouri.

Throughout the crusade, Mark would say, "Joe Jackson's coming, Joplin." Halfway through the crusade, Pastor Evers decided to fly back to Springfield, Missouri. Right in the middle of his message, I remember Mark saying, "Somebody start the plane, we're leaving." I never found out why he left.

Pastor Lyn Sahr, one of the organizers of the crusade, said, "Joe, you take over."

I said, "Take over what?" The crusade was supposed to last for three more days. If I took over, I figured that nobody would show up. I hoped he wasn't suggesting that I become the evangelist. I didn't have even one sermon prepared. Maybe I could give my testimony three days in a row. I'm not an evangelist; I'm a singer. Perhaps Lyn Sahr saw something too.

We prayed, the crowd came back, and His anointing fell. Sometimes other people see gifts inside of you that you can't see. After many unreturned calls to Brother Mark, I guess Joe wasn't going to Joplin. The next year, Lyn invited me to Ladysmith, Wisconsin to sing at the Nicky Cruz crusade.

In 1982 Doug, Marilyn, and little Dougie moved back to Tacoma. He opened a pizza shop and did quite well. Somehow he lost two fingers in a restaurant accident, but he still managed to make the best deep dish pizza in the neighborhood. He also ran for the city council in East Side Tacoma. Although he was Jewish, he was very active in the Church of God in Christ. Doug Delin died suddenly in 2005. I loved Doug and Marilyn. They were great friends.

In 1984 we had a concert at an outdoor event in Minneapolis called Soul Liberation. Each night different Christian bands and artists would perform, artists like Barry McGuire, Leon Patillo, The Winans, Larnell Harris, Andrus Blackwood and Company, Rosey Grier, and many more. Soul Liberation was an awesome annual week-long community event with great music and preaching to heal the broken communities and neighborhoods.

After we finished our set, Ed Johnson from the Billy Graham organization called me and asked if we could meet for lunch. I was thinking, *Wow, maybe he wants me to sing with the Billy Graham team.*

We met and, no, it wasn't that. He offered me a job as crusade coordinator. I told Ed that I was honored for consideration, but I'm committed to music ministry and felt that's where God was leading.

Years later, I realized what a tremendous opportunity I had passed up to sit under one of the greatest evangelists of our time. What was I thinking?

I may have missed it in 1984 with the Billy Graham team, but God didn't give up on me. He sent me to Phoenix to sit under one of the most anointed men of God I've ever known, Tommy Barnett. God always has a ram in the thicket with your name on it; just keep walking.

# Chapter 22: Athletes International Ministries

After five years of teaching in the Bloomington district, I was laid off. Abraham Lincoln High School and Portland and Penn Junior High Schools closed. Last hired, first fired, I guess. Again, I was at a crossroads. My band Refuge was pretty busy playing on the weekends. We were a working band with daytime jobs. There was no way I could make it financially with just singing. So from 1984-1987, I coached football, basketball, and track for the Burnsville, Minnesota school district. Those were good years—great administration and staff. I lived in Burnsville, so it was a short commute.

Had the Bloomington district not let me go, I'd probably still be teaching today. In 1969 Ken Johnson told me that God loved me and had a plan for my life. I asked God, "What's my next move?"

He said, "It's not a move; just be still and know that I am God."

In Minnesota, I attended the Bloomington Church of God. Their worship and doctrine are very similar to the Assemblies of God. The pastor, Mike Thompson, gave us access to the church, so our band practiced in their sanctuary. It wasn't the largest church in town, yet several Minnesota Vikings and Minnesota Twins were members, including Bobby Bryant, Greg Coleman, Karl Kassulke, Dick Stigman, Tim Baylor, and others. During my ministry, I began to cross over into the Assemblies of God camp.

An Assemblies of God pastor gave me the 1986 Assemblies of God national directory. I contacted pastors hoping to book services. Pastor Bob Cashatt pastored First Assembly of God in Waterloo, Iowa. He responded to my request and invited me to his church. At that time, I wasn't preaching, only singing, so I did a concert at his church. After my first song, a kid in the front threw up—which is never a good sign!

## A Big Decision

Bob encouraged me to reach out to Phoenix First Assembly. I had never heard of it, but he said it was the largest Assemblies of God church in America. I thought, *If that's the case, why in the world would they ever want me?*

Bob pressed me to call them, so I reached out to Phoenix First Assembly of God in 1987. My call was transferred to Pastor Larry Kerychuk. His voice and delivery were clear and professional, and I felt very comfortable talking with him. I told Larry about my experience, which consisted of singing with many of the current contemporary gospel artists, including Andre Crouch and Bill Gaither. Larry patiently listened, but I could tell he wasn't moved or impressed. The people in Nashville told me to divorce myself from any mention of my NFL career and stick to what God was doing currently through music ministry.

Larry said, "Bo or Joe, whatever your name is, I'm sorry, brother, we're booked through 1988."

I said, "Okay, man. No problem. Thanks for your time." I reminded myself what the people in Nashville said, but before I hung up I said, "There's something else I'd like to say. I did play defensive end for almost nine years in the NFL with the New York Jets and Minnesota, including Super Bowl XI."

Larry replied, *"What?* Man, you're just the guy we need!"

In May of 1987, Larry Kerychuk sent me an airline ticket to Phoenix. I sang in the main sanctuary during the Wednesday night service before Pastor Barnett preached, then spoke in Larry's college and career class. It was awesome!

Not only was Larry one of the pastors at Phoenix First, but he is also the founder and director of Athletes International Ministries (AIM). He also birthed Master's Commission. One of the highlights of AIM is the annual Phoenix Conference and banquet for professional and collegiate athletes, coaches, and family members. Since 1985, over ten thousand athletes and coaches have attended the AIM conference.

Before I returned to Minneapolis, Larry mentioned that I should pray about something. He asked if I would consider moving to Phoenix. I could operate my ministry out of Phoenix First Assembly of God and join the AIM team. He said I would work with Travis Turner, who played quarterback at Nebraska.

Travis worked with the college athletes. I said I would pray about it and let him know. Minneapolis was my home. The only thing I hadn't adapted to was lutefisk and lefse—and, of course, the harsh winter months. Other than that, it was a very livable city, a great place to raise a family or build a career. It's not like New York City but certainly not like Las Cruces. Maybe a little of both.

The Twin Cities is one of the most socially conscious and interracial communities in the United States. I always felt that there must be something in the water. After all, Minnesota does boast of having 10,000 lakes. However, I'm sadly reminded of the social unrest after the recent murders of George Floyd and twenty-year-old Duante Wright. Regardless of what's in the water, the issue is always what's in the heart of mankind (Matt. 15:17-20). Minnesotans are good people, and Minneapolis is a great city. Don't let the unconscionable actions of some determine your feelings about the entire populace.

When the Minnesota Vikings signed me as a free agent in 1976, my only thought was to make this football team. I was driven; that was my focus. Now with an NFL career in the rearview mirror, the Lord showed me His other purpose for my life—He would build a ministry, starting through music.

He revealed that I had other gifts waiting to be opened. I don't know if that could have happened the way it did in any other city than Minneapolis. Could my season in Minnesota be over? God will sometimes ask, "Are you traditional or transitional?" Will you take a step onto the water?

If you're a Minnesota Viking, you're always a Viking—regardless of how long you played or what other teams you played with. Minnesotans love their sports teams. Because I played with the Vikings, my transition from the classroom to full-time ministry was seamless. God opened doors for ministry throughout the state. I must've preached and sung in every small town and village from Owatonna to International Falls.

## Another Transition

Even though I was getting tired of lighting a pan of charcoal underneath my car to turn the crankshaft in the winter, Minnesota was home to me and my ministry was birthed there. Moving to Phoenix would be like starting over. Yet my spirit was restless. For some reason, I felt God was redirecting my path in another direction for the next level. What would I tell my band? Maybe they would come with me.

As I shared my feelings with the band, I hoped they might consider relocating, but it was like pulling teeth. I painted the best picture I knew how. Why didn't they get it? It was frustrating. I later realized that I was trying to take people who were not destined to go with me.

Moses let the people frustrate him to the point that he saw the Promised Land, yet he never entered it. And like Moses, I could have seen the opportunity at Phoenix First Assembly but never experienced it. I had to separate from some very dear friends.

We did our last concert at Pastor Randy Saatzer's church in January of 1988. Robert Edwards, John Hiiva, Pete Anderson, John Paavola, and Tim Skogen were more than bandmates; they were family. Saying goodbye was hard. Robert Edwards helped me to pack the moving truck as I headed back to the desert.

God closed the door and opened another on the path that led me to Phoenix. Still single at 38, maybe Phoenix would give me more than a new address; maybe this would be where I find my righteous fox. I arrived in Phoenix in my 1977 Mercury station wagon, pulling a trailer loaded with all my worldly possessions, including my grandmother's antique king chair. That chair traveled with us from Cincinnati, New York, New Mexico, Minnesota, and now Phoenix.

My transition from Minneapolis to Phoenix was more seamless this time than it was twenty years earlier. That 18-year-old boy who moved from Cincinnati to Las Cruces, New Mexico had matured. I was ready for all of the Mexican food I could eat! The hotter, the better. And I wanted to find a good country station to hear Charley Pride sing "Kiss an Angel Good Morning" or Freddie Hart's "Easy Loving."

My only concern was starting over again. I didn't know anyone in Phoenix except Larry. How would I get bookings? How would I survive financially? Larry said, "Don't worry. God will provide." Larry Kerychuk introduced me Larry Fosholt. He was a businessman who was recently divorced and lived in a huge, 6,000-square-foot home at Camelback Mountain. Larry let me live at his house for almost two years. It was an awesome location, only ten minutes from the airport and twenty minutes from the church.

In the late '80s, two interstate freeways came through Phoenix, I-10 and I-17. There were no loops or bypasses. The city's fathers wanted to keep Phoenix small. Warren Mecum was governor. Arizona was embroiled in controversy regarding a paid holiday for Martin Luther King, Jr. Day. Mecum preferred an unpaid holiday on Sunday. He described Black children as pickaninny, whatever that means.

In reaction to these events, Boycott Arizona was organized. I started question my decision. Was this the right move? I had gone from the more inclusive culture and political platform of Hebert H. Humphrey and Walter Mondale to the exclusive mentality of Barry Goldwater and Warren Mecum. The Super Bowl pulled out, and others businesses threatened similar action. Phoenix doesn't have many Fortune 500 companies; its biggest export was tourism. With this controversy, the snowbirds considered hibernating in Texas or New Mexico, which meant a blow to our economy. Mecum was impeached in April of 1988.

## Divine Appointments

It was perfect timing in January, 1988: 85 degrees and something called "Pastors' School." Every year Pastor Tommy Barnett would hold a three-day pastors' conference in February after the Super Bowl. Pastors from all over the world came to Tommy Barnett's conference to seek the

Lord and catch God's vision and dream for their life. This turned out to be a phenomenal resource for me to make contacts with churches.

Pastor Tommy would be speaking at the Tuesday morning session, and Larry asked if I could sing just before Tommy preached. After I sang, Pastor Barnett endorsed my ministry and encouraged pastors to schedule me to minister at their church. An endorsement from Pastor Tommy Barnett was all it took! I couldn't believe it. I was able to book most of my calendar during that conference. For the next twenty-six years, this was a great tool God used to fill my calendar.

I was reminded of the prophecy spoken over me at a small church in Grasston, Minnesota in 1983. Pastor Jim Brightbill gave the altar call and asked me to come forward. He laid hands on me and gave a prophetic utterance I've never forgotten. He said, "Joe, one day God's going to broaden your borders like Jabez, do you believe it?"

I said, "Yeah, man. I believe it." To be honest, I really didn't know who Jabez was. I thought he was talking about some street preacher from *the hood.* I said to myself, *Jabez is a cool name. Maybe I'll name my son Jabez Jackson. That's a great football name.*

In Minnesota, my borders were mostly in Minnesota. Rarely would I receive a call from another state. It was always a big deal to say we're doing a concert in Wisconsin, North or South Dakota, or Iowa. The prophecy said that God would broaden my borders.

Because of Tommy Barnett's pastor school conference, I have preached the gospel in every state and many foreign countries throughout the world. My vision is broadened as well as my ministry.

Phoenix '88 was my first Athletes' Conference. Nearly 700 athletes and coaches attended this life-changing, spirit-filled oasis in the desert. Mike Singletary, Meadowlark Lemon, Rosey Grier, Earnie Shavers, Madeline Manning Mims, Carl Eller, A.C. Green, Hollywood Henderson, and Coach Bill McCartney checked egos at the door and cried out to God in one voice. It was awesome to see the body of Christ look like it is supposed to.

Dr. Edwin Louis Cole was one of our speakers. Dr. Cole spoke about keeping your word. He hammered the phrase over and over: "Your word is your bond." Unknown to all was what the Lord was speaking to Coach Bill McCartney. Coach Mac was the head coach of the Colorado Buffalos. He realized the importance of a team—the forging together of young men from various backgrounds, colors, and neighborhoods. Coach Mac also dealt with the death of his star quarterback Sal Aunese, who fathered his grandchild. Coach recognized that any division could potentially destroy a locker room and team.

Coach Mac knew the value of a cohesive unit and the importance of molding one team with one purpose with love and respect for all. He saw men as the vehicle for this new dispensation. Promise Keepers was birthed at our Phoenix '88 conference. Like the Jesus Movement, Promise Keepers was radical.

Visions were birthed, men packed stadiums all over America, walls were torn down, and Christ was lifted high. Its impact will reverberate for years to come, maybe until Jesus comes.

In 1991 Coach Mac led the Colorado Buffalos to a national championship, beating Notre Dame in the Orange Bowl. Coach Mac was at the top of college football. In 1994 the Buffalos posted an 11-1 record. They capped off their season by beating Notre Dame in the Fiesta Bowl. At the end of 1994, Coach Mac retired from coaching at the age of fifty-four.

Coach Mac is a great friend of myself and Athletes International Ministries. He once told me, "Joe, I pray for you every day." He is a man of faith, a man of prayer, and a man of his word. I love Coach Mac.

When I was recruited by Michigan, Coach Mac was a young general agent on the Wolverines' staff. Many times I've thought, *What if?* Though Coach McCartney never coached me as a football player, he coached me how to be a godly man and how to be a champion.

# Chapter 23: Purple Rain and Big Chick

The movie *Purple Rain* was released in August of 1984. The Minneapolis music scene was put on the map. Everyone wanted the Minneapolis sound. Prince, Jimmy Jam, and Terry Lewis found a niche. Paisley Park was the new Motown Hitsville. Even gospel music exploded with the Sounds of Blackness.

Big Chick Huntsberry was the bodyguard for Prince and Bon Scott of AC/DC. They partied hard. Big Chick (Charles Huntsberry) stood six feet six inches and weighed around 330 pounds. Chick told me that after a tour ended, he and Bon Scott talked about picking up things when the next tour began. Bon Scott died a few weeks later. Big Chick once wrestled a bear and even pulled off a man's ear. He looked the part and was the part. *Rolling Stone* featured Big Chick in their April 6, 1989 article titled "Stand by Me."

I was singing in a Minneapolis church and noticed an imposing figure in the back. I thought, *Who in the world is that, a wrestler?* We met after the concert.

He said, "My name is Chick Huntsberry; I was Prince's bodyguard." We exchanged numbers and kept in contact. Big Chick was a natural and powerful communicator with a big heart. He was a big teddy bear who loved the Lord and people. He also loved his wife Linda and six children.

Chick accepted the Lord early in life but walked away from the church for the lure of the world. When he was no longer with Prince, God drew him back into the family of God. Chick repented, and God turned his life around. The Lord opened doors of ministry for Chick. He would speak in churches, prisons, and high schools, inviting the students to come back for an evening rally to hear his testimony.

I remember Big Chick sharing his testimony at Phoenix First Assembly of God during our athletes' conference in 1988. The church was packed with over 6,000 people in attendance. When Chick spoke, he said, "For years I protected a man named Prince. I watched over him, cared for him, led him through crowds, and provided for his needs. Now the Prince of Peace watches over me, protects me, and loves me. Jesus Christ is my Lord, and I love Him. Don't you hear me? I love Him, and I want to tell you something—if you don't know Jesus as Savior and you walk out of those doors, let me be the first one to call you an idiot."

That was Big Chick's style. The place erupted, and many came forward for salvation. Perhaps some responded just to avoid the wrath of my friend and brother Big Chick Huntsberry.

We were booked in high schools in St. Cloud, Minnesota to share our anti-drug and alcohol message through a program named the Super Star Competition. We would compete against six or seven of the schools' best athletes in five events—volleyball, tug of war, relay race, push-ups, and basketball.

Between events we'd share a five-minute testimony, keeping the program moving. Although we weren't able to share the gospel message, God always anoints the truth. We would invite the students back for an evening rally. I remember one evening rally in northern Minnesota where over a hundred students came forward to accept Jesus Christ as savior.

Heavyweight boxer Earnie Shavers, Bengals tight end ML Harris, and I were at our hotel in St. Cloud waiting for Chick's arrival. Earlier that week, Chick and I confirmed the date, time, and place. Where was Chick? He would never miss an opportunity to share his story. I called him several times only to reach his voicemail. I was concerned. He had recently gone through a battery of tests at the Mayo Clinic for chest pain. He once told me his heart was in bad shape and was failing, but his personality was so big I didn't think anything could slow him down. Big Chick had kicked his cocaine habit to the curb in 1985, and he was clean and filled with the Holy Spirit.

That morning I received a call from Larry Kerychuk. He told me the previous night Big Chick preached his final message at a church in Minneapolis. It was a great sermon. When Chick gave an altar call, his six children came forward and accepted Christ as their savior. He knew the end was near. His work was complete. Larry said sadly, Big Chick passed the next morning, April 2, 1990. He was only forty-seven.

# Chapter 24: I Don't Want a Singer in My Pulpit

I n the fall of 1991 I was asked to minister at a church in Nebraska. That Sunday I met with the pastor for breakfast. I usually don't eat breakfast, certainly not before I sing. We talked about the two morning services. He asked me about the subject I'd be preaching, and I said, "I don't preach; I sing."

He replied, "I don't want a singer in my pulpit for Sunday morning."

I was so ticked off with him for that statement that I could have head slapped him. Looking back, that was all part of God's amazing plan. The only sermon I'd ever preached was in May of 1978 at the Spanish Methodist church in Las Cruces. It was absolutely the worst sermon ever.

I excused myself from breakfast and started writing down some thoughts. In the first service I sang a couple of songs then started preaching. It was a disaster. I was so embarrassed that I wanted to hide. It had to be the worse sermon ever preached in the history of preaching. I felt like there was no way I was going to preach the 11:00 service. Somehow I dragged myself to the pulpit for the second service. I prayed and relaxed, and it was like night and day. I shared my testimony, and it was great.

Thank you, Jesus! I remembered that I could recover from a fall. It was another transition along my journey. The Lord used music to bring me to ministry. If He had told me to preach, I would still be running from the call. But He said, "Just start singing, and I'll show you My glory." I have come such a long way compared to where I began!

126

## Overcoming Fear

Someone left a copy of *USA Today* on a seat at Stapleton Airport in Denver. I was waiting to connect to Phoenix. I grabbed it and immediately turned to the sports page. To my pleasant surprise, there was an article written by my former teammate Alan Page. I thought, *Maybe he will say something about Big Joe in the article.* And he did.

Page was one of the greatest defensive tackles to ever play in the NFL. He's an NFL Hall of Famer, winning the NFL Defensive Player of the Year in 1971, and he earned a law degree in 1978 while playing with the Vikings. He became a Minnesota Supreme Court Justice. It was an honor to play with great people like Alan Page, Jim Marshall, Carl Eller, and Doug Sutherland.

The news we hear about entertainers, politicians, and professional athletes is usually negative—and sometimes for good reason. However, it was great to see something positive. Page was implementing a program to stimulate fourth graders to become better readers and comprehend what they read, inspired by something that had happened in the locker room. His article told the story that I remember so vividly. We had a new defensive line coach, Murray Warmath, who passed out the playbooks one day and asked each player to read a paragraph. My confidence level was near zero. When it came to my turn, I froze and stammered over a couple of lines about defeating a double team block. Alan Page made no literal mention of my name in the article; he didn't have to. The inference was deafening—I was one of the four. There was no problem with my reading. I could read; I'm an English Literature major. I had a problem overcoming fear. We know that fear can be our greatest motivator and also our biggest dream killer.

I'm glad I've overcome through God's grace. One of my favorite songs is "Your Grace and Mercy" by the Mississippi Mass Choir. That's my anthem. Doubt has often tried to convince me to chase another dream or remind me of my failures, but I had to keep pressing on like the persistent widow in Luke 18. She had every right and reason to quit, but she kept her faith, and God rewarded her with a breakthrough.

# Chapter 25: The Man
# from La Mancha

Athletes International Ministries continued to build its team. In June of 1991, Cincinnati Bengal M.L. Harris was our newest edition. M.L. played tight end for my hometown, the Bengals, who played the 49ers in Super Bowl XVI. They fought hard before losing 20-16. M.L. was another Buckeye from Columbus, Ohio, and we bonded immediately.

There wasn't a whole lot of room for office space at Phoenix First Assembly. Larry Kerychuk was paid staff and had an office in the administration building. The rest of us worked from home. To keep up with the growth of this ministry, we needed our own office. There was a vacant house near the church property that could be converted to an office. Someone from the church purchased the property, and it became the AIM house. We officed there for three years.

The church needed the AIM house for other ministries. Soon we were looking again for office space. Chuck and Diane Griffin owned the La Mancha Hotel and racquetball club. La Mancha was prime real estate, located right off of Central Avenue. Chuck and Di were great friends. Could this be a landing spot? Before we approached them, we prayed for God's favor.

We met and discussed the possibility of office space at La Mancha. I inquired about the cost.

They said, "We know you guys are a ministry. How does free sound?"

For the next nine years, the La Mancha Hotel and racquetball club was home to Athletes International Ministries. I even lived there for a few months. M.L. and I continued to do our high school drug and alcohol awareness program, the Super Star Competition. We probably went to over two thousand high schools and middle schools, doing three or four assemblies a day.

The thought of running down a basketball court and sprinting in a relay race is now only a great memory. Today my knees are shot and need to be replaced unless God does a miracle! The La Mancha was not only a racquetball club; it was a sports center that had a full gym, fitness center, swimming pool, and boxing ring. It was common to see NBA great Hall of Famers Connie Hawkins, Meadowlark Lemon, and Dan Marjerle walk past our offices.

## George Foreman

Michael Carbajal was an American five-time world boxing champion and silver medalist in the 1988 Seoul Olympic Games. His nickname was "Little Hands of Stone," and he was Phoenix's greatest boxing champion. Michael was trained by his other brother at La Mancha. It was exciting to see a world champion train right in front of your eyes. La Mancha also began to promote fights. They would draw local personalities like Earnie Shavers, Johnnie Tapia, and Earl Butler to help with the gate. For one big fight, George Foreman was scheduled to make a guest appearance, and I couldn't wait to see him.

In 1987 I was asked to sing at a youth camp in Zimmerman, Minnesota. They had already booked their speaker, so they didn't need me to preach. At the time, I was only singing anyway. The speaker did a great job and he related well with the youth. We shared the same cabin. After a long day and night of camp, it was finally lights out.

I was ready for bed, but the speaker wasn't; he was still preaching. I thought about saying in a nice and respectful way, "Hey listen, bro, I don't need another sermon, I'm ready to hit the sack." But I was smarter than that.

The speaker was the former heavyweight champion George Foreman. Yeah, the same George Foremen who knocked Joe Frazier down six times in two rounds—and I sure didn't want to be the seventh knockdown! Well, somewhere in the middle of our conversation, I was able to get in a few words.

I told George that I thought he should make a comeback. I said, "George, if you look at the heavyweight division now, there's no one out there. Man, I really think you could regain your title."

This would be our first meeting since that conversation five years earlier. Our offices were all glass so I could see everything. When George walked toward the lobby, I sprang from my chair. I called out, "Hey George, this is Joe Jackson, we did the youth camp together in Zimmerman, Minnesota in 1987."

He said, "Hey, Joe, I remember. How are you doing?" What he said next really was a shocker. He said, "Joe, I want to thank you for something you gave me." I figured he wanted to thank me for giving him one of my CDs. He said, "No, that's not it. I want to thank you for encouraging me to come back."

You see, on November 5, 1994, George Foreman, after not having boxed in nearly ten years and at almost 46 years old, knocked out Michael Moorer in the tenth round to regain the WBA, IBF, and lineal heavyweight championship of the world. This encourages me that I can make a comeback, too—not in the NFL, but I know I can get up and recover from a fall.

No matter how beaten and bruised you are, you can get up and fight again. Just remember, it's not your fight. You have an advocate. Don't let the enemy steal your future. Jesus says that He comes so you might have life abundantly (John 10:10).

We know the enemy always comes to steal our dreams, kill our vision, and destroy our future. Don't let him win. In the Foreman vs. Moorer fight, George took control of the fight and knocked Moorer down. In the war we fight, we know that the battle is not ours, but God's (2 Chron. 20:15).

In the fall of 1995, we expanded our ministry to Lambertville, New Jersey. With a large population of current and retired athletes living on the east coast, this would be a great resource pool. Hall of Famers Lenny

Moore and Marion Motley, Mr. Universe Dennis Tinerino, and Jake the Snake Roberts were honored at our awards banquet. This was the first banquet I co-hosted with Madeline Manning Mims. In the meantime, Larry and I had an opportunity to host our own television show on the TBN network.

Paul and Jan Crouch were looking for a show with an ESPN type of format. We had been guests on TBN in Los Angeles but had no experience in hosting a nationwide television program. They would provide the studio, camera equipment, director, and staff. We'd tape the show in Phoenix at a local TBN affiliate. Our program was called *Inside Sport*. Larry was a natural. He could have easily been an ESPN host.

Besides being a co-host, I was like a roving reporter interviewing athletes and coaches at different locations in the US. Even though I was a rookie and made my share of fumbles and wrong quotes, I loved it. When Super Bowl XXVI came to Minneapolis, it was exciting. TBN sent Jamie and me to cover the big game. Minnesota had never hosted a Super Bowl, so it would be very special.

The Washington Redskins and Buffalo Bills each had a strong representation of Christians, including Redskins head coach Joe Gibbs. I interviewed Redskin defensive tackle Charles Mann and asked about the influence their head coach had on the team. He said, "Yes, we are a reflection of our head coach, but he doesn't cram his faith down our throat; he just lives it." The Buffalo Bills' James Lofton, Tim Tasker, and Frank Reich were also strong believers. It was a unique experience to interview the Christian players alongside the anchors from other top news and sports networks.

Being in Minneapolis for the Super Bowl reminded me of how much I missed Minnesota and the Twin Cities. There are not a lot of generational roots in Phoenix. We're all transplanted from other states. On my street, there's probably not a single person (since my daughter moved) who was born in Arizona. Minneapolis proper contains America's fifth-highest concentration of Fortune 500 companies. Phoenix has one or two.

Where Minneapolis is urban, Phoenix is western. In Minneapolis, families and neighborhoods spawn generations within a five-block radius. Phoenicians are mostly transplants or snowbirds. It took a couple of years to fully complete my transformation to Arizona, and it was a harder transition than I anticipated. Gone were the 10,000 lakes, my Viking teammates, the Mall of America, the neighborhoods, the Minneapolis skyline, acres of farmland, and the absence of tax on anything that you can eat or wear. Don't get me wrong; I still detested the harsh and long winters, but I missed Minneapolis.

With nearly 300 days of sun in Phoenix, I no longer had to rely on tanning booths. I can lay out by my pool and get as brown as a glass of Pepsi. The Lord opened this door and confirmed a move to Arizona. I knew the He would give me His peace.

Some people miss the will of God because they give up too soon. I preach a message called "The Danger of Giving Up Too Soon." In our culture, we want everything immediately. You can go to a fast-food restaurant and be eating your dinner in five minutes.

It would take my grandmother hours to bake a blackberry pie. She would slowly drive her 1964 Chevy Corvair to the countryside, where I would pick wild blackberries, always watching out for snakes. When we returned home, she would wash the blackberries, make the crust, and bake the pie, all from scratch and never even using a recipe. No one does that anymore. It's easier to go to the store and buy a pumpkin pie for five bucks, even though it will never be as good as grandma's. I'm afraid "made by scratch" has been scratched.

Just like New Mexico, it took time for me to finally change my driver's license and plates to Minnesota. At that point, my season in Minnesota was over. I fulfilled my purpose and outgrew that chapter of my destiny. If you are the smartest kid in class, then guess what? You've outgrown your class. Had I stayed in Minneapolis for music, I'd probably still be walking that path. Minneapolis had a signature sound.

Flyte Tyme Productions enjoyed great success with their artists, including Janet Jackson, Rod Stewart, George Michael, Mary J. Blige, and many more. Our band was nominated for contemporary Christian artist of the year in Minneapolis.

Sharing studio time with Jellybean Johnson and Jesse Johnson was the norm. Even Prince's former guitarist Dez Dickerson filled in with our band at an outdoor event. If I wanted to stay with music, why would I ever leave Minneapolis at the height of this musical explosion? Because it was time to turn the page. When you know something in your spirit, you just know it.

The Lord gave me no sign; I heard no voice, I was just impressed to go. I came to Phoenix as a gospel singer, not an evangelist, because that's what I thought I was. That's how I saw myself. People told me I was a gospel singer. But the Lord said, "Trust Me, I have something more for you. I'm going to broaden your borders, not only geographically, but personally."

# Chapter 26: The Briefcase

One day I was walking through the Phoenix Sky Harbor Airport parking garage on my way to the gate. I was running late so I had to pick up the pace. From out of nowhere, I felt a whack on my hindquarters from what appeared to be a briefcase. I thought to myself, *Someone's gonna get hurt.* As I turned around, it was my pastor, Tommy Barnett, crouched over.

We had a good laugh and a short conversation. Just before I continued on to the gate, he said, "Joe, I believe God has His hand on your life; He's got something really special for you."

I said, "Thanks, Pastor. I needed that word."

He also said, "When you're in town, I want you to sit with the pastors at church. You're our church evangelist."

I thanked him and thought, *Church evangelist, wow, I am?*

Pastor Barnett saw me as an evangelist. He saw what I could become. At the time, I didn't see it. I only saw what I had done, not what I could be. From the foundation of the world, God called me to serve as an evangelist.

Larry and I were suffering for Jesus in Maui, Hawaii. We each had our own ocean-view condo. This was the perfect setting to watch the waves skip against the sandy beach. Brother Dave Morocco arranged for an outreach into several high schools. We would be joined by NFL players from the Pro Bowl and Super Bowl.

## A Surprising Response to Outreach

Washington Redskin Darrell Green, Steeler Tim Johnson, 49er Jesse Sapolu, San Diego Charger Leo Goeas, and others would participate in the Super Star Competition. Darrell Green held the title of the fastest man in the NFL. His hand-held 40-yard dash is 4.09. I knew that we'd be in good shape for the competition. Before we began our program, we gathered for prayer and final instructions. With the addition of the Pro Bowl players, the gymnasium was electric.

The principal and school superintendent thanked us for coming. We were cautioned not to share any personal Christian testimonies or anything religious. I assured them that our message was secular but positive.

The first event was the relay race. The whistle blew, and 300-pound Jesse Sapolu surprisingly kept it close. He passed the baton to Redskin defensive tackle Tim Johnson who made up some ground, but we were still trailing. Next was 290-pound Leo Goeas. Goeas huffed and puffed his way to the next runner, me.

For a big guy, I've always been able to run. I am blessed with fast-twitch muscle fibers; however, there was no way I would catch that high school kid. I passed the baton to Darrell Green, who was like a bolt of lightning. In twenty yards, he caught up to the other runner. When he made the turn, it was over. We won our first event! The next was the tug-of-war, which is usually never any competition. So to make it fun, we began to pull the other team toward the centerline. At the last second, I signaled the audience to help out their classmates. They emptied the stands, and it was no contest. We're all even.

Between the second and third events, one of the athletes talked to the student body. I was up first. I told the students that they were loved and destined for greatness. I stressed that regardless of how many times they've failed in life, failure's not failure, nor is it final unless you don't learn from it. I shared my story of lessons learned because of poor decisions, saying that the most important thing someone can do is to make good choices and to see themselves as someone with intrinsic value. You count; you make a difference. It doesn't matter what color you are, what neighborhood you live in, or who your daddy works for. If you have a dream and are willing to commit, who knows? Maybe one day you'll be playing in the pro bowl.

The next event was push-ups. Between push-ups and volleyball, another speaker addressed the student body. This time Darrell Green spoke, thanking the high school for the opportunity to share with the students. He talked about the Super Bowl win over the Bills and the effort and hard work it takes to be a champion. Then he shared his testimony. He shared how Jesus Christ is his Lord and Savior and how there was a revival among the Washington Redskins, and how their head coach, Joe Gibbs, is vocal regarding his faith in Jesus Christ.

Larry Kerychuk and I looked at each other and lowered our heads. We knew we were in trouble. Darrell finished preaching and gave the mic to Leo Goeas, who also shared his testimony. Next, we moved to the final event, basketball. After the game, Tim Johnson and Jesse Sapolu spoke. I guess they didn't get the memo either. They both shared that Jesus Christ changed their life and that He was the only way to find their purpose. They told the students that God has a plan for their lives.

Larry and I looked at Dave Morocco, who was sweating bullets. After the assembly, we signed autographs, took pictures, and congratulated the student athletes. I tried to avoid eye contact with Dave Morocco. I knew what he was thinking. He had arranged the assemblies assuring that our message would be secular. *I guess we blew it!*

I noticed Dave was talking to the district superintendent, who waved us over. Holding our breath, we walked over. The superintendent and principal shook our hands and said that the assembly was the best program ever to come into the high school. He couldn't believe how well the students behaved and listened to every word the athletes spoke. I was shocked. Dave had warned us not to say anything about our faith. I wasn't expecting that kind of response from the administration. Larry and I couldn't believe it. I had to repent of my doubt and fear.

# Chapter 27: Be a Doer
## of the Word

A thletes International Ministries has walked in God's favor. I will never forget when Larry Kerychuk and I went to Los Angeles to receive a check for one million dollars. God spoke to a businessman who was so moved by the testimony of the professional athletes that he sowed into the ministry of AIM.

We eventually were able to purchase the Phoenix Swim Club, where Olympians Gary Hall, Jr., Anthony Ervin, and NFL pros had trained, and the Outlaw Waylon Jennings would drop by for treatment.

From our club alone, thirteen medals were won in the 2000 Summer Olympic Games in Sydney. If our club were a nation, we would have won more medals than 43 countries. What a blessing to walk in God's favor!

Gold medals, promotions, health, and wealth are not always indicators of God's favor. In some of the darkest days in my life, I've felt God's favor because nothing can separate me from the love of God (Rom. 8:31). It's the love of God that leads me to redemption; it's the love of God that brings me through the desert. Romans 5:2-5 (ESV) reads:

> Through him we have also obtained access by faith into
> this grace in which we stand, and we rejoice in hope of
> the glory of God. Not only that, but we rejoice in our
> sufferings, knowing that suffering produces endurance,
> and endurance produces character, and character
> produces hope, and hope does not put us to shame,
> because God's love has been poured into our hearts

through the Holy Spirit who has been given to us.

My sports information director from New Mexico State, Sonny Yates, scheduled me to speak in a high school in Ft. Walton Beach, Florida in the early 90s. It had been at least twenty years since our last meeting. Sonny was a mover with a big vision and dream. After he left NMSU, he directed the Sun Bowl carnival in El Paso, Texas. Sonny was an innovator. He gave me my college nickname of Mad Mountain Jackson. It would be great to see Sonny again.

Sonny had booked interviews with a few radio stations and the local NBC. Sonny had hands in many pots. The interview started out the same—questions about the NFL, our connection at NMSU, and asking what I was doing now. Then, to my surprise, Sonny asked me to share my faith. He said, "Joey, tell the television audience what Jesus Christ means to you." It was evident that Christ had become real in Sonny's heart.

After the interview, he accompanied me to the high school and introduced me to the principal. After some small talk, we walked toward the auditorium. Just before introducing me, the principal said, "I don't want you to only talk to the students about your football career. These kids need God. Tell them your testimony." In over three thousand secular schools that I've spoken in, no principal has ever requested that!

If we were allowed more freedom to share the gospel, I wonder what our society would look like.

When I was in Sydney, Australia, I spoke in a dozen public high schools. I was able to openly share my faith and even give an altar call. I'm not sure how effective it was but at least the students had the opportunity to hear the word of God.

We know that hearing the Word is a start, but it takes more than that. The Bible says we need to be doers of the word and not hears only, deceiving our own selves (James 1:22). Connecting me with Sonny Yates reminded me of the early days in Las Cruces.

When I was in college, I was sometimes a hearer and a speaker of the Word. It's easy to hear and speak the Word, but it's harder to walk and live the Word. I learned early in my Christian walk that sometimes, there can be a fine line between commitment and hypocrisy.

My first year on campus, we ate at Milton Student Union. The athletes enjoyed a training table. I guess the football team ate so much that it was abolished after my freshman year. Beginning my sophomore year, the athletes ate with the general student body. One of the cashiers was named Maria. She always had a smile and a kind word every time I went through the line. She knew that I was a believer and would ask me questions about my faith.

One evening I went to the local convenience store for a snack. While I looked for a bag of chips, I picked up an adult magazine. Just then Maria happened to walk into the store. She said, "Hi, Joey, how are you doing?"

I said, "Fine," then quickly put the magazine down. It was too late. I'd been caught. I felt like a phony, so embarrassed. The next time I went through her line, I gave her a "four spiritual laws" track to ease my conscience. Instead of sharing that I had areas in my life that still needed work, I tried to justify my failure.

God says to be a doer of the Word and not only a hearer only. The Bible says that the hearer of the Word only deceives himself. I needed to get some Word in me so I could birth some real fruit. I learned that people look at how you live more than what you say. That missed opportunity with Maria still haunts me today. I would like to talk to her, but that moment's gone. I learned that when you miss a tackle, make a tackle on the next play.

Reggie White was the real deal; he didn't miss many tackles. He was one of the most dominant players in NFL history. There were many times when he couldn't be blocked, not even with a double or triple team—as they say, a man among boys. God blessed Reggie with a skill set that comes along once in a millennium. Reggie was a great friend and brother in the Lord. He attended our Phoenix Athletes Conferences and boldly shared his testimony whenever given the opportunity.

Toward the end of his playing career, I asked Reggie if he'd consider playing another year. At the time of his retirement, he was the all-time sack leader with 198 sacks. Certainly, 200 sacks were well in reach. He answered, "Joe, only if the Lord leads me that way." That's how he lived his life, following the path of the Lord. Sometimes the path of the Lord is the one least traveled. Reggie was bold. He stood on God's Word and never backed down. How could that happen? Some of his comments made him controversial. He appeared in a newspaper advertising a campaign to convince gays and lesbians that they could cease their homosexuality. As a result, CBS withdrew a five-year, $6 million contract for being a part of the *NFL Today* because of his statements. One of my biggest regrets is not honoring Reggie White at our athletes' conference.

If you stand for something, you need to be prepared to be controversial. Jesus was controversial; He said, "I send you out as sheep among wolves; I come not to bring peace but a sword." The days of timidity, indifference, and being a soft-spoken religious Christian who doesn't want to offend anybody are over.

It would have been an honor to play next to the minister of defense Reggie White. His legacy goes far beyond accolades and awards. On December 26, 2004, the minister of defense was called home. The following are members of the "All Heaven Team." Each of these people have attended our conference or been a part of the AIM ministry.

# Chapter 28: Hall of Faith

H ere are the names of AIM teammates who are now members of the Hall of Faith:

Meadowlark Lemon: Harlem Globetrotters, NBA Hall of Fame

Tom Landry: Dallas Cowboys head coach, NFL Hall of Fame, Super Bowl champion

Big Cat Ernie Ladd: San Diego Chargers, Kansas Chiefs, AFL Hall of Fame

Ernie Banks: Chicago Cubs' Mr. Cub, MLB Hall of Fame

Wayman Tisdale: Pacers, Kings, Phoenix Suns, College Basketball Hall of Fame

Marion Motley: Cleveland Browns, NFL Hall of Fame

Archie Moore: Light Heavyweight World Champion, World Boxing Hall of Fame

Wally Hilgenberg: Minnesota Viking legend

Andre Crouch: Gospel singer, father of contemporary gospel music, seven Grammy awards

Tom Sirotnak: USC Trojan defensive tackle, USC chaplain

Dave Dureson: Chicago Bears defensive back, Super Bowl champion '85 Bears

Jimmy Young: Heavyweight boxer, fought Muhammad Ali, Earnie Shavers, George Foreman, and Ken Norton

Big Boss Man: WWF

Aaron Pryor: Two-time lightweight world champion

Dennis Tinerino: Four-time Mr. Universe and Mr. America

Blue Moon Odom: Oakland As, World Series champion

George "the Animal" Steele: WWF professional wrestler

Marquis Cooper: linebacker, Tampa Bay Buccaneers, Minnesota Vikings, and Oakland Raiders

Big Chick Huntsberry: Bodyguard for Prince and Bon Scott of AC/DC

Armen Gilliam: Phoenix Suns, Charlotte Hornets, Philadelphia 76ers, New Jersey Nets

Coach Kay Yow: North Carolina State Wolfpack, 700-plus victories, Naismith Memorial Basketball Hall of Fame

Michael "Hawk" Hegstrand: one half of the team known as the Road Warriors

Coach Hank Stram: Kansas City Chiefs head coach, Super Bowl champion, NFL Hall of Fame

Isaiah Robertson: Los Angeles Rams

Dr. Edwin Louis Cole: author, founder of Christian Men's Network, favorite speaker at AIM conferences

Garry Lefebvre: Edmonton Eskimoa, Grey Cup champion, Canadian Football League

Karl Kassulke: Minnesota Vikings

Tom Skinner: Redskins chaplain, author, AIM speaker

Melvena Lay: Olympic sprinter

# Chapter 29: The Big Dipper, Rosey, and Evander

I first met Meadowlark Lemon at an AIM rally in 1987. He was gracious and reserved. It was surprising to see this side of Meadowlark. I was expecting to be splashed with a bucket of confetti as soon as I walked in the door because Meadowlark was known as the clown prince of basketball. It's hard to think of the Harlem Globetrotters without Meadowlark Lemon. I really miss Lark.

We became good friends. I will never forget the day he introduced me to Wilt Chamberlain. Wilt was my all-time favorite big man. To me, he was symbol of the sport. I couldn't wait for the chance to meet one of my heroes.

Lark said, "Joe, he doesn't like to be called Wilt the Stilt. Call him Wilt, Dippy, or the Big Dipper."

I asked Lark about his faith—was Wilt a believer?

Lark said, "Joe, I'm not sure, just keep praying."

I don't know if Wilt ever became a believer. I do know that whenever he was around Meadowlark, he heard the gospel.

My good friend David Ford was holding a crusade in Globe, Arizona. Globe is a smaller version of Las Cruces, located ninety miles east of Phoenix. He invited me to share my testimony and preach on Sunday morning. I said, "Great! I'll be there."

I brought a couple of friends with me—Meadowlark Lemon and heavyweight boxer Earnie Shavers. They ministered in the power of the

Holy Spirit. We had church, revival, and evangelism. God's Spirit fell on the stadium. The Lord put this together, and the crusade was a tremendous success because of prayer and fasting.

Meadowlark and I became golfing buddies. We'd play once a week. Neither of us was a threat to Tiger Woods. I couldn't break 100, and Lark shot somewhere in the low 90s. Whenever we played, I'd always have to keep score because he would sometimes forget to add a stroke or two. Being athletes, we were both very competitive.

Meadowlark, Rosey Grier, and Olympic gold medalist Madeline Manning Mims would host our AIM awards banquet. The banquet is like the ESPYs. Some of the greatest athletes and coaches in America are honored. Rosey would enter the ballroom from the back singing, and the crowd would erupt with the first note. By the time he reached the front, everyone was standing, clapping, and singing along.

In 1994, Evander Holyfield was the WBA, IBF heavyweight champion of the world. He's the only boxer in history to reign as the undisputed champion in the cruiserweight and heavyweight division. We heard of his strong Christian faith through Earnie Shavers, so we invited Evander to our athletes' conference.

I had arranged transportation for Evander from Sky Harbor to the Radisson Resort Hotel. Seeing and *hearing* Mike Tyson and his poise several years ago at LAX, I prepared for an entourage of handlers, security, and managers. I asked Pastor Bob Cashatt if he could bring his car to help transport Evander and his staff. We left the resort and headed to the airport. My 17-year-old twin girls (nieces) Keisha and Brandi were riding with me. They lived in Evander's hometown, Atlanta, and wanted to meet and greet the champ. With two sedans, I didn't think it would be a problem. We arrived in plenty of time and headed to the gate. Evander's plane was early and scheduled to land in five minutes, but somehow Pastor Bob ended up at the wrong gate.

I started to panic. How is this going to work? I can't fit eight or nine people in a five-passenger sedan. It was too late; Evander's plane just landed. *This is going to be a disaster.* To my shock, Evander walked through the jetway into the terminal with no bodyguards, handlers, or managers. Just himself and his brother. The heavyweight champion of the world travels without an entourage? You've got to be kidding me!

Although it was only Evander and his brother, five passengers could be a tight fit. I explained the mix-up about the other car. He said, "No problem, I come from a large family." My twin girls were in heaven! At the awards banquet, Evander shared his testimony, humble beginnings, and journey to become heavyweight champion of the world. It was a wonderful time.

# Chapter 30: Ministry Tales

B ill Bright was the founder and director of Campus Crusade for Christ. Bill Bright wrote *The Four Spiritual Laws*. In 1970 I attended my first Crusade conference with a good friend Jack Durkin. Jack was from Hatch, New Mexico. His father and my dad grew up in the same suburb of Cincinnati—Madisonville. What a small world!

Cliff Barrows from the Billy Graham Association was the evening speaker and led worship for the crusade. During the day, students were sent out to various locations to evangelize. Some hit the beach, others the streets, and some went to the airport. Jack and I hit the airport. We were dropped off at LAX. The airport was filled with students headed somewhere fun for spring break.

We prayed, asking the Lord to lead us to the right person. We noticed a student reading a newspaper who seemed harmless enough, so we approached him and asked if we could share something with him. He said yes. We used the same tract that Ken Johnson shared with me earlier. Jack took the student through the message of the tract. In the end, there are two circles that represent our lives—one with ego and self on the throne, the other with Christ on the throne. The final question is, "What circle best represents your life right now, Christ on the throne or ego and self?"

He said, "Ego and self."

We asked, "Which one would you like to have on the throne of your life?"

He said, "The one with Jesus."

I could hardly control my excitement and joy. We led him through the sinner's prayer. The very first person with whom we shared Christ gave his heart to Jesus.

Later, Jack and I were back on campus having lunch at the Milton Student Union. Everett joined our table. We began to share Christ with him just like we did at LAX. We were feeling confident that he would accept Christ as his Savior. Before we could get to the second law, Everett started cussing out God and the Bible and directed his venomous anger toward us. He called me an Uncle Tom for believing all of that crap. His rant was demonic. It was the most violent attack I ever experienced to this day.

Less than a week later, Everett was driving to El Paso on Interstate 10 when he somehow lost control of his vehicle and was decapitated. Saddened and shocked, I called Jack Durkin and told him what happened. I don't know if that was God's judgment or just a terrible wreck. I do know that the wrath of God is being revealed against those who suppress the truth (Rom. 1:18).

## Breaking in the Church

M.L. Harris and I drove to Tucson, Arizona where I was scheduled to sing in a small church. We arrived early, and the church was locked. I had a lot of sound equipment, so I wanted to set up the system and do a soundcheck. I walked around the outside of the building, looking for an open door. Finally, I saw a window that was unlocked. I opened the window, went inside, and opened the door for M.L., who asked, "Are you sure about this? Shouldn't we wait for the pastor to unlock the church?"

I said, "No, man, let's just get set up. He'll understand; he's cool."

We set up the sound equipment, and I ran through a couple of songs. A few minutes later, Pastor Steve came and wondered who let us in. I told him I crawled through a window then opened the front door.

He was upset and said, "You boys broke into my church. I could have you arrested!"

I said, "Pastor, I'm sorry. It takes about an hour to set up our equipment. I wasn't sure what time you would be arriving." I don't think he ever understood; I wouldn't either. I apologized again and asked for forgiveness.

## Pretending to Be a Pusher

I met the Greanwolds in South Dakota in the early '80s. They were a family of five. Their older son Lonnie started hanging around the wrong crowd. Nancy, his mom, was concerned because Lonnie had a call of God on his life for ministry. Somehow they found out that I was singing at a local church and contacted me. Nancy asked me if I could talk to her son, who was selling drugs on campus. He was attending the local university.

I said, "Yeah, I'll talk to him."

She wanted me to not only talk to him but scare him. She said, "Pretend you're a drug pusher from the underworld and scare the daylights out of him."

I said, "Wow, that sounds like fun. I'll do it."

I asked Pastor Jerry Hackett if he'd go with me. He said, "Yeah, let's do this."

We went to Lonnie's room and knocked on his dormitory door. Lonnie had heard that someone might be coming after him, so he asked some of his friends to be his bodyguards.

I was wearing a pair of shades, a fro, a black leather jacket, and had a full beard. They opened the door, and I told the bodyguards to "get the heck out of here." They scrammed.

I went into Lonnie's room and grabbed him by his shirt. I said, "You peed on somebody's feet." (I can't remember where I heard this phrase from, but it seemed appropriate.) "You owe me money, turkey, and I want it now." I slapped him across the face a couple of times to make it dramatic.

Earlier that morning, I was reading the Dakes Bible. I turned back to Pastor Jerry and said, "Dake, watch my back." I noticed an open Bible on his coffee table and asked, "Who does that Bible belong to? Do you read that stuff?"

Lonnie said, "It's mine. I read it sometimes."

Then I said, "Well, you need to start reading it more."

He looked at me and nodded yes.

That's when I decided to end the ruse and told him who I was. I said, "Lonnie, your parents really love you and are concerned that you're getting mixed up with the wrong crowd. You don't want to start to go down the wrong path." Shortly after that, I heard that Lonnie transferred to a Bible college. Lonnie needed another chance to make a good choice. He did and turned his life around.

## Memories of Earnie Shavers

Earnie Shavers has more knockouts than any heavyweight boxer in the history of that division. He moved to Phoenix in 1987. Earnie grew up in Warren, Ohio. His dream was to reign as heavyweight champion of the world. Because he was from Ohio, he was one of my favorite fighters.

He came close against Muhammad Ali and Larry Holmes. Ali said that Earnie was the hardest puncher he ever fought. He said Shavers hit him so hard that his ancestors felt the punch. Muhammad nicknamed Earnie the Acorn. When Earnie knocked Larry Holmes down with a left hook, we thought the heavyweight title would change hands, but Holmes recovered and won the fight.

I first met Earnie in 1987 at Phoenix First Assembly of God Church. It was great to meet some of these athletes I admired and cheered for, but it was even better to know that they accepted Christ as their Savior. Over the next few years Earnie and I would travel and speak in high schools, churches, and prisons. We participated in the Charles Colson prison ministry. This was a great vehicle that took teams of athletes into the prison system to share their testimony with the inmates. Some of the most powerful and anointed services I have experienced were in prison.

In 1968 or '69, I had my first prison ministry experience. I was a young Christian who hardly knew the difference between the Old and New Testaments. Steve, my dorm director at Garcia Hall, asked if I would go to jail service and speak to some of the prisoners early on Sunday morning. We'd speak for about thirty minutes. Someone would sing a song, and I would share what little testimony I had.

Although I've never been incarcerated, for some reason I've felt very comfortable speaking in prisons. Walking through some of the most dangerous prison yards in America seemed like a walk through the Botanical Garden in the Bronx. But for God's grace, I could be wearing that orange jump suit and all tattooed up, looking at life without parole.

Earnie and I were speaking at the Indiana Youth Reformatory, which houses over 1,400 inmates. During the evening service, Mike Tyson was brought into the meeting. There was a shortage of space in an adult low- and medium-security setting, so he was placed there. Earnie Shavers shared his testimony, and many of the prisoners prayed to receive Christ. I'm not certain if Mike Tyson raised his hand or not. I do know that when he was released, he joined the Nation of Islam.

Earnie Shavers had one speed—full speed. Earnie probably didn't play much basketball growing up in Warren, but he approached the game like a title fight. We were competing in the Super Star Competition in South Dakota in a basketball event. Earnie was running up and down the court, looking for an opponent to knock out. He was doing roll blocks into the student athletes.

The principal warned Earnie to take it down a notch. Earnie said yes, but continued knocking down anyone in his way. Finally the principal shouted, "Hey, if you do that again, I'm going take you out." Earnie responded, "Be quiet, Principal, or I'll take you out." So the game continued.

Another time we were at our office when Earnie stopped by. There was a youth evangelist named Gary there whom Larry and I were scheduled to speak with at Phoenix First Assembly that evening. Gary lived in Hawaii and was on tour on the mainland. He also said that he was a boxer. Then Gary started rapping a song about boxing. In the song, he expressed that he was a good fighter.

Earnie Shavers asked, "Can I see your jab?"

Gary continued his rap, not responding to Earnie's question.

Earnie asked again, "Show me your jab; show me your jab."

The guy finally stopped rapping and started shadow boxing. Bad decision. Somehow that triggered Earnie to start punching. In two seconds, the fight was over—pop, pop. Blood was everywhere.

My secretary, Melanie Bales, shouted, "Earnie, please don't kill him!"

Earnie's response was, "Man, you should have been wearing a mouthpiece."

Larry and I cracked up. We took the guy to the hospital to get stitched up. Needless to say, he didn't make it to the youth service that night.

Earnie and I did ministry in Montana, speaking on the Crow Nation Reservation. We visited Custer's last stand and learned a lot of history that you'd never read in a history book. It was a great week of ministry.

When we landed in Phoenix, we headed to baggage. Approaching me was my girlfriend, Christy. I didn't expect Christy to meet me at the airport. It was a nice surprise. *Maybe we'll grab something to eat.* As Christy approached me, I extended my arms for a hug. To my surprise, she raced past me into the arms of Earnie Shavers.

I said, "Hey, what the heck going on? I thought we were dating?"

Christy said, "Earnie and I are dating now."

I couldn't believe it. Earnie had never said a word that he and Christy had hooked up.

I said, "You can have her." Besides, I didn't want to contribute to his knockout record. I think they got married.

## Campus Ministries

In college, there were many campus ministries that reached out to students, including Campus Crusade for Christ, the Navigators, InnerVarsity, BSU, Chi Alpha, and the Fellowship of Christian Athletes.

Each of these ministries was unique. Crusade had the vision for evangelism with a simple but effective tool in the *four spiritual laws*. Navigators capitalized on scripture memory; InnerVarsity reached out to both students and faculty on the campus. Chi Alpha, despite its name, is not a fraternity or sorority; Chi Alpha emphasizes the five-fold philosophy—being a community of worship, prayer, fellowship, discipleship, and mission. And the Fellowship of Christian Athletes, FCA, seeks to evangelize the athletic community, recognizing the platform of the student athlete and coach.

I wasn't aware of FCA until my sophomore year of college. FCA brought me the balance I needed. It was the most identifiable and relational ministry that understood the needs of the student athlete. It really resonated, especially after seeing the strongest man in the world, Paul Anderson, confess his need for God in his life. I was blown away to see him take a penny nail and drive it through a two-by-four with his hand.

Billboard's number one hit song on Valentine's Day of 1962 was "Hey, Hey, Paula" by Paul and Paula. Paul was the young songwriter Ray Hildebrand and Paula was Jill Jackson. Ray played basketball for Howard Payne University. He had written that hit song by the request of teammate Russell Berry.

I met Ray in the summer of 1969 at an FCA conference in Michigan. Ray traveled for the FCA and became one of the pioneers/founders of contemporary Christian music. I guess Ray was the first real celebrity I ever met. Elvis Presley said that "Hey, Hey, Paula" was one of his favorite songs. Ray and I ministered in music together over the years.

In the summer of 1973, the FCA conference was held at Estes Park, Colorado. Roger Staubach and I would share our testimony, and Paul Anderson would preach. Roger and I both grew up in Cincinnati. He went to Purcell High School, which is a Catholic high school located only seven miles from Withrow High School. We scrimmaged several Catholic high schools during the summer, including Purcell.

After Roger and I shared our testimony, we waited for Paul Anderson outside the auditorium. I shared the story of stealing cars. Roger claimed that his 1954 Chevy Bel Air was stolen and blamed me. We all laughed. Paul Anderson was thirty minutes late. *Where is Paul Anderson?* Ray Hildebrand was inside, stalling the crowd as if using a four-corner delay tactic. Roger and I stood outside the auditorium and looked and waited for Paul Anderson. Thirty minutes seemed like an hour.

Finally, a brown 1973 Fleetwood Cadillac sedan raced up the driveway. It was Paul. He said his plane was late. I didn't care what the excuse was; I was glad he made it. Communication was not what it is today; there were no cell phones or text messaging back then.

After the 1978 NFC Championship game against the Cowboys, I embraced Roger and congratulated him on the win. The Cowboys were going to Super Bowl XII instead of us. Had our quarterback Fran Tarkenton been healthy, who knows how our season could have turned out? I asked Roger if he remembered that FCA conference in Estes Park in '73. Roger said, "Yeah, that was a long time ago."

I remember seeing our Championship game on ESPN classic and the shot of Roger and me embracing after the game. During the broadcast, Pat Summerall commented, "These two combatants are discussing the big game." Not exactly, Pat. We were talking about Jesus and our experience at Estes Park.

Paul Anderson wasn't tall in stature. He stood only five feet nine inches but weighed around 360 pounds. What he lacked in height, he made up in volume. Paul had a great personality. His voice was big and carried. Paul's presentation was like an illustrated sermon. He would press a 250-pound dumbbell ten times with one hand, then bench press 600 pounds. That was in 1973, but I remember it like it was yesterday.

FCA, Athletes in Action, and Pro Athletes Outreach laid the foundation and sparked a vision that led my path to Phoenix First Assembly of God Church. These ministries each made an imprint in my life. God's sovereign hand and timing help prepare and lead me to Athletes International Ministries.

## Phoenix Conference Memories

Ecclesiastes 8 tells us there is a timing factor in the will of God. Our Phoenix conference has not only had some of the top athletes and coaches, but we also enjoyed praise and worship from talented and anointed Christian artists.

Phoenix 92 was special for me. That year I was the recipient of the Pete Maravich award. I couldn't think of a greater honor given to an unworthier recipient. The Pete Maravich award is presented to the retired athlete who is now serving in full-time ministry. Pistol Pete Maravich gave his life to Jesus Christ shortly before he died. AIM reached out to Pete and invited him to the conference. He committed to coming but had another commitment he couldn't miss—the Lord called him home in 1988.

Some of the other recipients honored that year were Olympian Dave Johnson, Kansas City Chief Christian Okoye, and NBA great/jazz musician Wayman Tisdale.

Not only did AIM honor some of the greatest athletes in America, but we were also blessed with anointed and talented praise and worship. Some of the musical guests were The Imperials, Andre Crouch, The Katinas, Sherman Andrus, The Winans, Carmen, Greg X Votz, Eddie James, the Cruise Family, Israel Houghton, Billy Blackwood, and The Couriers.

For Phoenix '92, Andre Crouch and the Disciples would lead in praise and worship and whatever they wanted to do. We were so excited that Andre Crouch would be at our conference. On a couple of other occasions, Andre would just show up at our conference. Larry met Andre in the '70s in Canada while playing with the Eskimos. In 1983 our band opened up for Andre at the Jesus People Church in Minneapolis.

Negotiations weren't easy. I had spoken with several people from his camp. We would agree on an honorarium, and they would later come back and want changes. I never spoke to Andre, only his business partner. It was getting a little frustrating with all of the changes. I told Larry, "Let's forget it, don't think it's going to work." So I contacted them and canceled. The next day they called and said they wanted to come. I said, "Awesome!" We agreed on $5,000, which was a bargain for us. I'm sure they could make ten times that amount.

They were awesome in every way. We had no problems with Andre Crouch and the Disciples. When they sang the first verse of their first song, I looked at Larry and said they were *underpaid.* We were so blessed to have Daddy Crouch come with the family. This was the first time we heard Wayman Tisdale play the bass. He joined Andre's band and played left-handed like Jimi Hendrix, never missing a note.

Some of the speakers we've had were Tom Skinner, Dr. Edwin Louis Cole, Coach Bill McCartney, Jentzen Franklin, Jimmy Swaggart, Jerry Seville, Tommy Barnett, Denny Duran, Jack Wallace, Jim Willoughby, and Craig Lauterbach.

Sherman Andrus, who sang with Andre Crouch in the early '70s. taught me a '50s doo-wop song called "Jesus Is So Wonderful." Toward the end, I will stop the track and call someone on stage to sing a soulful riff. They're normally off key and can't hold a note. It's a lot of fun. One time I invited the WWE wrestlers. We put on sunglasses, had our steps together, and brought the house down. Another time I invited Coach Mac to join in. He wouldn't try to sing the soulful part.

My little brother Mike and I on my grandmother's front steps, tuning my guitar. Who would have thought that music would open the door to God's call?

Standing in my front yard dressed for church.

Mom and Dad's wedding day.

Lyon Jr. High School's football team. I'm on the first row, far left.

Withrow High School graduate

Coach Marv Merritt arguing my case to a referee who wasn't listening, Withrow High School, 1968. (Below)

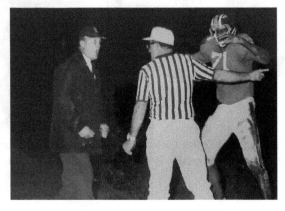

Standing next to Madisonville legends Tommy
Barnes (middle) and Lornie Starkey (right).

Greg Williams, my close friend who
left us too soon.

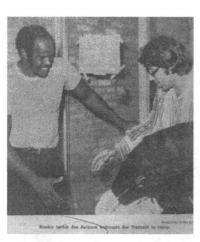

Meeting Joe Willy for the first time,
Hofstra University, 1972.

Joe Namath, Aunt Drew, Dad, and me at
Riverfront Stadium, 1974.

Buddy's bandits. First row: Mark Lomas, Bob Parish, Steve Thompson. Second row (left to right): Richard Neal, John Elliott, John Little, Buddy Ryan, me, and Eddie Gallagher.

Sacking Dan Pastorini. I got him twice that night.

Following Duck White on a Monday night game against the Miami Dolphins. Jackson #76, White #72.

JOEY JACKSON, D.T.
6-4    250    Cincinnati, Ohio

"The Mover" New Mexico State Aggie,
Joey Jackson, eventually moves into the
lineup with Viking Hall of Famers and
Purple People Eaters.

Carl Eller

Alan Page

"The Great" Jim Marshall

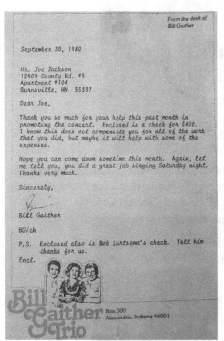

Picture with the Bill Gaither Trio and Marilyn Shandorf. I sang "The Blood Will Never Lose Its Power" in front of a sold-out arena at the St. Paul Civic Center, September 28, 1980.

Letter from Bill Gaither

Mom (far left) with Motown artist Freda Payne (far right), Gwen Gordy, Anna Gordy Gaye, and good friend Fredi Starkey.

My first revival meeting in Arizona. Pictured (left to right): Meadowlark Lemon, Harlem Globetrotters; Earnie Shavers, two-time heavyweight boxing championship challenger; and me, along with Evangelist David Ford, "Sheep Herder."

Singing "Can't Nobody Do Me Like Jesus" with Andrae Crouch.

ML Harris (Cincinnati Bengals), Earnie Shavers, and me doing a high school drug awareness assembly.

My wedding day

"Okay, okay, I'll sign."

Olivia's eighth grade
graduation. (right)

Welcome to the Jackson family.
(below)

Some teammates we've loved and lost.

Wally Hilgenberg, Olivia, Terill Jackson, Wes Hamilton, and me.
This was when Wally told me he had ALS and asked for prayer.

Matt Blair

Fred McNeill

Winston Hill

Paul Crane and others remembered
as great football players and humble
servant leaders who impacted my life.

## Some highlights from the AIM Conferences.

Me and George Foreman.

Gary Unger, St. Louis Blues; Larry Kerychuk, Winnipeg Blue Bombers; me; Wayman Tisdale, Phoenix Suns; Christian Okoye, KC Chiefs; Dave Johnson, Olympic Decathlon medalist;` and sister, Elaine.

Me presenting Joe Namath the AIM lifetime achievement award at Harvest Assembly of God Church.

My sister Mary, Meadowlark Lemon, and Mom.

Jim Marshall; Coach Mike Holmgren, head coach of the Seattle Sea Hawks; JD Hill, Buffalo Bills; and me having dinner at Don and Charlies.

BIG Chick Huntsberry (Prince's former bodyguard), me, and Ashley McQuinn.

Terill Jackson, "T Jack," and me, "Joe Jack," at the AIM Banquet.

Standing with Joe Bob Sellers and 100 pounds of award-winning brisket.

Paul Shaffer from Late Night with David Letterman offers me some coaching tips on 4-3 gap responsibility, while I suggest an 8-bar blues chord progression, Joe Namath Football Camp.

My sister Barbie with Fearsome Foursome great Rosey Grier.

Jim Marshall, Chuck Foreman, me, Paul Krause, and Tommy Kramer.

Rattlesnake in the front yard.

Bobcat in our backyard, Arizona desert.

T Jack's side gig—the unofficial team chauffeur.

Terill Jackson in Kona, Hawaii (love this pic)

Me and Jared Allen in Minnesota

Liv is not too crazy about Cincinnati staple,
Skyline Chili. No problem; more for me!

Emmett, my precious grandson and
future owner of an NFL franchise.

Enjoying my wedding day with my dear friend and brother Craig Lauterbach.

MLB Commissioner Bud Selig and me dining at our favorite restaurant, Don and Charlies.

The original "Jackson Five": Michael, Barbie, Mary, Jerry, and me. (below)

My twin nieces Bran-Bran and Kee Kee D.

Wedding Day for Joe Jack and T Jack, June 25, 2005.

# Chapter 31: The Buddy System/ Prime Time

I 've chronicled Buddy Ryan throughout this writing. His impact on my life reverberates today. In 1994 the Phoenix Cardinals were looking for a new head coach. I hoped that they would look outside the box and at least bring in Buddy for an interview.

Buddy served as head coach with the Eagles and defensive coordinator with the Houston Oilers. Some would say that he wore out his welcome in Philadelphia. He didn't always see eye to eye with management. He only had one way of doing things—the Buddy System. For the Houston Oilers, Buddy served as defensive coordinator.

In 1993 he helped the Oilers to an eleven-game winning streak. It was the last game of the 1993 season, a pivotal game against his old team, the New York Jets. Buddy was frustrated with the play calling of Houston Oiler offensive coordinator Kevin Gilbride. He referred to Gilbride's run and gun offense as "chuck and duck." As time was running out in the first half, Buddy felt that Gilbride should run the clock out. Instead, Gilbride called for a pass play. When the ball was snapped to Oiler quarterback Cody Carlson, he fumbled. This brought the defense back onto the field and, in the process, injured two of Buddy's defensive players. Buddy exploded and walked toward Gilbride. Both were yelling, cursing, and spitting in each other's faces. Buddy's emotions got the best of him, and he took a swing at Coach Gilbride's jaw. His punch came up a little short. Before more punches were thrown, players intervened.

I'm sure during the Cardinals' interview process, the fight was a topic of consideration, along with the bounty. Dallas Cowboys coach Jimmie

Johnson accused Buddy of paying his players to intentionally hurt opponents. Jimmie Johnson once said that he would beat Ryan up. There was some baggage that definitely had to be discussed before any serious consideration could happen.

To the shock of some fans and media, the Cardinals hired my old defensive line coach Buddy Ryan as the new head coach of the Phoenix Cardinals. After Buddy became the Cardinals' coach, the name was changed from the Phoenix to the Arizona Cardinals, which was a great decision.

When Buddy quickly settled into Phoenix, I reached out to him. We connected several times. I thought it would be a great idea to introduce Buddy to the business community and some of the local car dealers. My dear friend Louis Cowart was the general manager and part owner at the North Scottsdale Infiniti store.

I told Buddy that I could get him a loaner car to use for the entire season. All he would have to do is some advertising. We met at the Cardinals' facility, and we drove to the dealership. Mr. Cowart was a committed Christian with a kind heart. His southern drawl was a voice you could trust, which is rare in the automobile industry. Whenever I had an athlete come into Phoenix, Mr. Cowart would provide transportation. The Scottsdale Infiniti dealership was the number one store in America. After a short meet and greet, Mr. Cowart gave Buddy a brand new Infiniti Q45. All Buddy did was sign a few autographs and pose for pictures, and he was out the door with brand new $70,000 ride.

I said, "Wow, the richer you are, the more free stuff you get." I guess so because Buddy was also given a few other cars from dealerships throughout the valley.

Buddy called me and asked me to drop by the Cardinals facility for something. I thought maybe he needed another car? If I were ten years younger, I'd really be excited to play for Buddy again. I was too old for a tryout at forty-three, although I honestly thought I could still play.

When I arrived at the Cardinals headquarters, Buddy offered me a job. It would be a liaison position facilitating a close working relationship between the players and the organization. Even though I had commitments to speak in churches throughout America, I was very open to that position. I thought that I would be perfect for that job.

Buddy set up a phone interview with someone in Philadelphia. It lasted less than five minutes. The interview was a little weird. They were looking for someone with a degree in psychology or sociology, so I didn't get the job. I have no doubt that I could have done well in that position, but it wasn't part of God's plan.

In 1995 I played in the Arizona Cardinals' golf charity. I ran into Buddy and asked him if he needed a scout. He said, "Well, if I need anybody for you to look at, I'll give you call." That's the last time I had a conversation with Buddy Ryan.

In 1998 we honored Deion Sanders at our award banquet as NFL Man of the Year. Deion, Emmett Smith, and Michael Irvin were attending the Bishop TD Jakes' church, The Potter's House, in Dallas. We had a contact at The Potter's House who helped us get Deion. Sometimes with high-profile athletes, you have to pray for humility and patience. We weren't sure if Deion would come. He said he was committed, but I guess it was never confirmed.

What was confirmed was a lot of confusion. I went to Sky Harbor to pick up Deion. I wasn't completely sure if he would be there. His plane landed, and all the passengers got off. No Deion. Our banquet started in twenty minutes, and I was at least twenty minutes away from the hotel ballroom. Finally, I saw Deion being escorted through the terminal. As he came toward me, he was talking. I couldn't see the small microphone around his neck.

I asked, "Are you talking to someone?"

He said, "Yeah, do you think I'm talking to myself?"

I said, "No, I'm sorry, man."

There was very little conversation on the way to the hotel. When we pulled into the parking lot, Pastor Barnett had just arrived and was walking into the hotel. Deion noticed Pastor Barnett and called his name. They greeted each other, and everything was fine. Pastor Barnett had preached at The Potter's House the week before. Deion also brought Cowboys teammate Omar Stoutmire, which was a pleasant surprise.

Deion did a fantastic job in sharing his testimony. He took pictures, signed autographs for fans, and went out of his way to accommodate. On our way back to the airport, it was a different ride. He was very personable, talkative, humbled, and appreciative of his award. Several years later, we had a great visit at the Minnesota Vikings vs. Washington Redskins Thursday Night game. He was an analyst for NFL Network, and I was on the field. I walked across the field and introduced myself. We had a great conversation. I guess first impressions are overrated.

# Chapter 32: Runaway Bride

P hilippians 3:13 tells us to forget what is behind and strain toward what is ahead. Isaiah 43:19 says God is doing a new thing, making a way in the wilderness and streams in the wasteland. A *wasteland* is known as a land that is uncultivated or barren, a place devastated by floods, storms, or war. I was rocked by a storm in 1997.

I was preaching in a church in southwest Texas. After the altar service, I made my way to my product table. Someone from the church will normally help with sales. This time I was on my own. One lady patiently waited to purchase a shirt. Her name was Shari Foster. I sold her a couple of t-shirts, and she promised to come back to the evening service. I hoped so. She was pretty with long black hair. She came back.

After the evening service, the pastor and his wife took Shari and me to The Cheesecake Factory for dessert. Shari and I exchanged numbers and talked almost every day. I knew what they said about long-distance relationships, but I thought this would be different. Too late, I was smitten. She had been married twice and had two children. I knew if we got married, I would have to surrender my Assemblies of God license because she was divorced and because her two previous husbands were still living. Was this God's plan for my life? I sure hoped it was.

In my heart of hearts, I had my doubts but moved forward anyway. I introduced her to several of my minister friends with no red flags. I asked her to marry me at our athletes' conference. She said yes. We planned an October wedding. Invitations were sent out. Preparations were made. The week of the wedding my family members came to town. My mother purchased a new dress, thinking, *Finally, my boy's getting married.*

About five days before our wedding date, I called Shari but couldn't reach her. I left a message and waited for her call. Two days passed, and there was no call from Shari. I called Pastor Barnett and told him that I hadn't heard from my fiancée. I had a sick feeling that the wedding wasn't going to happen. It didn't. She never showed up. Embarrassed, hurt, and disappointed, I gathered my family and drove to Prescott, Arizona.

She finally called and said that her mother was sick and she needed to care for her. I was sick too—sick to my stomach. I guess I recovered because I gave her another chance—save the date, January 8, 1998, invitations sent out again, airline tickets purchased for Hawaii, hotels reservations booked. The same thing happened—no show. That's the last time I had any contact with Shari.

## Healing a Broken Heart

Well, where do you go from here? If I ever needed a touch from God, it was now. It was devastating heartbreak again, and I was in no position to preach to others. How in the world could I minister to anyone? I felt like someone should just lock me up in a closet, maybe cut a hole in the door to pass me a plate of food and a bottle of pop. I didn't want to face anyone, pray for anyone, or preach to anyone.

There was no refund on the tickets to Hawaii, so I gathered up enough strength to go on the trip. Maybe I would ask my mom to go with me. In those days, airlines did not require IDs. I once flew to Florida as Mr. Earnie Shavers.

My mom said, "Sure, I'll go to Hawaii with you as Mrs. Jackson." We strolled hand in hand on the island as if we were a newlywed couple. It was a sight to see!

Eventually, I had to get up and stop feeling sorry for myself. My calendar was booked. What would I tell the pastors who had me scheduled? Life is for the living. I was badly hurt but not dead. Life doesn't give you a pass for your circumstances, good or bad; you still need to move forward. Yes, I'm hurt, bleeding, and have a big dose of self-pity. But I got up and began to walk. Soon my pace picked up, and before long I was back in the race—and I still had my Assemblies of God ordination papers.

This was a process. It took time for the wound to heal. I'm stronger for what I went through. I do believe that God's timing is always right on time. He is in the business of divine appointments.

I was left at the altar, a beaten and broken man. No man likes the taste of rejection, especially from a woman. It was bitter, humiliating, yet the greatest blessing in my life. God loves us so much that He allows us to be hurt to guide us back onto His path. It's the will of God that always gives me peace, even in the storm; it's the will of God that settles my spirit; it's the will God that gives me the oil of joy for mourning, the garment of praise for the spirit of heaviness.

God doesn't have to take away the thing that breaks your heart for His joy to come upon you. It comes in spite of the loss, divorce, foreclosure, death, or no-show.

Later, many of my pastor friends told me they had a check in their spirit about the whole relationship. I asked, "Why didn't you say anything?"

They said, "You seemed to be so happy, plus you're six feet five inches and 270 pounds."

Well, God said something, and I'm grateful He did. He said, "You're going to see My glory in seven years." Keep walking the Jesus road. It's the path of a champion!

# Chapter 33: Is That Jim Brightbill?

I n 1998 Paul Krause and Mike Singletary were enshrined into the NFL Hall of Fame. Paul was a teammate, and I met Mike through our AIM conference. Although it took Paul almost twenty years, he finally received an overdue call to Canton. How do you overlook someone who played in four Super Bowls, four Pro Bowls, was named to the all-pro first team four times, and set the NFL record for 81 career interceptions?

What kept Minnesota Viking greats like Jim Marshall, Matt Blair, and Gene Washington from a Hall of Fame induction was not winning a Super Bowl. Yet Marshall's statistics alone are undeniable. Hopefully, he'll receive his call from Canton one day. It's easy to see why Singletary was a first-round ball Chicago Bear for twelve years. Mike was a leader on and off the field. On the field, his eyes were full of expression and fire. They seemed to burn right through opponents. He was a fierce hitter who saw every game as a celebration. You would often hear him say, "I love this kind of party."

I contacted a church in Akron to see if I could schedule a service for Hall of Fame weekend. I didn't want to miss their induction. I was able to connect with First Assembly of God and booked a service. After my plane arrived in Akron, I collected my baggage then went to the curb to wait for my rental car. This would be the first time I ever attended an NFL enshrinement, and I was very excited about seeing these two friends receive their gold jackets.

After about fifteen minutes, I called the rental car company to find out when the van would arrive. They told me it was five minutes away. I waited five minutes and still nothing. I was becoming more frustrated at seeing every van but mine. I didn't want to miss any part of the ceremony. Former NFL players have free access to most of the events, including the Hall of Fame game.

I called a third time and was told again that the van was five minutes away. I said, "That's what you said the last time I called!" I was getting ticked off, steaming mad. "Where are those jokers?" I shouted. *This is ridiculous.* I flew all the way to Akron, Ohio, only to be left at the curb.

I took a deep breath and turned to my left to see if I could get a better angle to spot the van—nothing but a flight crew walking toward me. As I turned away, there was something about the captain of that flight crew that looked familiar. My mind quickly flashed back to a face I once knew in Minnesota. I thought, *Oh my goodness, could that be the pastor who prophesied that God was going to broaden my borders like Jabez in 1983?* I knew that he flew in the navy and once told me that he wanted to pursue a dream to fly for a commercial airline, but there's no way—that can't be Jim Brightbill. We hadn't seen each other for over twenty-five years.

As he approached me, I thought, *Oh, my goodness, it's him!* I said, "Jim, how you doing, bro? This is Joe Jackson. You gave me a prophecy at your church in Grasston, Minnesota. You said that God would broaden my borders like Jabez. Well, I moved to Phoenix and now serve as church evangelist with pastor Tommy Barnett. God has opened doors for me to minister all over the world. Your prophecy has been fulfilled." He seemed pleased but even more shocked.

If the rental car van had picked me up thirty seconds earlier, I would have missed this divine appointment with Jim Brightbill. That's the last time that I saw Jim. I don't know if he's still flying or retired or maybe back in ministry. That was definitely a Championship Sunday appointment!

# Chapter 34: T-Jack, My Righteous Fox

There's a biblical significance to the number 7. We know that God rested on the seventh day (Gen. 2:2). Jesus mentions the seven woes on the unrepentant in Matthew 23; the seven letters to the seven churches in the Book of Revelation (Rev. 2-3); the seven trumpets (Rev. 8); seven signs given in the gospel of John; Naaman was told to dip seven times in the Jordan River (2 Kings 5:10); and there were seven pairs of clean animals received into the Ark (Gen. 7:2). Elijah sent the servants back seven times to check for rain (1 Kings 18:43-44). To add to that, I was born on the 7th of May. The number seven is known as a number of divine perfection or completion.

Almost seven years to the day, in the summer of 2004, I was working out at the Pure Fitness Gym (now LA Fitness.) I had just finished working out biceps and triceps and was ready for cardio on the Life Step machine. Before I could jump on a machine, Julie Sanders asked if she could have a minute. I knew Julie from Phoenix First Assembly of God Church, but we'd said nothing more than hello. Julie asked if I was married.

I said, "No, what's up?"

She said she had someone she wanted me to meet.

*Oh no, another fixup*, I thought.

She told me her friend's name was Terill Robertson, she was thirty-eight, pretty, never married, very funny with a crazy sense of humor, a single mother of a ten-year-old daughter named Olivia, and a member of Phoenix First Assembly. That was a red flag.

Pastor Barnett highly suggested that I not date women from the church, even though Phoenix First was running well over 15,000 people. For the most part, I followed his suggestion. But by now I was 53 years old—and not getting any younger.

I gave Julie my number and waited to hear something back from Terill. Several weeks later I followed up with Julie and said, "Hey, Julie, what's the deal? I haven't heard from your friend you wanted me to meet."

Julie checked and found out that Terill had no desire to connect with me. Terill was raised Catholic, so when Julie mentioned that I was an evangelist and a former pro football player, Terill thought that I was some wild screamer with an ego the size of Texas and had shoved my number to the side of her desk, one inch away from the shredder.

Julie told her, "Terill, I understand your concern. Can I give him your number?"

Terill said okay. She told Julie, "We'll do lunch because there's a beginning and end to that."

The next time I ran into Julie, she gave me Terill's number. I called Terill and asked if we could meet for lunch. She said fine. Unfortunately, I was a few minutes late. Once I turned the corner and saw her face, I said, "Wow, she's pretty and special."

Lunch was followed by a walk to her car. Before departing, I asked the question of questions, "When can I call you again?"

Her answer was "in about thirty minutes." I didn't expect that, but it was the best response I ever could have received!

I was so excited that after our second date, I called my Minnesota Vikings teammate Jim Marshall and said, "Jim, you got to meet this girl. Please say hello to Terill. She even has her own American Express credit card."

Terill called her brother, Todd, who is a huge Raiders fan. She told him we were dating and that I played with the Vikings and had a Super Bowl ring.

When Todd heard that, he immediately said, "Drop him, that guy's a liar. He's no good for you." He knew the Vikings had never won a Super Bowl. What Todd didn't know is that the Viking NFC Championship ring says Super Bowl XI. It doesn't say World Champions. To us, that's our Super Bowl ring.

Terill and I met Pastor Barnett in his office. He heard that I met someone from the church, so I scheduled a meet and greet. We had an awesome visit. Pastor gave his approval and was very encouraging. He even volunteered to perform our wedding.

Olivia, Terill, and I flew to Cincinnati to meet my family. They loved her. We hit a couple of my favorite restaurants, Skyline Chili and United Dairy Farmers. She loved UDF but not Skyline.

Terill grew up in Spokane, Washington. She graduated from Eastern Washington University with a communications degree. That's the school with the bright red football field. She came from a family of eight—three girls and three boys, their names all beginning with the letter T: Tracy, Troy, Todd, Terill, Trina, and Trent. The blessing and favor of God is always worth the wait.

# Chapter 35: Guess Who's Coming to Dinner?

I t was time for me to *meet her parents*. Terill's father, Steve, was a retired state trooper, and her mother, Rosey, was a huge cat lover. I think she had twelve cats at the time. Olivia was in Spokane on spring break. Terill's older sister, Tracy, had arranged a surprise visit. Terill and I would fly to Spokane, pick up Olivia, and meet the parents.

My conversations with Steve were always warm and friendly. He said, "Joe, I can't wait to meet you. Glad you're going to be a part of the family."

Tracy met us at the airport, and we drove to their house. She suggested that I surprise them. Tracy said, "When they're home, they never leave the front door locked; just walk on in and say, 'Guess who's coming to dinner?'"

I agreed and walked slowly to the door. It was about 8 p.m. Earlier that evening, the usually quiet Spokane Valley neighborhood rumbled with the loud sound of hip-hop music. Spring break was in full throttle. The drunken and wild party-goers were now dancing in the street.

Sergeant Steve Robertson observed someone staggering toward his house. Before the guy turned into their front yard, he passed out near their driveway. That's all it took. Steve shouted, "Hey, what the heck is going on out there?" He called the sheriff and reported the disturbance. In a few minutes, cops were everywhere—party's over.

As I approached the door and turned the handle, it wouldn't budge. I knocked twice, and Steve came to the door. The expected greeting of

"Hey, Rosey, look who's here!" was replaced with a deep intimidating voice that asked, "Can I help you, Mister?"

This wasn't the same friendly voice that said he couldn't wait to meet me. Steve later told me that he thought I was hitman sent to even up the score. Tracy and Terill were hiding in the bushes. Thank the Lord, they sprinted to my rescue and shouted "Surprise."

Finally, Steve yelled, "Rosey, look who's here!"

Rosey said, "Shoot, you're even better looking in person than in your picture." I guess that was a compliment.

Steve is a handyman who can fix anything. His shop is like a hardware store with every imaginable tool. Rosey's love for animals is what movies are made from. They gave me a thumbs up and welcomed me into the Robertson clan. I couldn't have asked for a better father- and mother-in-law. Besides the cats, I also met Steve's brother, Bob, who was visiting from Oregon. Our visit was too short.

## Love and Marriage

Wedding plans were made. We had the time, date, and venue. The only thing lacking was the ring and official proposal. On my calendar was a date to preach at Christ Chapel in Woodbridge, Virginia. This would be a perfect time to bring Terill with me. Pastor Bill Roberts had built a great multiethnic congregation. It was a church that was making a difference in their city and beyond.

I shared with Brother Bill that I was finally getting married. He said, "Praise the Lord, have you shopped for rings yet?"

I said, "We've only window shopped."

Pastor Bill mentioned that one of his members owned a jewelry store and suggested that we check it out. Their diamond rings sparkled with brilliance and were within our price range.

What happened next had nothing to do with purchasing the rings or the reality that I was surrendering my bachelor card. As we looked at rings and talked about the price, from out of nowhere came symptoms of a migraine. I knew if I didn't get to a pharmacy quick, a full-blown migraine would follow.

I said, "Terill, I'll be right back." I had to locate a drug store, which took longer than expected because I didn't know the area.

Terill wondered, *What happened to Joe? Did the prices freak him out? Did the reality of marriage want to send him through the back door?* I can imagine how she felt. I should have at least told her that I needed to pick something up at the pharmacy.

Well, we had the rings, but still no official proposal. Pastor Bill invited me to speak at an Assemblies of God district event for pastors. He told the pastors that I was getting married in June. They gathered around Terill and me, laid hands on both of us, and prayed.

After they prayed, I dropped to a knee and proposed to Terill. She said yes!

We planned to get married during our athletes' conference. This would be a first—planning a major conference and banquet is one thing, not to mention a wedding too. Terill didn't know or care anything about the conference. This was our wedding and where her focus needed to be. My focus was two-fold—the wedding and the conference.

I still had the responsibility of hosting the awards banquet. One night we talked on the phone about food for the reception, and I mentioned that we could have the same menu that the conference would be having—and that's as far as the conversation went.

She said, "I'm sick and tired of hearing about the conference. This is my wedding!" The next sound I heard was the dial tone. She hung up on me. The conference may have been a great idea to have a wedding, but Terill didn't understand anything about the athletes' conference.

I had to host a major banquet Friday night then sing my wife down the aisle for my wedding Saturday at 2 p.m., June 25, 2005. The wedding came off without a hitch except for a panic attack I experienced the morning of our wedding. Somehow I misplaced Terill's wedding ring. I looked everywhere and couldn't find it. Could it be in the ballroom, the trash can, my car? I contacted the front desk to see if it was turned in—nothing was turned in.

Whenever I got a panic attack, I would take off running. Even though the temperature was 109 degrees, I always found relief in running. I laced up my Nikes and took off. I'm not sure how long I ran, but eventually the panic attack stopped, and I was able to relax. When I came back to the hotel, I was exhausted. I collapsed on the bed and closed my eyes for a second. I prayed, "Lord, I need to find that ring, please help me." I rolled over and felt something against my side. It was Terill's wedding ring! I shouted, "Thank you, Jesus." All the fret, worry, and panic for nothing. The ring never left the room.

My groomsmen were from the NFL and pastors or both—Bengals, M.L. Harris and my brother Mike Jackson; Browns and Bills, J.D. Hill; and Larry Kerychuk of the Eskimos. Pastors Tommy Barnett, Craig Lauterbach, Jim Willoughby, and Gary Blair. This was the greatest day in my life, and I had no doubt that this would not be a runaway bride.

Tracy suggested that I sing "If It Wasn't for Your Love" as Terill walked down the aisle. I had never heard of that song before. I bought the CD and liked it right away. I looked for the music but could not find it. A good friend Wayne Reece produced and mixed a track for me and it was awesome. You can find our wedding on You Tube: Wedding Day Bliss32.

The next morning, Mrs. Terill Jackson and I went to Phoenix First Assembly. Pastor Tommy Barnett commented from the pulpit that "anyone who comes to church the day after his wedding deserves to preach." I had nothing prepared, but God gave me a word.

Monday, we flew to Hawaii and honeymooned at Turtle Bay on the North Shore. During our honeymoon, we met up with Sherman and Winnie Andrus. Sherman was reunited with The Imperials, who moved from Nashville to Hawaii. They were doing the Elvis Presley tour.

Being married to the right person is worth the wait. Now I'm not suggesting that you wait until you are fifty-four. Just don't marry because you're twenty-four. I often thought that if I could do my life over again, what would I change? Sure, I would love to have a fifteen-year NFL career, sign a hundred million dollar long-term contract, win a Super Bowl, and be inducted into the NFL Hall of Fame. But as corny as this sounds, I wouldn't do it without Terill.

If I could not have her in my life, forget it. She's my completion and gift from God. I wouldn't do it. Terill (T-Jack) is special, yet we don't have a whole lot in common. When I started college, she was only three years old. She's frugal, I'm a free spender; she's a healthy eater, I'm a chicken and ribs man; she drinks water, I'm a Pepsi guy (diet of course); I'm a car guy, she wouldn't know Benz from a Buick. Her idea of dessert is an apple, and mine is an apple pie; her favorite store is Traders Joe's, mine is Costco. Besides our love for each other and our Christian faith, we don't have a lot in common except the important things. The Lord brought us together, and our love is unshakable and undefinable. On our second date, I told her that she is my *last* girlfriend. The transition from 54 years of bachelorhood to husband was seamless.

After getting married, there have been no major adjustments, except now I have to take a shower immediately after I work out and don't leave the toilet seat up. Also, I have more than three pairs of underwear.

The transition to becoming a father was a little more challenging. Our daughter, Olivia, was and is strong-willed and extremely bright. Her career choices are limitless. Though we butted heads a number of times, she knows I'm her father, and I love her. I think one of the major issues was converting a twosome into a threesome. For eleven years, it was just Terill and Olivia. Now she has to share her space and her mom with a stranger. We both said things we regret. Sorry, Liv! We made the transition and are on a great path.

When my dad married my mother, she had a son, my older brother. Their relationship was indifferent at best and volatile at worst. One night my dad was arguing with my mother, and my brother intervened. They got into a fight, and my brother left and never came back. At dad's funeral, Jerry was a no-show. He told me he couldn't afford to purchase an airline ticket.

I promised myself that if I ever married a woman who had children, I wouldn't be like my dad. I'd spend time with that child, nurture that child, and train that child up in the Word of God; I'd be the godly role model. It turned out that, in some ways, I was just like him—pointing out the negative and ignoring the positive, good was never good enough, finding fault instead of grace. My grandmother once said if you're looking for a booger, you can always find one.

The NFL off-season is the longest of the four major professional sports in America. For some teams, it can be almost seven months. I look forward to the start of each new season for the NFL and college football.

In September of 2005, the fall meant the kick-off to a new season. I was excited to start tracking my favorite teams. It was also the beginning of the new school year. Terill and I encouraged Olivia to consider sports, music, or some extra-curricular activity. Whatever she choose, we wanted to assure her that she had our support. She selected orchestra and tennis. We were excited about her choices, and she immediately began taking viola and tennis lessons. She quickly made good progress and her first concert would be in a few weeks. We could hardly wait!

Since school started in early August, they had several weeks to practice. The concert schedule was announced, and, to my great surprise, all the concerts were scheduled for Monday nights. That's right, the same night as Monday Night Football. They would begin at 6:30 PST. There was no debate. My priorities were to support Liv, but it wasn't easy.

Many of the sixth-grade students did not have breath or finger strength when playing string, woodwind, and brass instruments. Some nights it was a real challenge, but I got through it. Of course, I recorded the game, but you always want to watch it live.

I picked up Tony Dungy's book *Quiet Strength* and later I realized that it was more important for me to be an all-pro dad than wondering who would be the next NFL all-pro great. I've said this before—life is about finishing strong. I have so many examples from football. You can recover a fumble and change momentum. Sometimes changing momentum starts with saying, "I'm sorry, let's try it again." I'm determined to get it right.

# Chapter 36: I'm Brett, I'm Jared, I'm Joe

B rett Favre's last year with the Minnesota Vikings was 2010. In 2009 he guided the Vikings to the NFC Championship game against the New Orleans Saints. When I heard that Favre could possibly be coming to Minnesota, I wasn't too happy. Don't get me wrong; I knew Brett had a lot left in the tank. But how would this play out with the Vikings fans? Suddenly the leader of your biggest rival is now the face of *your* franchise. It's not the same as signing an offensive guard or left tackle. This was quarterback Brett Favre.

The year before, Brett played with the Jets. They started out great but trailed off. In 2009 he retired, then had a press conference and unretired, which resulted in some confusion. At that point, Brett had nothing to prove; he was a sure first-round Hall of Famer. He certainly didn't need the money. But he needed to prove something, and he did.

Terill and I were on hospital visitation. The Vikings vs. 49ers game was on television. The Vikings had the ball but were trailing with a few seconds left on the clock. Brett rolled and scrambled to his right. He was nearly sacked. Somehow he spotted Greg Lewis in the back of the end zone. He had a small window. It would be like threading a needle. While throwing off the wrong foot, seconds were ticking down. Running for his life, he found Greg Lewis skirting across the back of the end zone. Lewis made a great catch and managed to stay in bounds. A Viking win! I love me some Brett Favre.

Brett had a great year in 2009. He threw 33 touchdowns and only 7 interceptions. Some counted him out, but he came back and proved his critics wrong. In 2010 I met Brett Favre at the Minnesota Vikings chapel before we played the Bears. Brett was the first player to arrive, followed by 25 other Bible-packing Vikings, including Adrian Peterson and Jared Allen. I was introduced as a former Vikings defensive end who now lives in Phoenix and travels as an evangelist. After the chapel service Jared Allen told me that he also lived in Phoenix during the off-season. We exchanged numbers and planned to get together after the season.

In 2012 Jared set the single Minnesota Vikings franchise record for most sacks by a Viking, with 22, only half a sack short of tying Michael Strahan's all-time season record of 22.5.

Since his retirement, Jared is very visible and busy in the community. He created his own charity—the Jared Allen Homes for Wounded Warriors. These are men and women who were severely wounded while serving in Iraq and Afghanistan. Jared is a great friend and supports my ministry. We try to do lunch about once a month.

## A Lesson about Love and Grace

It was lunch at our usual Italian spot. Jared ordered a salad, and I ordered a meatball sandwich. The Minnesota Vikings' training camp would open soon, so Jared went light on carbs. After lunch, I went back to my office at Phoenix First Assembly of God. The last thing I remembered was opening my laptop. I blacked out for thirty minutes; I don't remember anything.

Larry Kerychuk called 911, and they rushed me to the hospital. Larry thought I was a goner. The next thing I remembered is opening up my eyes at John C. Lincoln Hospital and looking at Mary, our secretary. She said I had a grand mal seizure.

The neurologist thought the seizure was the result of head trauma playing football. I never had a seizure until I retired from the NFL. The first one happened in June of 2001. This was my second seizure. After lunch, I could have easily driven the 45-minute drive home to Gold Canyon. Instead, I drove to my office, which was only five minutes from the restaurant. God is good.

They ran all kinds of tests to find out why I had the seizure, but the MRI revealed very little. When I played football in college and the NFL, one of the pass rush techniques I used was something called a head butt. You would use your head as a weapon, butting the head of the offensive lineman. This is a jarring jolt that we were taught to do. I supposed I've used this move a thousand times. I remember my high school coach telling me that I was the best nose blocker on the team. There was zero concussion protocol back in the good old days, plus the helmets weren't very good.

After two days in the hospital, I was more than ready to check out. I had ministry in Tampa coming up the next day. The doctor told me not to drive for 90 days.

I said, "No way. I'm driving from Miami to Tampa tomorrow. I've got to preach."

My wife said, "You're in no condition to preach, not to mention driving from Miami to Tampa." She said, "You're not going anywhere."

I said, "Babe, I can't let these people down; they're expecting me."

Finally she gave in with one stipulation: "You call someone to drive you to Tampa. You're not driving."

I agreed, and I didn't drive for 90 days, except for driving a golf cart.

A two-day stay in the hospital cost over twenty-two thousand dollars. We had no health insurance. So how was I going to pay this hospital bill? I didn't know what to do, so I reached out to the NFL. They directed me to NFL Cares. NFL Cares is a program to assist former players in improving their quality of life. They paid my bill. I've never been very positive about how the NFL treats former players. Sometimes it seems like they're only waiting for us to die. Our retirement is the worst of the four major professional sports. It should be the best because of the high rate of injuries and mortality, especially for the linemen. NFL Cares came through for me. I don't know how I would have been able to pay that hospital bill without them.

Someone substituted for me. NFL Cares paid a bill that they didn't owe. I owed it. They paid my bill so that I could have the freedom I did not deserve. I deserved the responsibility to pay the cost. But I couldn't pay for it. That's why Jesus died. He paid a debt He did not owe. We owe it so that we could have freedom that we do not deserve. That's called love and grace.

# Chapter 37: A Small Cloud

The bubble burst in 2008. Terill lost her job with Schindler Elevator where she worked for five years. They laid her off. Churches tightened their budgets for guest speakers, evangelists, and missionaries. My love offerings were down thirty percent. Coupled with cancellations, I fell behind on all of my accounts, including my first and second mortgage. Quickly I was six months behind on both mortgages. The bank threatened to foreclose. I tried to keep this from Terill, but it came out. I felt like a failure.

We had built our house and moved in one month after we married. I asked Terill, "What are we going to do?"

She said, "No, what are *you* going to do?"

I went to my office and prayed. "Lord, help me. What am I going to do?"

I started reaching out to my friends. In an hour, the Lord brought in $8,000, which was what we needed.

I'm sure they would rather I not mention their names, but if it wasn't for Viking teammate Jim Marshall and good friends Dr. Dana McQuinn, Pastor Jim Willoughby, Pastor Craig Lauterbach, Mark Reicks, Jack Carey, and businessman Tom Blackwell, we would've lost the house.

God always makes a way in the desert. For Elijah, it was a small cloud arising from the sea like a man's hand. It had not rained in Israel for three years. They were in a drought. Ahab was now king of Israel along with his crazy wife, Queen Jezebel. Ahab was one of the most godless of all the kings of Israel. He destroyed the altar and killed many of the prophets of God, replacing them with the false prophets of Baal. This thing was an abomination to the house of Israel.

The prophet told a servant to go and look because rain was coming. At the time, the sky was clear and blue. After being sent back several times, the servant saw a tiny cloud rising. Then what began as a small cloud like a man's hand proved to be a storm. Don't despise the days of small beginnings. With that seemingly small and insignificant information, Elijah warned King Ahab that there was a storm in the forecast. "Get thee down that the rain stop thee not" (1 Kings 18:44 KJV).

Perhaps it was there, but the servant didn't see it because he was looking for the wrong sign. Or he was sent back until he came into agreement with what the Lord already confirmed. Even though it hadn't rained in three years, Elijah told Ahab to prepare. Do you see a small cloud? Prepare for your miracle, for your breakthrough. It's gonna rain. You have to walk out what you believe.

When Peter saw Jesus walking on water, he said, "Lord, if it is You, tell me to come to You on the water." Peter got out of the boat and walked toward Jesus. But when he felt the wind, he was afraid and began to sink. That's what fear does. Your confidence begins to sink, your hope begins to sink, your dream begins to sink, and your faith begins to sink. Peter called out to Jesus, and He pulled him up. Jesus asked, "You of little faith, why did you doubt?"

# Chapter 38: United Flight 93

In 1980 our quarterback Tom Burnett led the Bloomington Thomas Jefferson Jaguars football team to a championship runner-up trophy. It was my second year of teaching and coaching. Tom Burnett was an all-around great athlete and honor student. Tommy had many college offers, but he decided to play football at a small Jesuit college in Minnesota named St. John's University.

He played two seasons before an injury ended his career. Tommy graduated from the Carlson School of Management at the University of Minnesota. It was a privilege and honor to coach and teach Tommy Burnett. I lost track of Tom Burnett. As a gifted athlete and student, I knew his future was bright and that with hard work he'd reach his goals. I later discovered that Tommy moved to San Ramon, California. He was married and the father of five-year-old twin daughters. He worked at Thouro-Tech-Corp where he was vice president and COO.

Tommy was on a pleasure/business trip through Minnesota and New Jersey. On September 11, 2001, Tommy boarded United Flight 93 from Newark to San Francisco. Forty-six minutes into the flight, terrorists breached the cockpit and overpowered the crew. Tom called his wife Deena four times. In his last words to her, he said, "We're all going to die, but there's four of us—Todd Beamer, Jeremy Glick, and Mark Bingham—who are going to do something. I love you, honey."

The hijacked plane, United Flight 93 was now headed for the Capitol. Because of the heroic actions of Beamer, Click, Bingham, and Tom Burnett, United Flight 93 crash-landed in an empty field in Stoney Creek Township in Pennsylvania. Tommy Burnett boarded United Flight 93 without knowing that this would be his last flight or that he would never see his family again; that he and 42 other brave souls would sacrifice their lives for the greater call.

As a teacher and coach, you try to lead your students and athletes to greatness—that regardless of failure, greatness is attainable. Greatness never comes cheap. It always comes with a price. You have to earn it. It was unfathomable to me that the same hand I put on Tommy's shoulder encouraging him to lead the Jefferson Jaguars to victory is the same hand that touched the engraved letters on Tommy's name at the ground zero memorial. Tommy Burnett paid the ultimate price on United Flight 93.

When Tommy said, "I love you, honey; we're gonna do something," he and the others were saying what Jesus said in Matthew 26:42, "My Father, if it's not possible for this cup to be taken away unless I drink it, may your will be done." His sacrifice was in obedience to the will of His Father. In Hebrews 12:2 (NIV), we read, "For the joy set before him he endured the cross," because *something had to be done.* He said, "No one takes my life from me. But I *lay it down of my own accord*" (John 10:18).

Jesus could have summoned 72,000 angels. Burnett's last words were, "I love you, honey; we're gonna do something." John 3:16 is the heart and soul of the gospel: For God so loved you that He did something, He gave His only begotten Son that whosoever believes in Him should not perish but have everlasting life.

The question, "What have you done since 9/11?" is relative. For a moment, strangers became friends as Americans briefly united. Churches were filled, prayer vigils were observed, and people became more patient and caring. All lives mattered—Black lives, white, red, brown, yellow, and those dressed in blue.

For a while, we were one party—one united America. For a while, we were all one family, all patriots (not the team, the country). Gradually the campfires died out and the chorus of "Kumbaya" was drowned by the old familiar tune of self-preservation. "Us" and "we" were replaced by "me" and "mine." Some say nothing much has changed since 9/11. It came, it went, we wept, we prayed, and we moved on.

Today in 2021, we're more fractured along the lines of race and class. Police officers don't feel the respect of the community anymore. Christianity has become a watchdog of who's right, who's wrong. To some, Christian faith is determined by which news organization you watch, Fox or CNN. Fox, you're a believer; CNN, you're a lost reprobate. Maybe it was Fox News that died for our sins. Maybe it was CNN.

We shouldn't be in the business of dividing the family. We should be in the ministry of restoration and building His church. This nonsense only serves to widen the racial gap and ignite political polarization that seeks to divide America and the church. Divide and conqueror. People are so wrapped up in the issues that they lose sight of what America stands for. It's simple—one nation under God with liberty and justice—and *Jesus* for all!

Football is the ultimate team sport. You're forced to unify. One missed assignment can spell defeat or victory. Jerry Kramer blocked Jethro Pugh just enough to enable Bart Starr to find the end zone in the Ice Bowl. That put the Packers on the path to three straight world and Super Bowl championships. That team had players from Alabama, Grambling, Mississippi, Fernander Smith, Arizona State, Notre Dame, and Georgia.

The great Jim Brown said it best recently. The discussion was about taking a knee during the playing of the national anthem. Brown said, "You need to decide if you're a football player or an activist. These owners pay you millions of dollars to play football. They didn't bring you to the San Francisco 49ers because that is the best place to launch your social platform."

These owners are billionaires whose first priority is not their players' social platform. They care about the financial success of their franchise. Division can tear up a locker room. I fully understand injustice and racial profiling, but what do these players expect to accomplish? Kneeling during the National Anthem is not going to compel justice for all. It won't bring about social change. Yes, it does create awareness. But we know what the problem is; we don't need more awareness; we need radical change. It always starts in the heart. We need transformation (Rom. 12:1-2).

There's nothing more radical than the change of heart—the change from Saul of Tarsus to the apostle Paul. Paul was convinced that he needed to destroy Christianity. He was on his way to Damascus to seek letters from the high priest so that he could aggressively pursue and capture as many Christians to be arrested, persecuted, prosecuted, and eventually executed.

Paul hated Christians. He didn't care if they were male or female. But God did a work in Paul's heart. God knocked him off of his beast onto his hindquarters and Paul accepted Jesus as personal Savior. The scales were removed from his eyes. God changed Paul into one of the greatest champions in the New Testament.

Paul's transformation was so radical that God had to first convince the church that he was really converted. That's what the love and power of God will do. He'll change your path and, like Paul, He'll put you on Straight Street.

It breaks my heart when I hear that another Black child is shot and killed for no legitimate reason other than looking suspicious. You look for justice, yet it's not to be found. I can understand the conclusions that are drawn. The death camps of Chelmno, Auschwitz, and Treblinka shout in vivid horror that certain lives didn't matter; 6,000,000 Jews were gassed in chambers for something called ethnic cleansing. From 1619 to 1865, *two hundred and forty-six years*, Blacks were owned and sold like a piece of property, murdered without consequence, and women were raped and beaten just for being Black. Do Black lives matter?

You better believe Black lives matter. Black, white, brown, red, yellow, and blue lives all matter. God gave His only begotten Son and nailed the sin of racism, hatred, and bigotry on the back of Jesus Christ because you matter. Why would God send His only Son to die for someone who had no value, no potential, and no soul?

Paul hated Christians throughout the death, burial, and resurrection of Christ. Today he would be considered as a modern-day terrorist, an insurrectionist. The Lord did a work of grace in his life. It took the revelation of Christ for Saul to see that all lives matter.

Footnote: When I was with the Vikings, Bud Grant would line us up in training camp on the sideline. Our helmet in our right hand, left arm to our side—all Americans, all Vikings. Someone would turn on the PA, and the National Anthem would play. We practiced standing at attention until we got it right. Football is the ultimate team sport. Get it right, America. Let's sack the sin of racism!

# Chapter 39: Are You Steve Harvey?

Has anyone ever told you that you look like somebody famous? I was in the Admirals Club in Dallas, waiting to connect to Phoenix when I noticed a lady peeking at me. It's not unusual; people always think you're somebody. She finally came over and asked, "Are you Steve Harvey?"

I said, "No, ma'am."

She said, "Yes, you are."

I said, "No, ma'am. I'm not Steve Harvey."

She said, "I know you're Steve Harvey, I won't tell anyone."

I finally just said thank you.

While working out at LA Fitness, a man walked by and said, "I love to watch your show TV show with the kids."

TV show? I just said "thank you" and moved on. Please! I'm taller than Steve Harvey, bigger than Steve Harvey, better looking than Steve Harvey, and my mustache is not as thick as Steve Harvey's. I'm not rich like Steve Harvey either, but it would be nice!

Mankato State University was the training camp location for the Minnesota Vikings. I am eternally grateful that Buddy Ryan recommended me to the Vikings. It was hard to believe that I played alongside Jim Marshall, Alan Page, Carl Eller, and Doug Sutherland, the famed Purple People Eaters. I had Carl Eller's poster on my bedroom wall when I was a kid, and now these great players were my teammates. When I lived in Minnesota,

I was often mistaken for Jim Marshall. I told Jim about that once, and he said, "You don't look anything like me."

A couple of years ago, Terill and I flew back to Minneapolis for the Vikings' alumni weekend. I wasn't able to attend the game because of a commitment I had in Grand Rapids, Minnesota. As we deplaned and walked through the terminal to baggage, someone said, "Hey, Jim, how you doing? Can I get an autograph?"

I said, "I'm sorry, I'll give you my autograph, but I'm not Jim Marshall." He gave me that look and almost a wink that said, "Sure, okay," as if I were trying to keep my identity a secret.

I said, "No, I'm serious. I'm not Jim."

That evening I had dinner with Jim and some other Viking teammates. I told Jim what had happened as I walked through the terminal. I was ready for Jim's response, "You don't look anything like me." Instead, Jim motioned other teammates to come over and hear what I had just told him. Now that we've gotten older, I guess it's okay for Jim to be compared to someone fourteen years younger than him.

## The Great Jim Marshall

During training camp we'd take the team bus or catch a ride to the airport or stadium. It was my first year with the Vikings, and Jim Marshall asked if I needed a ride to the airport. I couldn't believe it; I'm riding in Jim Marshall's brand new Mercedes Benz to the airport. I agreed. Who would miss this opportunity? I wondered why the veteran players choose to ride the bus rather than ride with Marshall. This would be my first time riding in a Mercedes Benz. I couldn't wait to buckle up. And I'm glad I did. We made the hour and a half trip from Mankato to Bloomington in 47 minutes. Next time I either took the team bus or rode with my roommate, tight end Steve Craig.

As an 18-year-old defensive end at New Mexico State University, I revered the Purple People Eaters Alan Page, Carl Eller, Gary Larson, and Jim Marshall as my heroes. They were one of the most feared defenses in the NFL. I especially admired defensive ends Carl Eller and Jim Marshall.

Never would I have imagined that I would be teammates of one the greatest front fours in the history of the National Football League.

Carl Eller was mean and powerful. His nickname was Moose. I admired Jim Marshall's first step of explosion coming off the line of scrimmage. His hands were extremely strong. At six feet five inches and 245 pounds, he dominated left offensive tackles with quickness and technique. I was exactly the same size and tried to pattern my game after his. In high school, I even wanted to wear number 70, but it was taken by an upperclassman so I settled for number 71.

The life and near-death stories of Jim Marshall are legendary. He has come through multiple surgeries, an ultralight plane crash on our football field at Thomas Jefferson High School, a gunshot wound, a ruptured artery that gave him only minutes to live; he was trapped in a blizzard where he burned money to survive only to wake up the next morning to find one person in his camping party frozen to death.

There wasn't another player in our locker room who was more admired and respected than the great Jim Marshall. Including playoffs, Jim Marshall played in 302 consecutive games. His consecutive regular-season mark stands at 282. That record stood until Brett Favre broke it in 2009. During a 20-year career, he was the NFL's version of the quintessential iron man. Coach Bud Grant loved Jim Marshall and elected him captain in 1967.

Grant credits Jim Marshall for the Vikings going to four bowls in a nine-year span. He says the image that best represents the Minnesota Vikings' 56-year history is a picture of Marshall standing on a muddy, snowy football field glaring down at a quarterback KO'd by a Joe Louis right hand.

After the ultralight plane crash, I visited Jim in the hospital. He was hurt pretty bad. For a little while it was touch and go. He broke almost every bone in his bionic body. We had a word of prayer, a short visit, and he had a long recovery. By God's grace and mercy and Jim's amazing will, he pulled through.

Ten years later, I would learn of an extraordinary phenomenon in the annals of Jim Marshall. He had an amazing out-of-body experience. Jim says that as he floated outside of his body on some spiritual plane, he saw me grab his hand and begin to pray for him. That's exactly what happened during our hospital visit. Oddly enough, when I moved from Minneapolis to Phoenix, our friendship became closer.

In 1992 I was honored with the Pete Maravich award at the AIM athletes' banquet. I asked Jim Marshall if he would present me with this award. Jim graciously said, "Yes, I'll be there." Our banquet is much like the ESPYs. After a video presentation, the presenter will announce the award recipient then share personal comments and highlights of his or her career.

In the natural, you would think that it should be the other way around, me presenting an award to the great Jim Marshall. I was more than humbled to receive this honor presented by a living legend who should be in the Pro Football Hall of Fame. In 2000 we honored Jim Marshall as NFL Man of the Year. The favor was returned as I introduced Jim.

When I became a Minnesota Viking, Jim Marshall was nearly forty years old and Carl Eller was thirty-six. I didn't get to play with them in their heyday, but as seasoned veterans they were feared and respected by quarterbacks throughout the NFL. These two greats have amassed 257 quarterback sacks between them—more than any other pair of defensive ends who ever played the game.

Throughout my high school, college, and NFL career, I've had great coaching. At Withrow High School, Coach Marv Merritt trusted his instincts on a 15-year-old sophomore. At New Mexico State, Coach Don Kloppenberg motivated a young freshman to heights I never dreamed, while Buddy Ryan, the genius, told me that I could beat anybody on any given Sunday. However, the best coaching I ever received came through watching Moose, Alan, and Jim for two years.

# Chapter 40: I Know You'll Pray for Me

Wally Hilgenberg was a Minnesota Vikings legend. He played outside linebacker with one speed only—full speed. He started in all four Super Bowls. Wally never backed down from any fight or challenge during his 16-year NFL career. Some say that he had a mean streak. One reporter went so far as to classify him as a dirty player. To us who played with Wally, he was never a dirty player, but he didn't mind getting his hands dirty. If you're slinging mud, he will sling it right back at you. He was an awesome teammate.

The Minnesota Vikings had a great core of believers on the team. Wally's wife Mary prayed that Wally would give his heart to Christ. During the 1978 off-season, Wally accepted Jesus Christ as his personal Savior. With the same tenacity and enthusiasm, he was a warrior for the kingdom of God. He told everyone he met that Jesus changed his heart.

In December of 2006, I brought Terill and Olivia to Minneapolis for the Vikings' alumni game. This was Terill's first visit to the Twin Cities. We stayed at the downtown Hilton. Our hotel was decorated with Christmas spirit. There's nothing like Christmas in Minnesota. Although the temperature was below freezing, you didn't need a coat, gloves, or a hat when shopping in downtown Minneapolis. Many of the retail stores are connected by the Twin City Skyway.

Even though Terill never saw me play, when we attended these alumni games, she fit right in with the players' wives. It's a great feeling. I introduced her to many of my former teammates, including Chuck Foreman, Carl Eller, Coach Grant, Bench Warmer Bob, and Wally. I asked Wally and Viking guard Wes Hamilton if they would pose for a picture with my family.

After we took several pictures, Wally pulled me from the group and said, "Joe, I haven't told very many people, but I know you're a man of faith, and you'll pray for me. I have ALS." ALS (amyotrophic lateral sclerosis) is a fatal disease affecting the nerve cells in the brain and the spinal cord. It's pretty much a death sentence.

Wally's words sent a shockwave through me and broke my heart. How could this happen? I knew what was ahead for him. Thank the Lord that he had a support team to walk down this path.

I can't remember who we played that week and even less about who was inducted into the Minnesota Vikings' Ring of Honor. I do remember the Viking alumni gathered on the field in a line or semicircle. As we lined up, I was standing next to Wally. I put my arm around his shoulder and started quietly praying for him. I had no idea the effect that would make for Wally. Don't get me wrong, I know God hears and answers prayers, but the fact that we would pray during the halftime celebration had a great impact on Wally Hilgenberg.

Almost eight years later, I had one last visit with Wally. He was seated in his wheelchair on his front porch. His wife Mary, his daughters, and other family members were gathered. After we prayed, I gave him a hug, a smile, and a tear. It's sad to see my brother barely hanging on. He said, "Joe, I want to tell you this." With almost all of the strength he could find, he told me something I'll never forget.

He said, "Do you remember when I told you I had ALS and you prayed for me on the field at the Metrodome?"

I said, "Yes, I sure do remember."

He said, "Let me tell you something. Of all the things that have happened to me on a football field, the big games I've played in, including four Super Bowls, my greatest moment on a football field ever was when you put your arm around me and prayed for me."

That wasn't what I was expecting to hear. In over 340 games Wally played in his 16-year career, including preseason and postseason, that prayer was the highlight of his NFL career! Wow, I was humbled and blown away. The prayer of faith meant more to him than any big play, big game, or any big victory.

Wally had his priorities in the right order. His faith and his family came first. We prayed and said our final goodbye. Two months later, on September 23, 2008, the Lord called him home.

At his funeral, Wally preached his going home service. There wasn't a dry eye in the church. Teammates, Coach Bud Grant, family, and friends were there for his homecoming celebration. As they pushed the casket to the hearse, Vikings players were lined up on each side of the hallway. This created an open path and gauntlet with footballs raised high as a final salute to a great Minnesota Vikings champion, Wally Hilgenberg.

Wally reunited with fellow Vikings Chuck "Goodie" Goodrum, Karl Kassulke, Fred McNeill, Curtis Bobo Rouse, and Grady Alderman. We'll meet again, brother. We're all on our way!

# Chapter 41: Who's That Guy?

Matt Blair was inducted in the Vikings' Ring of Honor in 2012. He went to six straight pro bowls from 1977-1982. He still holds team records for blocked kicks and sacks for a linebacker. Many of his teammates came back for his induction ceremony, including linebacker Fred McNeill. Matt and Fred were great friends. They came into the league at about the same time. I hadn't seen Fred for almost thirty years.

Fred loved music. At training camp, we would sing after practice in the dormitory stairwell because of the echo. We even recorded ourselves and played the tape in his car. It sounded pretty good. I was looking forward to seeing my old friend Fred McNeill.

On alumni weekend, players and coaches relive stories that get better every year. Who could forget Moose and the pancake uproar? We were in Atlanta having our game meal. Moose (Carl Eller) wanted pancakes. Pancakes were not on Coach Bud Grant's menu. Moose talked a waiter into dishing up a stack of buttermilk pancakes.

When Coach Grant got wind of this, the special order was immediately cancelled. The waiter went to Moose and told him that Coach Grant nixed his order for pancakes. Moose exploded! He kicked a tray of plates and dishes that bounced off of the 25-foot-high ceiling. Then he stormed out of the room and walked past Coach Grant steaming mad. That's the last time we saw Moose that weekend. He didn't even play in our game against the Falcons. You had to be there; we could have used some of that aggression during the game.

Fred McNeill looked the same as he did almost 30 years earlier. He earned a law degree and was practicing in southern California. Fred was in great shape, and I recognized him right away. I walked over to him and said hello. We embraced and looked each other over as if we were fishing for a compliment on how good we looked since our playing days.

I said, "You look great!"

He said, "You look great too." But the more we talked, the more I realized something was wrong. Sadly, Fred had no clue of who I was and no memory of why he was here. I felt the need to pray with him right there. I prayed, and then he prayed. In his prayer, he referred to me as "this young man." It was discovered that another Viking linebacker had ALS. Fred McNeill died two years later at the age of sixty-three. Another Viking linebacker. First Wally, now Fred.

## More Memory Issues

Matt Blair was never satisfied with labels. He was more than a Minnesota Vikings linebacker; he was an entrepreneur. Matt loved photography and took the team photos for the Vikings program and press guide. Matt had endorsements before Jordan turned Nike around. He had many interests and talents. In June of 1995, I received a call from Matt. He asked if I would be interested in coming to Jacksonville for the Jaguars inaugural football game.

The Jags and Carolina Panthers were the two NFL expansion teams. The NFL would sponsor thirty players and their wives or girlfriends for a weekend of golf, good food, and a football game. Where do I sign up? It was a great weekend and a great memory! I met Deacon Jones, Merlin Olsen, L.T., and many other NFL Hall of Famers.

That same year, Phoenix would host Super Bowl XXX. Matt arranged a Super Bowl package of hospitality for corporate executives and heavy hitters. He put together a package that included Super Bowl tickets, food, hotel, access to the NFL experience, and golf. Dallas beat the Steelers that Super Bowl 27-17. Matt's a great golfer, so I arranged a golfing outing at Superstition Mountain whenever he came in town. I looked forward to seeing Matt and Mary Beth at the alumni weekend.

Two years ago at the alumni weekend, we visited the Vikings' training center. Their weight room and training facility were very impressive. Back in the day, the only piece of weight equipment we had was an old-school universal gym machine that no one ever used.

They served us lunch and gave us an opportunity to visit the facility. I passed on that and waited for the bus to the hotel. While I waited, Matt Blair walked into the training site cafeteria. He and Mary Beth came over and joined Terill and me for lunch. There were a few Vikings teammates in the cafeteria.

I thought Matt was joking when he asked, "Joe, who is that guy? Who is that guy?"

I said, "Matt, quit playing around."

He said, "No, I can't remember their names, Joe."

I was shocked by the many teammates he didn't know. Mary Beth didn't say anything. She didn't have to. She knew he was battling the early stages of dementia.

The next year, Terill and I came back to the alumni weekend. Matt and the Ring of Honor members were recognized. Matt was in a wheelchair. I said, "Hey, Brother Matt, what's going on, man? How are you doing?"

He didn't answer, only smiled. Three months earlier, a local Minneapolis television station featured a story about Vikings great Matt Blair. The story revealed that Matt had dementia. Mary Beth said he recognized faces but didn't know where from. He would smile and think everyone was his friend.

Here was another Viking linebacker with cognitive memory issues. It just makes you wonder. One thing I don't wonder is that if Wally, Fred, and Matt were asked would they do it again, they all would say, "Yes, absolutely."

God gives out gifts for a divine purpose. Most are used for self-gain, fulfillment, and pleasure. When you play a team sport like football, there's no room for individual selfishness. Matt was an ultimate teammate and champion. The last time I saw Matt Blair was September of 2019. He was a resident in an Alzheimer's care facility. On October 22, 2020, Matt Blair joined his mother and brother around that blessed table in heaven.

# Chapter 42: Singapore

After riding 17 hours in coach, my knees needed to repent for cussing me out. Finally, welcome to Singapore! What a reprieve. After clearing customs (which surprisingly only took a few minutes), I headed for baggage claim. I wasn't sure who would pick me up, but I was sure they'd recognize me. I don't think anyone in Singapore stood over five feet eight inches, and at six feet five inches, even Ray Charles could see me at night.

Pastor Ang and Jenny greeted me at baggage. They were very friendly. We loaded the car and headed to their home. I would stay with them for a night then check into my hotel in Batan, Indonesia the next day. Pastor Ang arranged a tour in several Assemblies of God churches. This would be the first of several trips to Singapore.

Singapore is a global commerce, finance, and transport center. It is the most technology-ready nation in Asia and ranks highly in education and health care. The official language is English. If you own a car that's over ten years old, you must sell it, and you'll pay a hefty price for a driver's license. Don't expect to find Wrigley's Orbit chewing gum—or any gum, for that matter—in Singapore. However, if you have a taste for American food, you'll find everything from Burger King to Taco Bell.

If you're in a parking garage, you have to back into your parking space. Because the range of humidity is between 73 to 96 percent, you shower and change clothes at least twice a day. A lot different than Phoenix with its arid, dry temperatures. The shortest route to Batan is a 35-minute ferry ride. Some areas in Batan are third-world. Garbage stacked seven or eight feet in the air, high population of the homeless.

The main transportation is by motorcycle. It's not uncommon to see a family of four riding one motorcycle. My hotel was a destination for prostitutes. Every morning you'd hear whistles and catcalls. Unfortunately, in 2017 300,000 workers were laid off. Islam is the majority religion in Batan with 76 percent, followed by Christianity at 17 percent.

Our three-day revival was promoted by posters and word of mouth. There had been some persecution of Christians, so I was told that the organizers of the outreach decided it would be safer to remove all of my promotional materials. Someone beheaded a Christian pastor the week before I arrived. Thankfully, I experienced no issues in Batan and returned the next year for a youth revival.

Pastor Ang introduced me to Pastor Dominic Yeo. Pastor Dom is senior pastor at Trinity Christian Center. Although his vision is global, he believes that all ministry is birthed out of the local church. Trinity Christian Center serves as a beacon of refuge and hope to lift up a light in a dark world.

Like Tommy Barnett and Phoenix First Assembly of God, their ministry cuts across denominational and cultural lines that seek to divide. Find a need and fill it, find a hurt and heal. It is more than a motto—it's their heartbeat. Under the leadership of Pastor Dom, the church has grown to more than 6,000 members.

Pastor Dom scheduled me for a spring revival the following year. This time my accommodations were in a high-rise hotel in downtown Singapore. I even had a king-sized bed. I love the people of Singapore and Trinity Christian Center. During the revival, there was an awesome move of God.

Singapore and Trinity Christian Center should be a destination on everyone's bucket list!

# Chapter 43: Sydney and the All Blacks

I n 1997 I flew to Sydney, Australia for an outreach. Another long flight. My knees held up better. They and I were younger at the time. We landed in Sydney and proceeded to baggage claim. While we waited for our bags, I noticed a man wearing sunglasses. He looked like an actor or a rock star. We nodded and continued to wait. After we picked up our bags, the cool guy with shades was quickly moved into a limo and taken to the Ritz Carlton. I was picked up in a station wagon and taken to a home. My schedule was full. They booked me into seven different Assemblies of God churches and high schools in ten days.

Pastor Williams, who moved from the US, pastored one of the Assemblies of God churches in Sydney. They invited me to their home for dinner. His wife Sandy made the best apple pie with homemade ice cream. I would go back to that church just for the apple pie.

In Sydney, I learned that the *All Blacks* had nothing to do with skin color. They were the premier rugby team in the world. I met several players and even went to a game. Those players are great athletes; there's no equipment needed for rugby. For you ladies, there's also an All Black women's rugby team.

They found me a gym to train in. It wasn't LA Fitness, but it was okay. The weights were measured in kilos, which threw me off. I adjusted the weight to what I felt was right and stopped comparing everything to the United States. The more I traveled internationally, the more I learned how spoiled Americans are. I was upset because I couldn't find a Circle K or

QT with a soda dispenser. I also discovered that we Americans like ice. I also never got used to driving on the right (wrong) side of the car.

I brought my golf clubs and played a round at a public course. I remember slicing a shot into a weeded area. I went to look for my ball and quickly abandoned the search. A 12-foot python was resting in the weeds. Search over!

Later that week, I found out who the cool dude in the airport was. It was lead singer Michael Hutchence of the rock band INXS. He was found dead on November 22, 1997 in his hotel room at the Ritz Carlson. Hutchence's death was ruled a suicide while depressed and under the influence of alcohol and drugs.

During my assemblies that week, I wanted the students to understand that name, game, and fame are not what bring real meaning and purpose in life. Michael Hutchence had it all, yet he felt he had nothing to live for. Life is not about having; it's about knowing. The word *know* or *knowledge* appears almost 950 times in the Bible. To know God is not to struggle philosophically with His eternal essence but rather to recognize and accept His claims.

# Chapter 44: Joe, You'll Have to Fly This Bird

M y first trip to Bethel, Alaska was in August of 1993. Pastor Ralph Liberty invited me to his church to preach a four-day revival. Bethel is a strange place. It's a city of almost 6,000 residents. Most don't have cars, and there are hardly any affordable transit options. You either walk or take a taxi.

No roads lead in or out of Bethel. The cost of a car is about double what you would pay on the mainland. Bethel has one paved road. For that reason, when entering someone's home, you remove your shoes first thing. The only paved road in Bethel is the one I'd run to the airport and back every morning.

For the native Alaskans and locals, it's their way of life; for me, it was like living in the Alaskan bush. There was maybe one motel in Bethel. Pastor Liberty had a room in the church attic that served as my evangelist quarters. The ministry was anointed, and I was able to preach in the Bethel jail.

The Lord has opened many doors. Who would ever think I'd be speaking in Bethel, Alaska or Auckland, New Zealand? Not me!

On this journey, I'm discovering that the family of God comes in all shapes and sizes. We don't all look the same, talk the same, or vote for the same candidate. What makes us family is not being members of the same political party; it's being members of the sanctified party by faith in the Lord Jesus Christ. Whether you're in Bethel or the Bronx, it's the same

Jesus who works His grace and mercy in our lives and transforms us into His image.

Bethel may not have paved roads, but who needs that when you're fishing on a glassy lake full of salmon? It seems everyone in Alaska has a pilot's license. One of the members at the Bethel Assembly of God church asked if I wanted to go fishing. I said yes!

Dwight Leffler had a small plane and knew the best spots for catching the big fish. We loaded up his plane with our gear and headed for a day of salmon fishing. Dwight landed on a short dirt runway about twenty feet from the shoreline. I was praying, *Lord, let this plane stop before the runway ends.* This was my first flight in a Piper J-3 Cub. The fish were biting, and we caught about one hundred pounds of salmon in a few hours.

On our flight back to Bethel, Dwight told me that he had a heart valve replaced. He had just been medically cleared to fly and felt fine. We loaded the fish and took off. As we neared the airport, Dwight groaned, grabbed his chest, and said, "Oh no, Joe, you'll have to fly this bird."

I said, "What?"

He laughed and said, "I'm just kidding."

Dwight and Glenna Leffler are some of the beautiful champions I met along my journey. Since that time, they have both been called home.

# Chapter 45: Mr. Universe, Barbecue, and Barnett

L arry Kerychuk and I drove to Tucson to watch James Jones and Lenny Davis compete in Greco-Roman wrestling. They won their matches against the Russians and were both training for the '96 Olympic Games. On the other side of the gym, you couldn't help but notice someone with the physique of Arnold and Lee Haney. Was this another wrestler? Later we found out who it was. It was the reigning Mr. Universe, Martin Downs.

Martin stood about six feet three inches and was 265 pounds. He was considered tall for a heavyweight. I said, "Larry, we have to meet his guy and invite him to the conference."

At the time, we had no idea who he was. We just knew that he had to be an athlete. He was very approachable and introduced himself as Martin. He said he lived in Tucson but was thinking about moving to Phoenix or Los Angeles to pursue acting. He had small parts in several Hollywood movies. We encouraged him to come to Phoenix and join the AIM team. He could start going to schools and sharing his amazing story. I'm not sure he had one. At that time, I honestly didn't really know if he would even consider Phoenix. I guess my sales pitch worked. In a month, he moved to the Valley of the Sun and joined the AIM team.

Our first outreach was my old stomping grounds of Las Cruces, New Mexico. Earnie Shavers, M.L. Harris, Martin, and myself were invited to bring our drug and alcohol awareness program to the Las Cruces public school system.

It was great to be back in Las Cruces. Many of my close friends were still living there, including Johnny Pickett, who was now the senior pastor at University Press. Johnny grew up in Las Cruces. He and I attended New Mexico State around the same time.

We arranged our schedule so each athlete would preach or share a testimony at a different church. Las Cruces Detective Joe Bob Sellers and PAL also sponsored our outreach. Joe Bob smokes the world's best beef brisket. If you're ever in Las Cruces, look for Joe Bob's trailer, and you'll taste what I mean. Also, Joe Bob and Mary Sellers are the pastors of Latter Rain Harvest Fellowship Church.

This was Martin Downs' first outreach. He fit right in and was doing a fine job. He had a great speaking voice and was a natural communicator. Very impressive.

M.L. and I were doing some high school assemblies in northwest Ohio. Somehow we ended up on the campus of Bowling Green University. We noticed a crowd of students had gathered around an outdoor stage listening to some wacko activist speaking very negatively. He was cutting down women and the church, saying, "Everyone's going to hell; all the jocks are fornicators, nothing but phonies." I should have ignored him and walked away, but I just couldn't take any more. I went up onto the platform, grabbed the mic from him, pushed him aside, and started preaching the gospel. The crowd roared. That's what happens when the anointing of God either falls upon you or you're in the flesh. Either way, Jesus was glorified.

M.L., Martin, Earnie, Rich Jessup, and I did hundreds of high school assemblies. We'll never know what kind of impact we've had. Even though we weren't allowed to preach the gospel, I know that God will anoint the truth, even if it's secular or physical truth.

Speaking of Martin, Earnie, M.L., and myself—we all love barbecue. There was a brand new barbecue joint named Texas Joe's Real Barbecue Ribs. It opened not too far from my office. One afternoon the four of us went to try it out. The owner recognized us and said everything would be on the house if we would sign an autographed picture that he could use to promote his new restaurant. We signed pictures and enjoyed some free barbecue.

No, it wasn't the best I've ever tasted, but it was free, and it was barbecue. Pastor Tommy Barnett is from Kansas City, the home of some of the best barbecue ribs on the planet, and Pastor Tommy loves barbecue. One day he took some of the Phoenix First Assembly of God staff members out to lunch at Texas Joe's. He noticed our pictures on the wall and a strong endorsement. He was confident that this was the place.

Several weeks later, he cornered me in the sanctuary. He said, "Joe, I want to tell you something. You soul brothers don't know anything about good barbecue."

I said, "Pastor, what are you talking about?"

He said, "I went to Texas Joe's. I saw your pictures on the wall saying that this was the best barbecue you've ever eaten. It was awful!"

I said, "Pastor Barnett, I know, you're right, it wasn't the greatest. I just said that because it was free."

He said, "Let me tell you, you need to go to Arthur Bryant's in Kansas City. That's real barbecue."

I went to Bryant's. It was really good. It seems like every pastor has his favorite barbecue house. When in Anchorage, Pastor Gary and Alice Morton take me to Rib Land; whenever in El Paso, Texas, the State Line; Alabama, Dreamland; Cincinnati, K and K Barbecue; New York City, Texas Barbecue House; Las Cruces, Joe Bob's Beef House. For me and my house, I'll choose Honey Bear's BBQ right here in Phoenix.

The two questions pastors generally ask: Is your hotel okay, and what do you want to eat? My answer is always the same: barbecue or Mexican. When Terill and I were dating, we'd go to my favorite barbecue and Mexican restaurants, either Honey Bear's or Carlos O'Brien's.

After we were married, I'd say, "Hey, babe, let's get some barbecue."

She'd say, "I don't like barbecue."

"You don't like barbecue? You did when we were dating, now all of a sudden you don't like barbecue! Well, let's go to Carlos O'Brien's," I would answer.

"I don't like Mexican food," she would reply.

"You did when we were dating!" I would say.

She said, "No, I only went to those places because I knew you liked it."

I wish she would have told me that before we got married. *Maybe I would have...* Nah, just kidding! Terill and I obviously have a mixed marriage. Yes, some might say unequally yoked, *and* we do have a color issue. Her people love the Raiders' silver and black; my people love God's Vikings' colors, purple and gold. In spite of our differences, we try and live a normal life—except during football season.

# Chapter 46: The Unit

I referenced Paul Krause earlier. He played free safety for sixteen years in the NFL, four with the Washington Redskins and twelve with the Minnesota Vikings. He set the NFL record with 81 interceptions, which he picked off from 45 different quarterbacks. Paul was inducted into the NFL Hall of Fame in 1998, and it was well overdue.

The first words I ever remember from Paul Krause were, "Hey, Joe, when we get to the Cities, I'm going to get you a unit."

I said, "What are you talking about, Paul?"

He repeated, "I'm going to get you a unit." He explained that he wore a hair unit and could fix me up with one.

I said, "You're kidding, you're wearing a hairpiece?"

He said, "Yeah, man, and I'm gonna fix you up. It won't cost you anything either."

I said, "Great, thanks a lot."

When I was about 19 or 20, my hair began to recede on the top left and right side of my head. For a young man, this is like the kiss of death. While everyone was wearing Afros, I was wearing a hat. In the ninth grade I remember my white teammates spraying something in their hair. I once asked what it was and they said, "It's called Concort. It keeps our hair in place."

I had an idea. *I'll cut some hair from the back of my head and place it on the front, then spray some of that Concort onto the new hair, and no one will know the difference.* Brilliant! Not exactly. If you ever did find time for a little romance in your life, you'd have to be careful that your date's roaming hands didn't go past your neck. A light flip of her fingers and that fake hair would be gone.

Maybe a hair unit was the answer. I contacted Celebrity Hair Stylist and made an appointment. Two weeks later, I had some hair. I will never forget walking into the Vikings' locker room, and Coach Bud Grants spotted me and said, "You're starting!" In two years, that's the only time he ever spoke to me except when he cut me. And it was only a joke when he said, "You're starting this week."

I wore that hair unit (toupee, piece, rug, wig) for 26 years. I thought that maybe I would feel better about myself and then other people would too, that I'd feel more confident around the ladies and eventually find a wife. That worked to a certain degree. But it seemed like some of the women I met were a bunch of odd ducks.

The hair unit wasn't always secure. Whenever I played in a game, it would get loose in my helmet. Basically, it was glued to the hair you have and taped to the bald spot in front. I was never comfortable diving in a pool, riding on a roller coaster, or going outside on a windy day. You always felt the stare of someone looking, trying to figure out if you were wearing a toupee. What I thought would free me up, bound me up.

When I moved to Phoenix I had to find a new stylist. I found a few but was never comfortable with them. I remember once hanging out with dear friend Craig Lauterbach. We were at a waterpark in Phoenix. He encouraged me to take a ride down a giant water slide. Without thinking about what would happen when I hit the pool going 90 miles an hour, I said, "Sure, let's do this." Bad decision! I hit the water, and my wig popped off as I sank to the bottom. I was so embarrassed that I could have died. I wanted to hide forever. All those people around, including my twin nieces. Worst of all, Pastor Craig said, "Ah, Joe, forget about it; everybody knows you're wearing a piece." Thanks, Craig, you really made my day.

Another time, I tried to curl it myself. I bought the curling strips and rollers. I put it in the oven at a low temperature, just like they told me. I went to the gym to work out and I must've forgotten that the wig was in the oven. When I came back home, I noticed a smell. My wig had almost melted. It had shrunk to about the size of my mustache. That was a sign that it was time to retire that wig. Even though I knew that the wig had worn out its welcome, it was hard to take off the mask.

As bad as that wig looked, I thought the alternative was much worse. After shaving my head, I thought *Lord, this was a mistake. What are people going to think?* I know that Earnie Shavers, Marvin Hagler, Telly Savalas, Michael Jordan, and others shaved their head for years and looked great, but as bad as that wig looked, it was a crutch and mask I hid behind. I knew in my heart that it had to go. Still, it was one of the toughest decisions I ever made as an adult.

After I removed the mask, some pastor friends said, "Praise God, I'm glad you finally got rid of the nappy-headed thing. We were praying that you'd take that wig off your head." I thought no one knew, but it turned out that the only person I was fooling was me.

When Jesus healed the man who was blind from birth, He spit on the ground, made some mud, then anointed the man's eyes. The man went and washed his eyes out in a pool and came home seeing.

That seems like an unusual method of healing. How bad do you want a breakthrough? How bad do you want your miracle? Maybe you need to take off that wig you're standing behind and allow God to do something His way.

My way wasn't working. I came to the point when I said, *Lord, I don't care what people think or say. I want my miracle. I want the Lord to bring someone special into my life. God, at 51 years old and never married, I want a wife. Lord, let's do this thing Your way.*

Two years later, and as a *bald man*, I met Terill. I took off the mask. It's not easy to take off a mask. We think that maybe people won't like us when they see the real us. Maybe they won't, but so what? You don't need those people in your circle anyway. I learned that lesson in my twenties— how I see myself is more important than how others perceive me. You're destined for God's greatness.

You may have come into this world under the most horrid, heinous, and hideous circumstances known to man. You may be the offspring of gang rape. You may been dropped off at the circus in a basket as a baby. You're destined for greatness.

You are not some wild onion growing on the side of a hill looking for someone to find you. You are not the pollination of two bees buzzing around a flower looking for someone to pick. You are not some accident that happened who spends the rest of your life looking for someone to like you. You are not some lost shoe kicked to the curb that no one wants (Jer. 29:11-13). You are the divine result of a God who knew you before He formed you in the womb (Jer. 1:5).

When I towered over my friends as a sixth-grader, I often wondered why I had to be so big. I was 176 pounds—by the sixth grade. Was I some kind of freak? Why couldn't I be like everyone else? I didn't like being labeled "overgrown."

God gave us each a unique skill set and DNA. He has something very special for you to do like no one else can. In twenty years of football, I scored only one touchdown, the result of falling on a football in the end zone. The only other legitimate touchdown I scored was in high school. We were playing Hughes High School and I out-jumped the defensive back in the end zone and scored. It was called back because Billy Jones was penalized for holding. After all these years, I think I've forgiven him—I think.

Even though only one career touchdown will show on my resume, I was still vital to the success of the team. Without my position, there would not have been many victories. You have value, and you make a difference. Along the path to the quarterback, I learned many life lessons. My value is not determined by someone's opinion, good or bad—that's called subjective value. My value is intrinsic, meaning that my qualities are uniquely designed for my success and incredible destiny. The same is true for you!

# Chapter 47: The Ram in the Thicket

A t Phoenix '89, Coach Tom Landry spoke during Athletes' Sunday at Phoenix First Assembly of God. He flew his private plane to the conference, and after checking into the hotel he handed Larry Kerychuk a check for a thousand dollars. Coach had just been fired by the new owner Jerry Jones. He never contacted Coach Landry until the media broke the story. Not even a fax. Coach Landry heard about his firing just like we all did, watching television.

Coach could have been at any church, political rally, or venue in the country. That Sunday morning he was at Athletes' Sunday at Phoenix First Assembly of God. He spoke to the congregation and simply said, "You may have heard that I was fired by the Dallas Cowboys. After thirty years, I won't be on the sidelines anymore. But please, no pity for me. You see, the bottom has dropped out from my life. The foundation I'm standing on is something that cannot be shaken. My faith is grounded in the unshakable truth that God loves me and has a wonderful plan for our lives."

How about them Cowboys! I've never been a Cowboys fan but I'd play for Coach Landry on any given Sunday. In 1998 the San Antonio Spurs finished with a record of 56-26. They made it to the West semifinals, losing to the Utah Jazz. That year we honored David Robinson as NBA player of the year. He is one of my all-time favorite NBA players. The year before, his teammates David Wood and Avery Johnson attended our athletes' conference.

They told David about the conference and encouraged him to come. After the playoffs David had arthrosporic knee surgery. Because of the recent surgery, the Spurs' medical staff advised David not to attend our conference, but David insisted he was going. I had rented a Lincoln Town Car for him so he could stretch out in the back seat.

Walking with a cane, David Robinson and his family came to our conference. At the awards banquet, he shared a powerful testimony of what the Lord means to him. It was brilliant, classy, and moved everyone in that ballroom. It's such an affirmation to see someone so accomplished yet so humble express their love for God and strong desire to impact their team and community.

The admiral spoke with integrity and genuine love for God. David, A.C. Green, Terry Cummings, Avery Johnson, Paul Westphal, David Wood, Kevin Johnson, Armen Gilliam, the Van Arsdale twins, Connie Hawkins, and other NBA greats had a lasting impact on my life and Athletes International Ministries.

## J.D Hill

J.D. Hill and I are brothers, but it hasn't always been that way. J.D. played wide receiver with the Buffalo Bills. He was a gifted athlete out of Arizona State University. Had the NFL not worked out for J.D., he could have had a career in Major League Baseball. He was selected in the first round by the Bills, the third overall pick. J.D. was not only skilled with hands and lightning speed, but for a wide receiver he was a tremendous blocker.

The Bills had some great players, so it was only a matter of time until they were a playoff contender. J.D. will never admit this, but I can remember playing the Bills at War Memorial Stadium back when the crackback block was *semi*-legal. During that game, the Bills ran 37 sweep right. I had a great pursuit angle on O.J. Simpson; then from out of nowhere, J.D. planted the side of his helmet into the side of my right knee. Juice bolted for 65 yards while I limped off the field with a hyperextended knee. Every time I bring up that play, he claims he doesn't remember.

J.D. Hill has come a long way down redemption's road. His story is well documented. He became a cocaine addict and was homeless, living in crack houses. He knew the Lord had a calling on his life. He tried different treatment centers, Teen Challenge, even religion. Nothing stuck.

Larry Kerychuk arranged for J.D. to live at the Los Angeles Dream Center. J.D. said he would try it for one year. His wife, Carolyn, was praying. She knew J.D. had a strong anointing on his life if he could only stay on God's path! The Lord did a miracle in J.D. Hill's life. Although J.D. is no longer catching passes in the NFL, the Lord gave him the ministry called Catch the Vision. He caught the vision of what God intended for him from the foundation of the world. J.D. has strong communication skills and can relate to any audience. He caught the vision of surrender and accountability.

Today he serves as a teacher, preacher, and counselor at the Phoenix Dream Center. He also works very closely with Athletes International Ministries and is one of the hosts at the AIM banquet. He's on a new path. He also was one of my groomsmen.

## The NFL Super Bowl Gospel Choir

J.D. is also a board member of the NFL Super Bowl Gospel Choir, which is comprised of current and former NFL players and performs in concert at a venue on Friday before the Super Bowl and is televised on BET.

Our first concert was Super Bowl XLII in 2008. You may remember this was when the New England Patriots were pitted against the New York Giants. With a record of 18-0, the Patriots were heavy favorites over the Giants, who finished the regular season at 12-7.

That Friday, the choir backed up Donny McClurkin. The concert also featured Patti LaBelle, Marvin Winans, and Ce Ce Winans. We had about thirty players from nearly every NFL team.

Some of our choir members were J.D. Hill, Ray Lewis, Sydney Justin, and David Tyree. Former Los Angeles Ram Sydney Justin is also the lead singer of Motown legends, The Miracles. David Tyree was the only player from the Giants or Patriots to participate in the concert—and we know the contribution that he made in that game. It was an exciting weekend!

Several members of the Super Bowl choir were asked to sing the National Anthem prior to the Tampa Bay vs. Washington Redskins game in 2015. There were three leads parts, and I was given a solo. Every time I was asked to sing the National Anthem, I said no. However, singing with the choir would be something I could do. We were given different parts so I'd have to sing harmony as well.

Singing harmony is a weakness for me. It's much easier for me to sing the melody than to find my harmony part. I practiced my harmony part and stayed on key. We rehearsed at Church Without Walls for two days. This would be a great opportunity for the choir and me.

Leslie Frazier was the new head coach of the Tampa Bay Bucs. I made sure he knew I'd be singing. I called friends to let them know I'd be doing the National Anthem. Of course, I didn't tell them it would be with the choir. Heck, let them figure it out.

When I arrived at the stadium I headed for the green room. Just before the door opened, one of the organizers said, "Joe, I hope you won't be mad at me."

I said, "What's up?"

She said, "The pastor of the church wants to make a change. He's one of the sponsors of this weekend's event, and he wants one of his choir members to sing your lead part."

I said, "No way."

She said, "Yes way, he's going to sing your part."

I asked, "Why? I've worked on this part for two solid days."

She said, "That's the way it is."

I said, "You can tell that preacher that I don't care what he said."

I walked out of the Buccaneers' stadium mad as a nest of hornets. I had no idea where I was going. The temperature was around 95 degrees and humid. I was sweating bullets. My cell was ringing, but I wasn't answering. I just walked around Tampa, as lost as a ball in high weeds. It was super hot, plus I was dressed in all black. Finally, I went to a restaurant to cool off and recharge my phone.

The hostess said there was about a 15-minute wait. No problem, I'll wait. People were texting me, but I was determined not to go back. *The nerve of those people. It would be one thing if I were replaced by another NFL player, but this person was a member of the church choir. I thought this was the NFL Super Bowl Gospel Choir.*

My fifteen-minute wait turned into thirty. I thought, *Forget it; I'll find another restaurant or take a cab back to the hotel.* On the corner was one of my all-time favorites, Burger King. Once inside, the only seat left was at a high-top table. Not my favorite, but at least I was out of the heat. *Maybe I'll get a couple of double-meat-and-cheese whoppers, large fries, and diet coke.*

Just before I placed my order, I heard a voice call, "Hey, Joe."

I thought, *Gosh, they sent someone after me to entice me to come back. I'll tell them exactly what I told them before. I'm not coming back.* I turned to the voice and didn't recognize the face.

He said, "Joe, what are you doing in Tampa? Are you going to the game?"

I mumbled something like, "Uh, ah, ah yeah, yeah, I'm going." I wasn't prepared for what he told me next.

He said, "It's me, John. Several years ago you preached and sang at the Lakewood Church of God. You sang a song called 'Your Grace and Mercy.' You were really a blessing to me."

I said, "I was?"

He said, "I hope you'll come back."

I said, "Thanks, John. Good to see you again." He thanked me again before we parted ways.

John didn't need me, but I needed John. John was the ram in the thicket that I needed. Had I stayed at the other restaurant, I would have missed the encouragement I needed. I lowered my head and began to weep. The Lord's timing is always perfect. It's amazing how much He loves us. No, I still didn't go back to the stadium. My self and self-pity took a cab to the hotel. We hung out and watched the game. Should I have gone back to the stadium and sung? Yes, I should have.

Coach Leslie Frazier asked, "What happened to you? I didn't see you on the field."

I explained there was some type of mix up then quickly changed the subject. Hopefully, I can learn from this and remember that it's not about me.

Larry and Wendy Kerychuk were battling serious health issues and decided it would be better to cancel the conference until they regained their health. Wendy is a tireless servant who is important to the success of AIM. She'll work twenty straight hours for the success of the conference. Wendy and Larry are two of my dearest friends. We decided that the AIM banquet and golf tournament would be our focus.

Although the banquets were very successful, it wasn't the same without the athletes' conference. I told Larry that we needed to start having the conference again. Larry was fighting pneumonia and lacked the energy needed to produce a major conference, and I had some health concerns as well, yet we each knew that God birthed this ministry and there was more to do.

Although it seemed that we were on the Jericho Road, beaten, robbed, and left for dead, we were still alive. So we started talking about what it would take to have our 30th annual athletes' conference. We had lunch at Oregano's and wrote on a napkin which athletes we wanted to invite.

We set the bar pretty high with names like Joe Willy Namath and big George Foreman. I've worked with George before in the past and Joe's my old quarterback. Why not give it a shot?

Starting in May, George was shooting a new television show called *Better Late Than Never*, so he regretfully declined. How about Joe Namath? We're friends, so I reached out with a text.

Joe usually gets back without delay. A week went by with no response. I sent another text and still nothing. Finally, I called him. He answered and says, "Joe, I guess you're wondering why I haven't answered your text or called you. I am really thinking about coming to the conference, and you're on my list to call. My family says I should go. Tell me more about it."

I told Joe that since 1985 AIM has honored some of the greatest athletes and coaches in America. I said, "You've been selected for a lifetime achievement award for having the Joe Namath football camp for forty-six years."

Later that week, he said, "I've prayed about it and I'll be there."

We have had many superstar athletes, coaches, and entertainers attend the AIM conferences, but this would be the most anticipated conference yet. Everyone was excited about Joe Namath coming to our conference. Even though Joe hadn't played football in almost forty years, what he accomplished in Super Bowl III combined with the endorsements, movies, playboy image, and late-night talk show appearances gave him a celebrity status that is still relevant today.

On Friday, June 30, Joe Namath woke up at 2:00 a.m. and drove two hours to the Miami airport for a 7 a.m. flight. He arrived in Phoenix at 9:00 a.m. to be available for pictures, autographs, and conversation. Then he attended the banquet, pretending to enjoy a cold piece of steak, received the Hall of Faith Award, smiled for more pictures, autographs, and hugs before heading back to Sky Harbor Airport for a 12:20 a.m. flight Saturday morning. All that and he said he would come back the next year!

Other award recipients were New York Jet Eddie Bell and New Orleans Saints defensive end Cameron Jordan. Cam couldn't make it because of a prior commitment as best man at a teammate's wedding. His father, Minnesota Vikings great Steve Jordan, accepted his award as NFL player of the year. Also on hand was Joe Namath's Super Bowl teammate Bishop Earl Christy. There's no one like Earl Christy.

After a five-year hiatus, it was one of the best conferences ever. God really showed up. John and Sharon Williamson led morning prayer, and Denny Duron and Pastor Tommy Barnett were our conference speakers. Need I say more? That conference rekindled the fire in Larry, Wendy, and myself, and we started planning for the next year's conference and beyond.

# Chapter 48: I Don't Believe It

I n 1974, the New York Jets started out 1-7, then won six straight games to finish 7-7. This would be the new head coach, Charley Winner's, first year. During the streak, we beat playoff-bound Miami Dolphins and the Buffalo Bills.

I was ready for the off-season and my trip to NMSU. On my way back to Las Cruces, I stopped in Camden, New Jersey to visit my college roommate Jeff Smith. A leg injury ended his NBA career with the Seattle Super Sonics. He had several offers to play in Europe, but the money wasn't right, so he turned in his Converse All Stars for a badge and a gun. This began a long career as a man in blue.

Unfortunately, Jeff and I lost touch. Our path had not crossed in 44 years. I had no idea where he lived or if he was married. We dated sisters in college, and I was the best man at his wedding in 1970.

In March of 2017, I was booked to preach at the Atlanta Dream Center. Pastor Paul and Patty Palmer birthed the Atlanta Dream International Center Church in 2003. The Atlanta Dream Center serves as a bridge for homeless men and women, connecting them with long-term care they need in a Christ-centered environment.

My family also lives in Atlanta, so it's become my second home. This would be Terill's first visit to Atlanta. I told her that the culture would be more racially diverse than Phoenix, and the hospitality and food would be southern. It was a great visit, and she loves Atlanta. On my way to my sister's house in Conyers, Georgia, we looked for a QT convenience store. I saw a sign for a QT at exit 52 on my right, but I was in the middle lane and couldn't get over. Good thing that Atlanta has a QT on practically every corner.

Another sign said that a QT is at exit 54, so I switched over to the right lane to make my exit in time. We exited onto Flat Shoals Road and pulled into the QT. I had my usual 52-ounce diet Pepsi and a bag of flaming hot Fritos.

As I was waiting to check out, I noticed a tall brother standing to my right. He stood around six feet eight inches. Every time I see someone taller or bigger than me, I size them up in my mind. *What move would I use to get to the quarterback? Would I use strength or speed, or both?*

As I walked back to my car, I heard a voice call, "Joey." Normally if anyone calls me Joey, they're either from Cincinnati or Las Cruces. In 1974 NBC sportscaster Charlie Jones asked me, "What do you want to be called, Joey or Joe?" With names like Bubba, the Deacon, Big Cat, Moose, and the Hammer, I thought Joey was too soft for an NFL six foot five inch, 265-pound defensive end. Call me Big Joe.

*Who was calling me Joey? Could it be one of my relatives?* I turned around, and it was my college roommate Jeff Smith, whom I had not seen since our visit in Camden, New Jersey 44 years earlier. One exit earlier, and our paths would not have crossed. He even said that they planned to go to McDonald's. God's perfect timing is always on time. I introduced them to Terill and met his beautiful wife, Shirley.

They came to the Dream Center where I preached Sunday, met the rest of my family, and then came to our athletes' conference in June. It turns out that they attend a great church in Atlanta. What a God-ordained encounter! Another miracle, another champion. It's amazing how these miracles continue to happen in my life!

# Chapter 49: Take This Job and Shove It!

J ohnny Paycheck topped the country music charts in 1977 with the hit "Take This Job and Shove It." About every four or five weeks, I want to quit. I can't believe I've been treated like this. I preached five times, paid $500 for my own airline ticket, rented a car, and got a $400 offering. *This is ridiculous. I'm not doing this for the money, but how am I supposed to live? These guys better be glad I'm a Christian.* A familiar echo!

The call and office of the evangelist is a person with a special gift and calling from the Holy Spirit. Evangelists are God's gift to the church, an office of the church. He or she is a reaper in a harvest field. When someone says, "I think God is leading me into full-time evangelism," I tell them to think again and pray.

They say there are five signs that you are a natural-born evangelist.

- Number one: You value the lost.
- Number two: You love to share your testimony.
- Number three: It's easy for you to connect with new acquaintances.
- Number four: The gospel excites you to the point that you just keep talking about it.
- Number Five: You've led people to the Lord.

There should be a number six: Don't count on churches and pastors to call you back; they won't.

It's amazing that out of the thousands of emails and letters I send to pastors, there are very few who call you back or reply to your email. One pastor told me, "Pastor Jackson, please remove me from your mailing list. We're not interested."

*Wow, I thought we were on the same team.* Sometimes I was treated better when I was selling light bulbs for Jewell Electronics.

No, I've never been a pastor, and I'm sure their plate is full with requests from evangelists, missionaries, and musical groups. Not to mention raising a budget and putting out fires, smoothing out bruised egos, and hurt feelings because the pastor didn't mention them in his message. One pastor told me that his monthly budget is around $900,000—and that's *after* they burned their mortgage deed!

Today's evangelist has a small window of opportunity to minister in a church. Gone are Sunday night services and Wednesday night services. With the pastor only preaching once a week, I can understand why there are limited opportunities. In some churches, Wednesday night is small group or family night. Pastors tell me that their people won't come out on Sunday nights anymore.

## Evangelist: A Hard Calling

Pastor Tommy Barnett tells me there are very few evangelists out there today. It's not easy. The evangelist not only must prepare a message to preach or teach; he must build his ministry as you would build a small business, passing out business cards, building a website, and attending pastors' conferences and conventions to connect with different churches. There are many reasons why a person must be sure that they heard from God when accepting the call. Remember whether the doors are open or closing up, you heed the call of God because that's what it is—God's calling.

I've learned that the Lord will always make a way for your gift. Methods change. What worked well when my grandfather preached may be outdated today. You're not an evangelist because you need to make a house payment, car payment, or keep your house. You're an evangelist because God has called you to serve as you go (Matt. 10:7). You're an evangelist because, from the foundation of the world, God set you apart for this five-fold ministry anointing, regardless if there's only one chance for you to preach. I haven't started talking about love offerings, no offerings, being stranded at airports, sleeping in airports, and negative letters and emails sent to my pastor.

I preached a weekend of ministry in Moab, Utah in 1988. The pastor sent a letter to my pastor stating that I offended his people. How about the time a pastor gave me a church check that bounced and never made it good, or the time a pastor received an offering for me then said to the congregation and myself, "Man, this is a good offering. I don't think brother Joe will mind if I keep this and buy myself a pair of shoes." True story!

Then there are so many other times I can't even mention when the Lord has blessed me over and above, so many great pastors who encouraged me in my darkest moments. In 2016, Pastor David Sanville of Faith Assembly of God in Bethel, Vermont received a Sunday morning offering and wrote me a check for everything that came in. Pastor Wade Mumm of GreeneWay Assembly of God in Orlando, Florida encourages me every month with support. Pastor Gary and Alice Morton at First Assembly of God in Anchorage, Alaska have given me an open door to their pulpit any time. Pastor Ken Lang of Calvary Chapel, Pastor David Hernquist of Van Nest Assembly of God, and Pastor Craig Lauterbach from River of Life Assembly of God continue to support my ministry, even through the pandemic.

Some churches and pastors have come and gone. The relationship was seasonal. They were there when they needed to be. I am grateful for them too. When you come from a megachurch, it's easy to think that no one's doing anything for the Lord but you and the people you know. The traveling evangelist has a window into a larger picture of what God is doing in different parts of the kingdom. Every challenge, cancellation, and method change has shaped and molded me to remember why I do this and for whom. Sometimes this is very hard to remember.

## Chris Won't Quit; You Shouldn't Either

Have you ever felt like quitting? Let me introduce you to Chris Hogan. I met Chris at the Joe Namath football camp in 2014. Chris attended Big

Ten powerhouse Penn State where he played varsity *lacrosse*. Then he transferred to tiny Monmouth College in West Long Branch, New Jersey where he played one year of football. Monmouth has an enrollment of 6,700. In 2011, Chris Hogan was an undrafted free agent wide receiver. He ran a modest 4.5-6 second 40-yard dash.

Chris signed a contract with the San Francisco 49ers and received a $17,000 signing bonus. He lasted for three weeks. They cut him. The New York Giants picked him up, and he lasted another three weeks before they cut him. The Miami Dolphins picked him up and the same thing.

At this point, Chris had never played in a regular-season NFL game.

In 2012, Chris signed with the Buffalo Bills, where he was on the practice squad for the entire season.

After three years with the Bills, he caught the eye of New England Patriots coach Bill Belichick, who signed Chris to a multi-million dollar contract. Chris was a prisoner of a dream. He wouldn't allow failure to discourage him. His persistency and faith paid off. Chris knew he could play in the NFL; all he needed was an opportunity.

When I met Chris in 2014, I encouraged him to keep working hard and keep a good attitude. His hard work and perseverance eventually earned him a starting job on the New England Patriots. In the 2016 AFC Championship win over the Steelers, Chris caught 9 passes, ran 180 receiving yards, and scored 2 touchdowns, which set a team record.

Overcoming the odds is not always measured by talent, gifts, and skill set. If you don't have heart, a good attitude, and a strong "want to," talent, gifts, and skill are merely potential. They won't carry you very far in the NFL. The NFL is not the next level after college football; it's another dimension. There are many athletes who succeed on every level yet can't make a 53-man NFL roster. With 4:5.6 speed, Chris Hogan won't take the top off of a defensive secondary, but he can find a hole in a zone. His tenacity earned him a world championship Super Bowl ring. Congratulations Chris!

For 11 years and 22 seasons, my brother-in-law Troy auditioned for a chance to be a cast member on the CBS television hit show *Survivor*.

He failed to make the cut every year but never gave up. In 2013 he finally got his big chance. He was picked and flown to some remote island to compete for the one million dollar prize. Although he didn't win the big check, he did win the hearts of many who are holding on to a dream. In 2016-2017 he was invited back again. This time he finished in third place. A champion is not someone who never fails—a champion is someone who knows that failure is not failure, nor is it final unless you don't learn from it.

# Chapter 50: Roommates, the Mover, and the Mack

My roommate in my junior year was from Baden, Pennsylvania. He was a hard-nosed, no-nonsense offense guard named John Edmondson. Standing six feet two inches and weighing 260 pounds, John had the perfect credentials for being named to a national magazine's super freshman team. Had John stood an inch or two taller, he possibly could have had a long career in the NFL.

Baden, Pennsylvania is a borough in Beaver County along the Ohio River. The area's early economy was driven by boat building and steel mills. John came from a strong Italian Catholic family. He boasted that his grandfather's spaghetti and meatballs were the best in the county. I don't know if it was the best in the county, but it was the best I ever had.

Beaver County is also the birthplace of NFL stars like Joe Namath, Mike Ditka, Tony Dorsett, and Darelle Revis. Sports information director Sonny Yates nicknamed John "the Mower" for his power and me "the Mover" for my speed and quickness. The last time I remember seeing John was in the spring of 1973. We united again for the NMSU alumni spring football game. Since the alumni spring game, we saw each other several times and tried to keep in touch through Christmas cards.

## Saving My Life

In 1990, I traveled for ministry in Saver, Pennsylvania and contacted my old roommate John. We met for lunch at a Mexican restaurant. I ordered my usual nachos supreme. We enjoyed catching up and talking

Aggie football. I invited him and his wife, Nancy, to the church service where I would be preaching.

As I was stuffing chips and dip in my mouth, something caught in my throat that I tried clear. It was a small piece of a chip lodged in my throat. I couldn't breathe. I started to panic and instinctively stood up and raised my arms. John immediately got behind me and performed the Heimlich. After three abdominal thrusts, it popped out. John saved my life, and I am eternally grateful. I probably wouldn't be writing this book were it not for my former roommate, the Mower.

When I flew over the Bermuda Triangle, we hit turbulence, and I thought we were goners. It was twenty minutes of sheer terror. I didn't think the pilot could recover, but we did and landed safely. However, there's nothing scarier than the feeling of choking to death. They say that's a one-time experience. I know I didn't eat for three days because I couldn't swallow.

## The Mack

Big Ray Mack and I roomed together my senior year. Mack was a big defensive tackle from Hearn, Texas. He was also a junior college all-American at Blinn Junior College, the same college as Cam Newton. Big Mack was an intimidating force who knew one speed, and that's full speed. His front four teeth were missing. Mack had the loudest growl. You could hear him for days.

Mack would always talk about Blue Bell Ice Cream, claiming it was the best ever. Outside of UDF, he got no argument from me. Before we could buy it in Phoenix, I would have the factory ship me a gallon of burgundy cherry and butter pecan on dry ice. Big Mack loved the Lord. His faith and heart were as big as his home state.

# Chapter 51: From Boys to Men

O ver the last twenty years I've gradually transitioned from speaking in high schools to men's ministry. It happened when I turned fifty. Instead of pastors booking me into the local middle and high schools, I'm now asked to speak at a Saturday men's breakfast. This was nothing that I initiated.

It seemed like a natural, supernatural progression. The Lord was leading me along a different path. One of the keys to keeping in step with the Spirit is knowing when to switch (Gal. 5:16). A two-year-old memo or a ten-year-old newspaper was relative then. Companies closed their doors because they couldn't adapt to the new software, and marriages end in divorce because no one's willing to take the first step of submission.

NFL powerhouses are now cellar dwellers because their coaching schemes are outdated. The switch is the ability to transition. When the quarterback hands the ball off to his tailback, it's the tailback's responsibility to gain yardage—to fight for every yard and continue the drive toward the goal line.

When Pastor Tommy Barnett handed the ball to his son Luke Barnett, the vision never changed, but some of the methods did.

Replacing Pastor Tommy Barnett is impossible. But God's vision and purposes are larger than one man. When Pastor Barnett had surgery to repair a valve in his heart, Luke was already in place. We knew Pastor Tommy would come back; in the meantime, Luke took over the duties of preaching and the responsibilities of lead pastor. As Pastor Tommy Barnett recovered, he felt there needed to be a switch in the direction for Phoenix First Assembly.

It seems that the natural path of a church is birth, growth, and then a slow death. Pastor Tommy once looked at the choir and asked Pastor Dale Lane, "What do you see up there?"

Dale said, "I see a choir in robes."

Pastor responded, "I see a choir with old white people singing old songs."

A switch was made. Pastor Tommy is still the senior pastor, but Pastor Luke is the lead pastor. The church continues to grow and two more campuses have been added. God also blessed Dream City Church (formerly Phoenix First Assembly of God) with a property in Colorado City that was once used for sex trafficking.

The switch is not always seamless. Some don't make the transition. When Coach Bud Grant retired as head coach of the Minnesota Vikings in 1985, some might argue that the Vikings have never been the same.

What's wrong with the Old Met Stadium? After all, we went to four Super Bowls in the '70s, and not once since. Good point! If it weren't for the Green Bay Packers and the Chicago Bears, the NFC would have no remnants of the once-storied Black and Blue division (the NFC North). Everybody wants a billion-dollar dome.

It's seems like one of the reasons you build a billion-dollar stadium is to attract final fours, political conventions, or to host a Super Bowl. I thought the main goal was to win a Super Bowl. The owners will tell you that the main goal is to win championships, but if they're honest they will also tell you they want to make money. That's their acumen.

The owners are billionaires, not necessarily ex-coaches or jocks. They are Harvard educated and graduated from some of the top business schools in America. They know how to run a multi-million or billion-dollar company and show a profit. They have a keen sense of building a business and are very competitive.

The NFL has a combined value of over 40 billion dollars. That's more value than the national GDPs of Afghanistan, Cambodia, Nicaragua, Jamaica, and more than 115 other countries. The NFL owners recognize the value of having a stadium that is a multi-purpose facility. What NFL owner would build a 1.1 billion dollar stadium that's only open for business ten to twelve days a year? That's not a smart business model. So bring on the Barnum and Bailey Circus, final four, political conventions, Super Bowl, and a tractor pull.

I still prefer outdoor stadiums with natural grass and the marching band for halftime entertainment. You guessed it; I'm old school. Back in the day, only the superstar player was given endorsements to earn a six-figure income. Today, almost every NFL player has a sportswear or shoe deal. The era when I played required that you find an off-season job. In my entire eight-year career, I never made more than $400,000 total.

There weren't too many million-dollar contracts in the '70s and '80s. In 1978, Coach Bud Grant told us that we are in the entertainment business. To me, that sounded weird. Gone is the time when football was only a game. Coach Grant was right. It's entertainment.

Today a good Super Bowl is measured by the commercials and who's performing at halftime. It seems like more people remember Prince performing Purple Rain in the rain than the historical significance of two Black American head coaches in Super Bowl XLI. There also weren't as many football players in the headlines for rape, murder, abuse, and suspensions for performance-enhancing drugs.

Don't get me wrong; I'm glad the Vikings are not playing in the Old Met. That stadium is an antique. I can remember playing the Rams at the Old Met in January. During halftime, Wally Hilgenberg said, "Hey, Joe, stuff this hot rock from the sauna in your pants. You probably won't get in the game, but you can make a contribution to the team effort." I hope I made a difference.

Remember the question that the Lord will ask. Are you transitional or traditional? A transition takes us out of our comfort zone. Do you have the radical faith to find a new way to the end zone? He'll lead you; come follow.

# Chapter 52: You're Dreaming

P art of the attraction in the free-agent market is the organization. When a sought-after free agent or young recruit considers his options, the stadium could be a deciding factor between the storied Lambeau Field or billion-dollar US Bank Stadium. I'll never stand in the way of progress. I just remember that visiting teams would shudder at the thought of a January playoff game in Minnesota. The name *Minnesota* sounds cold—it creates a reaction. It gives a player one more thing to think about, which could make all the difference between just finishing and finishing strong.

I spend a lot of time looking backward, and I still dream that I'm playing in the NFL. It's the same dream—I come out of retirement and sign with the Minnesota Vikings. We're in training camp, and the other players think I'm in my early thirties. Bud Grant, our coach, knows I'm in my fifties but never brings up my age. Then I wake up.

Another dream is that I'm in college at New Mexico State, yet Buddy Ryan is my defensive line coach. Coach Ryan has demoted me to second string. I'm so discouraged because this is my senior year. I feel like quitting, but I'm waiting for my chance to get in the game. Then I wake up.

When I see my teammates enshrined into the Hall of Fame or the Ring of Honor, I wonder what I could have done differently. Did I make the best of the opportunity that God gave me? Speculation about the past won't change one thing. As much as I would want a do-over, it's not going to happen. That's why I tell young people that you get one chance to live a life. Take advantage of the opportunities that come to you.

I thank the Lord for the open doors, passion, and talent that He gave me, but I know I could've accomplished more. When Buddy Ryan became our defensive coordinator, the new defensive line coach was Dick Voris. He was an old-school coach. We never bonded, and I didn't have much success under him. Yet when the Eskimos waived me, Voris called me and offered me a contract with the Tampa Bay Buccaneers. I arrived at the start of their training camp ready to sign a contract but didn't.

This all stems back to that wrong decision I made in 1979 that I mentioned earlier. Had I not signed with the Eskimos and just waited two weeks longer, just maybe things would have turned out differently. You can second guess yourself until Cleveland wins a Super Bowl, but that won't change anything. Yet I know in my heart of hearts that the steps of a righteous man are ordered of God (Ps. 37:23). I would have missed the people and opportunities had I gone another direction. All things work together for good.

Walking by faith is not the easiest mode of transportation. It's also not sitting on your hindquarters waiting for a blessing to slap you in the face. We know that faith without works is dead. Faith is sort of like repetition in practice. How many times have I heard this from a coach? Run it again, run it again. Faith is trusting, and faith is doing. Faith is planting seeds hoping that a harvest will yield, believing that God will make a way where there is no way.

When I played, they could cut you anytime. In some ways it's the same in the ministry. Although I don't sign a contract with a church that invites us to minister the Word, there is a commitment that we make. Arrangements are made, airline tickets purchased, it's on the calendar; then you receive a call telling you that you're canceled.

I guess they think that the Lord will open another door, even though churches plan their schedules months and sometimes years in advance. You're right, I've never pastored, and I don't know what's on their plate. I just know there's not going to be much on my plate with getting canceled. Yet I know the Lord meets every need in our lives, and He always makes a way. David said he had never seen the righteous forsaken or his seed begging for bread (Ps. 37:25).

## Van Nest Assembly of God

In 2008 I spoke at the New York Honor Bound men's conference in Binghamton, New York. One of the other speakers scheduled was New York Giants running back Lee Rouson.

It's an awesome experience to see hundreds of men praising and worshiping God in freedom, spirit, and truth. The Lord broke down walls and barriers as men humbled themselves and repented of sin. They made commitments to walk as godly fathers, husbands, men, and servants of Christ. It was a powerful manifestation of the Holy Spirit.

Men's director Will Fox arranged for me to preach at a church in the Bronx named Van Nest Assembly of God. The pastor, David Hernquist of Van Nest, attended the conference and drove me to my hotel in Queens. Pastor Hernquist always wears a suit.

He's white and stands about five feet eight inches and probably weighs around 138 pounds; not my impression of the inner-city pastor. The church is multi-ethnic—Black, white, brown, red, and African. He loves his congregation, and they love him. Van Nest is packed for all five Sunday services. If you give the people heart and the love of Jesus, it doesn't matter how tall you are, what color you are, or your last name. The love of Jesus draws them. It is one of my favorite churches in which to minister.

It's always an adventure when I come to the Bronx. My wife works full time so she doesn't have the flexibility to travel with me as much as I would like. However, when I mention that I'm going to New York or Alaska, her schedule finds a way to open like the parting of the Red Sea. Sometimes we'll stay with Mike and Yvette Corbin. Mike is music director at Van Nest Assembly of God, and Yvette is the director of women's ministry.

They have a brownstone with an apartment in the basement. The apartment is rented out or used as an evangelist's quarters. When you're a guest speaker at Van Nest Assembly, expect to work. On a typical weekend, I'll preach seven times.

The houses are tightly built in a row, and the neighborhood is generally safe. Terill and I once walked back to the apartment from the Botanical Gardens. I didn't think I'd enjoy looking at flowers, but it was something different, and it gave me a great idea for a sermon. Other times we've walked to the apartment from the grocery store and even at night from the subway station.

On Sunday morning. I'm usually picked up at 7:30 a.m. for the first of five services. Terill will join me for the eleven o'clock service and our friends Jules and Mark from Van Nest will pick her up.

One Sunday, it was a warm summer morning so Terill went for a walk in search of a coffee shop. She was walking straight, then took a right, a left, then another left, and continued to walk. Soon she realized that she made the wrong turn and she was lost. I was in the pulpit preaching when she called me. The call went to my voicemail.

She called the church and reached Pastor Hernquist. Pastor asked his wife Mary to help Terill find where she was located and to get her back to the apartment. Mary soon realized that Terrill wasn't in a very safe area and told her to find a grocery store or someplace to wait inside while they sent someone to pick her up.

After the morning services, we went to lunch with Pastor Hernquist and Mary. I questioned him about the area where Terill had made the wrong turn. I thought that he told me that it was a safe neighborhood. He said, "No, I said semi-safe." I guess there's a marked difference between safe and semi-safe.

Two years ago, Pastor David and his wife Mary were honored for 25 years of ministry at Van Nest Assembly of God. It was a wonderful and long evening. Everyone wanted to thank the pastor and Mary for their service. I was supposed to speak around 2:00 p.m., but I didn't get the mic until around 6 p.m. The Hernquists were showered with love, appreciation, and gifts. One of the gifts was a week on a sandy beach in Hawaii. They politely declined and said, "We're not beach people; we'd rather go to see some of the historic national monuments." It was a great evening.

Two weeks later, I was in Alaska at another church for a similar function. This pastor and his wife also celebrated 25 years of ministry. However, the celebration was much different. The church gave him a $50 gift certificate at a restaurant. This couple had worked just as hard as Pastor David and Sister Mary. I was disappointed and voiced my opinion. They told me it's no big deal, that they were there to serve, grateful to be the Lord's servants. They reminded me of what Jesus said: "I come not to be served but to serve and to give my life as a ransom for many" (Matt. 20:28). I still think the church should have done more. Both servant leaders love the Lord and their church. One showered with testimonials of gratitude and gifts. The other not so much. Both are not reward-driven. They're kingdom builders, never losing focus on priorities.

# Chapter 53: I'm a Sheepherder

I've never seriously thought of ever pastoring a church, although I'm often asked. At Phoenix First Assembly of God (Dream City Church), I was recognized as the church evangelist by Pastor Tommy Barnett for 27 years. The evangelist travels from town to town and from church to church, spreading the gospel of Jesus Christ. Pastor Barnett has the heart of an evangelist as well as a shepherd. The Good Shepherd is the image used in the periscope of John 10:12, in which Jesus Christ is depicted as the Good Shepherd who lays down His life for the sheep.

In the late '80s, I attended a men's breakfast. Each man was asked to introduce himself and tell what he did for a living. There were professionals, educators, blue-collar workers, farmers, and even the homeless.

When it was my turn, I proudly stood up and announced that "I'm a gospel singer." Pastor Tommy Barnett followed me and humbly declared himself as a sheepherder, someone who looks after the flock.

Why am I an evangelist? Is it because I have communication skills and a story some can relate to? Is it because I can motivate and create a stirring within? Or is it because I'm a sheepherder who loves God and loves people?

No matter the response I receive after a high school assembly or how packed the altars are, I've never forgotten Pastor Tommy Barnett's humble response. Yes, it is a tremendous feeling of personal satisfaction when you're appreciated by others. How many times have I heard and laughed at the statement when someone says, "Joe, we don't get that kind of good preaching here." I guarantee you that what I've preached is no different than what their pastor preached two Sundays ago, the only difference is the deliverer and maybe the delivery.

When an evangelist comes in, they may have the gift of music, preaching, humor, great personality, and discernment. They will either do a great job or wreck the church by some whacked-out theology. They might take up an unauthorized offering before heading out of there.

On Monday morning, the shepherd comes and has to clean up the mess left by the evangelist and love on their sheep. The evangelist loves people, but he doesn't shepherd them. He can't because he's on his way to the next church. That's the difference between an evangelist and a sheepherder.

There are many evangelists who transition into the pulpit as a lead pastor. There are also pastors who've transitioned from the pulpit to the field. At nearly 84 years old, Pastor Tommy Barnett is evangelizing all over the world. I just try to remember that it's not what I do, it's who I am—nothing more or less than a sheepherder.

## Airport, Hotel, Church

I had just landed in JFK at 5:30 a.m. on the red-eye flight from Phoenix. I wasn't upgraded to first class for the five-hour flight, but at least I had an aisle seat in coach. As we deplaned, I was welcomed by a text message from the pastor. "Brother Joe, welcome to New York City. No one can pick you up until noon. Could you rent a car? Also, you can't check in to the Hampton Inn until 3:00 p.m."

So it looks like it's breakfast and lunch in the Admiral's Club for the next six hours. Welcome to the world of the traveling evangelist. I love it.

One of the smartest purchases I've ever made was in 1989. America West Airlines was born in Phoenix, Arizona in the mid-'80s. I had never heard of America West. In Minneapolis, I mainly flew Northwest Airlines. As America West Airlines grew, they offered amenities to keep pace with the highly competitive airline industry giants. America West Airlines opened its first lounge in 1989, the America West Club.

Deanne Druse, an agent in the club, asked if I wanted to buy a lifetime membership for $500. The annual membership cost was $275. At first, I thought it was too much money, but later I bought the membership. Today you can't buy a lifetime membership. If you were able to, it would cost around $3,500. This lifetime membership has transferred from America West to US Air to American Airlines. It was the best investment I ever made!

I love to travel—meeting new people and discovering new places. It's still exciting to arrive at the airport in anticipation of my next trip. Will my flight be on time? Who will I sit next to? Will I be upgraded to first class? Since I've been cleared for pre-check, I can usually avoid the long security lines. My elite status allows me to check up to three bags at no charge. When I arrive at my destination, I'm greeted with, "Joe, how was your flight?" The answer I love to give is "Routine." When you fly on a commercial airliner, all you want is routine.

To my knowledge, I don't remember too many close calls. Once I was flying from Phoenix to Tampa on Continental Airlines. As we prepared to land, I fastened my seat belt and raised my seat back to the upright position. We were almost on the ground when the pilot gunned the engines, and we began to climb. For what seemed like an eternity, we heard nothing from the flight attendants or cockpit.

Finally, the captain announced that there was something called a vortex that caused the landing to be aborted. He said we probably could have safely landed, but he played it safe. We made a second attempt, and everything was routine. This also happened in 2003 when flying over the Bermuda Triangle. That was scary.

In the NFL, it's all about routine—practice, practice, practice. When we travel for an away game, it's a sequence of the airport, hotel, and stadium. As an evangelist, it's the airport, hotel, and church. Strangely enough, the NFL helped to prepare me for the work and call of the evangelist.

The players receive the scouting report on Tuesday or Wednesday, and you get ready for your opponent. For a traveling evangelist, it's always an away game. You go to the airport, fly to another city, check into a hotel or motel, then go to the church. Your game plan is the Word of God. You listen to the Holy Spirit. He'll speak to your heart and confirm the message you need to preach. Even though the evangelist's message may be the same from week to week, you always seek the Lord for a fresh anointing. You're never comfortable with last week's victory. You're always hungry for a fresh move of God. It might be the same message or the same song, but it's always different.

In some churches, the pastor will tell you that suits and ties are not required. You'll find many of today's pastors in casual apparel—jeans, polo shirt, and maybe a jacket. I don't own one pair of jeans. Several years ago, you wouldn't be allowed to preach on Sunday morning without a suit. Gradually, the norms have changed. I think churches are more seeker-friendly today. I visited a church recently, and to my great surprise, the person I thought was preaching was only a hologram. I couldn't believe it.

For this baby boomer, that was spooky! They're trying to attract potential members through the less traditional door so that the church doesn't seem to be so "churchy." Announcements are a production; offerings are received when the plate is passed, or via text, or by online giving. The church has stepped up to the twenty-first century with a savvy technological transition. Same as the NFL. However, for me, Sunday is game day, practice is over. You've prepared for the big game. In college or the NFL, you don't put on your practice uniform to play on Saturday or Sunday. Only your Sunday best will do. It's special; it's game day, baby! That's part of the reason why I wear a suit and tie in the pulpit.

I'm not legalistic about it. I've preached in casual clothes before, it's just not my preference. Being on the cutting edge as far as methodology is concerned gets no red flag from me. But when churches feel like they need to adapt not because of technology but only to keep pace with First Baptist, then it's not a matter of methods; it's a matter of motive. I notice a lot of churches and pastors today are afraid of tradition. That is a very dangerous place to be, especially when you walk by faith and not by sight. When you enter some of the less traditional sanctuaries today, one of the first things that I notice is how dark the room is. It's almost like you're going into a movie theater or a bar. As if they're trying to create a certain effect.

How do you separate faith from tradition? Faith is the substance of things hoped for, the evidence of things not yet seen. Somehow the word *tradition* has been waived from the Christian experience like a twelve veteran right tackle who lost a step. I know that church doesn't have to look like a traditional church with a steeple, pews, choir loft, and baptistery to *have church*. I've preached in many barns, bars, warehouses, converted movie theaters, office complexes, and arenas and felt the power of God stirring hearts. Maybe what I'm suggesting is a little balance.

Several weeks ago, I was visiting family in Atlanta, Georgia. My college roommate Jeff Smith invited me to visit his church, the House of Hope Baptist Church. It could have easily been named House of Style Baptist Church. The folks were dressed to the nines. It looked like the BET fashion show. Even the young people weren't wearing jeans. Gone were baggy pants with rips and tears; there was an attitude of reverence, respect, and honor.

A week before that, I preached in a church where the communion was served by ushers wearing shorts and sandals. So what's the difference? In the Black church, I think the style of dress has something to do with pride; that we can look as nice as anyone else. How people dress does make a statement and maybe places you on equal footing, at least when it comes to Sunday. During the time of slavery, the Black church gave the slaves a perspective that one day there will be a brighter day.

Perhaps one of the reasons why the services are longer in some Black churches is because, historically, who would want to go back to an old shanty slave quarter full of injustice and false reminders? The slaves were told that they didn't even have a soul, they were lower than a donkey, and if they were "lucky" enough to go to heaven, it would be for the sole purpose to serve the white man.

In Bob Dylan's anthem "You Gotta Serve Somebody," he wasn't talking about man. He said that it might be the Lord or the devil. Spending eternity with the Lord has nothing to do with being lucky enough. Dylan's right— either you're living in this world's system or you're tracking a faith journey with Jesus.

# Chapter 54: God's Grace and Mercy

My ticket to JFK was purchased, and promotional materials were sent in advance. In less than two weeks, I was scheduled to speak and preach at a Saturday men's breakfast and preach Sunday morning. Pastor John and I spoke several times since we confirmed the date six months earlier. We were both excited about this outreach. I'm still amazed, humbled, and grateful when a pastor invites me to speak at their church.

While waiting to connect for my flight home to Phoenix, my cell phone rang. It was the pastor from the church in New York State. I could immediately tell from his voice something was wrong. It was a familiar, unwanted tone that you never welcome. He said, "Joe, we have to cancel."

I said, "You're kidding! We have less than a two-week window; besides, I've already purchased my airline ticket."

He apologized and said, "There's only ten men signed up for the breakfast. I'm so sorry. I'll reimburse you for your travel and send an offering."

Sometimes cancellations invariably happen, and you have to start believing what you preach.

This happens about once a year, but never with this short of a notice. What am I going to do? I began to pray. I immediately reached out to friends in the New York area for any church I could contact to schedule me on such short notice. Sometimes the Lord moves this way. One of the pastors I contacted was Pastor Dave Hernquist of Van Nest Assembly of God. Dave gave me the name of Pastor Ed Jones in Poughkeepsie, New York.

I emailed Pastor Jones and waited for his response. One day before my scheduled departure to JFK, Pastor Ed Jones called me and extended an invitation to preach at Faith Assembly of God in Poughkeepsie. He said he spoke to the church that canceled me and to Pastor Dave Hernquist. He said that he rarely brings someone he's never had before on such short notice; this was a first for them. Faith Assembly of God is a large church, and their sanctuary seats around a thousand. They have two Sunday morning services. Pastor Jones recommended that I wear a suit and tie. He said, "We're conservative around here."

For the early service, I had 35 minutes to speak. I've learned how to preach a message, sing two songs, and have an altar service within whatever window they give me. The last thing I wanted to do was go beyond my allotted time. I wanted the pastor to know that he could trust me to stay within the time zone I was given.

The second service had no time restraints. We had an awesome, powerful, and anointed service. The Lord's presence filled that sanctuary. Faith Assembly of God was where I was supposed to be from the beginning. It was ordained by the Holy Spirit. You could feel the presence of God in that sanctuary. The altars were packed, and hearts were stirred. The freedom of the Spirit was flowing in the anointing of God. Pastor Ed Jones affirmed that I was supposed to be at Faith Assembly, saying, "This is no accident. God doesn't make mistakes; His timing and purpose is always perfect." He never pushes, He guides.

If I had not reached out to Pastor Hernquist, I would have missed God. I would have been home, moaning a familiar blues cut named "How could this happen to me again?" The Lord used the cancellation of another church to open up this opportunity to guide me onto the place where He wanted me to be at that moment since before the foundation of the world. I had no idea that I would find a church to preach with such short notice, but I had to keep pressing on. Something in my spirit said, "Don't quit, Joe." I think my former football career taught me to never quit and to keep fighting until the final whistle blows.

I've never forgotten that 49ers vs. Vikings game on December 4, 1977. One of my favorite songs that I sing is "Your Grace and Mercy" by the Mississippi Mass Choir. God gave me a public sign. The enemy thought that I'd cave in: "No one will book you, Joe. It's too late. God's not in this; how could He allow this to happen and still claim His love for you?" The two-minute warning was right ahead. All these distractions and voices just cause us to take our eyes off of Him. No, the fire didn't fall from the sky, but the Holy Spirit did fall on the hearers as God opened a door that the enemy wanted closed and locked.

The taste of victory is so much sweeter when it's seasoned and tempered with perseverance, endurance, sweat, trust, and pain. Sometimes the Lord will remind you that you're still pretty special, and His hand is always where it's been, guiding your every step.

This is the message of the gospel. God gave the world a public sign over 2,000 years ago. Jesus died a public death on a public cross, then rose from the dead four days later. The prayer of Elijah is just as relative today as it was then. The three-year drought was real—our world thirsts for cool waters. Proverbs 25:25 (NIV) says, "Like cold water to a weary soul is good news from a distant land." The good news is that your thirst can be satisfied from the well that never runs dry (John 7:37-39). Just take a drink. Taste and see that the Lord is good; blessed is the one who takes refuge in Him.

The ministry had been good at Praise Assembly of God—good preaching, good people, and a good love offering. We had a Saturday men's breakfast and two great services on Sunday. I always look forward to *going to* and *coming back*. As effective as the ministry is in my evangelical call, my first call is to my family. It's always special to come back to T-Jack.

I buckled into my seat belt on my American Airlines flight from Toronto to Phoenix. Before boarding every flight, I thank God for the person I will be sitting next to. I pray that He'll give me an opportunity to start a conversation that will lead to something more significant than today's headlines.

Just before we took off, the lady sitting in the window seat greeted me with a smile and a warm hello. She said, "I bet you're glad to have an aisle seat."

I said, "Yes, ma'am, I sure am. My knees aren't very good."

As the plane climbed to cruising altitude, we asked the usual ice breaker questions to begin a conversation. Her name was Lynn. She was married with several grown children. Lynn and her husband were flying back to Phoenix but weren't able to sit next to each other. He was seated on the other window side. I offered to move, but she declined.

I mentioned to her that I played in the NFL and travel as an evangelist. As soon as I said the word *evangelist,* she waved at her husband to change seats. I thought maybe she didn't feel comfortable sitting next to athletes. Her husband switched seats and introduced himself as Mike Ortel.

Mike had pastored a Seventh-Day Adventist church in Arizona. He now had an executive position with that fellowship. Mike is a man's man who loves the Lord. He is an encourager and full of the Holy Spirit. He always wears a smile and greets you with a hug. Mike could have been a CEO or a professional coach who knows all the right buttons to push. I gave him my brochure and contact information.

He said he'd contact me and follow up with a lunch. How many times have we heard, "Hey, let's get together, I'll give you a call," only to never hear from that person again? However, I felt that Mike would follow through. And follow through he did. We had lunch and enjoyed great fellowship. He asked if I would be available to speak at a men's retreat in Prescott, Arizona.

My calendar was open, and we confirmed the date. At the retreat, I met men who loved God and walked in His power. The theme for the conference was Armed and Dangerous. I shared a message titled "The Battle Is Not Yours." As believers, we are armed and dangerous when we use the weapons that are not of this world's system. Our weapons have divine power to demolish strongholds (2 Cor. 10:4). The Word of God is our ammunition. If we were not armed with the Word, then we're only dangerous to ourselves.

The weekend was amazing. It would have been easy for me to feel like an outsider, maybe a little intimidated and judgmental, but there were no walls of division. They received me as a brother in Christ. All the other keynote speakers seemed to flow in one accord. That's what I love about the body of Christ. Jesus says, "I am the way the truth and the life, no one comes to the Father but by Me."

Today in the NFL, the offensive tackles are bigger, the running backs faster, but my love for the game is still the same. It was this motivation that enabled me to keep my dream alive. The desert and western environment was a greater opponent than West Texas State running back Eugene Mercury Morris or Duane "the Train" Thomas. It was hard to drown out the voices and distractions of the land where the Aggie Mountain and the Rio Grande were the new normal instead of the Cincinnati skyline and the Ohio River.

With every ounce of willpower I could summon, I fought the good fight and held to the belief that this was somehow the plan for my life. By God's grace and mercy, I was one of only four freshmen who graduated from the senior class. All the others dropped out or transferred to another college. The importance of finishing strong and listening to the right voice has proved invaluable in goal setting.

The Lord gave me a skillset and a strong passion for playing football. These are vital keys to the fulfillment of a dream. But without commitment and character, *talent and natural gifts are only potential.* Potential has never caught a pass, sacked a quarterback, or won a case in a courtroom. Some of our greatest sources of talent and potential are found in prisons, rehab centers, and cemeteries. It was said that Joe Jackson possesses all the tools; however, if the tools stay in the toolbox, what good are they?

## All the Right Stuff

I don't know what possessed me to buy a race car in 1974, but I did. I love cars, and having too much money and not enough sense may be the reason. Ed Jordan sold me a 1964 Chevy 11 Nova. It was set up for the quarter-mile. The Chevy 11 had a small block 350 with two 660 Holley carburetors on a tunnel ram manifold. The rear end had a twelve bolt, 480 gears with traction bars and slicks. It had all the right stuff.

That car was tricked out to do a quarter-mile in under ten seconds. At the drag strip, I never won a race and never broke fourteen seconds. This same car with another driver won several races. I had the goods and all the tools but lacked confidence. I didn't trust my ability to take the car to its limits. I was afraid that I might lose control and crash. I didn't want it bad enough.

All I wanted was a fast car but not a dragster. I eventually drove the car on the streets, roll bar, uncapped and all. I remember driving to El Paso with a full tank of gas. Las Cruces is only about 43 miles from El Paso, Texas, but I ran out of gas just outside the city limits. When training camp started, I sold is the car for $800. Lesson learned.

I realize that confidence is born out of experience. Like the saying goes, the more you do something right, the more you do something right. As a defensive end, I know that if I beat an all-pro offensive tackle once, I can do it again. It won't happen every time, but it can happen again.

Behind the wheel of the dragster, I lacked confidence. I was afraid to push the car to its limit. I was afraid to get beat, and that's exactly what happened. Overcoming fear is a make-or-break obstacle in pursuit of a dream. During my first year of teaching at Bloomington John F. Kennedy High, I had no vision, only a goal. A goal to overcome the fear of public speaking and become a more confident English teacher. In the bigger picture, God saw this as a beginning of not only a goal to be reached but a vision that He would soon birth. After five years of teaching, my confidence grew. I was tracking a master's, then God closed that door and opened another.

# Chapter 55: Barriers Broken

D r. Wade Mumm is the lead pastor at Greeneway Church in Orlando. Greeneway is a dynamic church that crosses racial, economic, political, and social barriers that divide a community. Brother Wade believes and understands the value of team and family— many members, yet one body. His vision is not just to build a great church but to build God's greatness in every individual.

Under his ministry and leadership, the church has grown from 175 to over 1,500 members. I first met Dr. Mumm in 2012. He responded to an email I sent to many churches. Most churches never replied, but Pastor Wade did. I've heard pastors say that they receive too many requests from missionaries, evangelists, drama teams, and musical groups to respond to every inquiry. Some probably delete my email before they even open it.

Thirty-five years ago, God called me to travel cross-culturally as an evangelist. He told me to trust Him to meet my needs. He's never failed me. Greeneway Church is one of only three churches that support me financially every month. I am grateful for the relationship I have with Dr. Wade Mumm and Greeneway Church, another champion I've met along my journey.

Recently I preached at the Church on the Greens located in Sun City West. Sun City West was the 1960s vision and brainchild of developer Del Webb. To be honest, my expectations were low. Sun City is the retirement community that offers golf, MLB spring training sites, and sunshine. The Church on the Green was once the Del Webb headquarters. It's conveniently located off the ninth fairway. My good friend Pastor Mitch King was the main contact for me to minister there.

I've known Mitch for nearly thirty years. He arranged for me to speak at their men's breakfast in the past. The church is comprised of mostly seniors. In the fall and winter, they run over 600. However, when the snowbirds leave, attendance drops to around 500. I was looking forward to preaching to the entire church family. Just before they called me to the pulpit, Mitch whispered, "Joe, I forgot to tell you that there are for-ty-three retired preachers here, and the former general superintendent of the Assemblies of God is here today." I just about made my exit to the parking lot upon hearing that!

It turned out to be a great service in every way. The church was a tremendous source of encouragement just when I needed it. They really blessed me! You never know who the Lord will bring across your path to remind you why you do what you do and who you do it for. My dear friend Pastor Mitch King left us in 2020. Because of COVID, I wasn't able to say goodbye.

For an evangelist, December can be a difficult month to book a ser-vice. With all the Christmas programs and musicals, churches don't have time for special guest speakers. If I were only singing, I believe more doors would open.

I remember in the late '70s, even before I sang with the Gaithers, I was asked to play the part of one of the three kings. At that time, I was attend-ing Hope Presbyterian Church in Richfield, Minnesota, led by senior pas-tor Bob Dickson. Pastor Bob was a tremendous communicator who loved God and walked in His power. Several Minnesota Vikings attended Hope Church, including Grady Alderman and Milt Sunday. Grady and Milt played on the offense during the Vikings' glory days. Somehow the word got out that I was a singer. At that time, I was not a singer—I only liked to sing. I guess that was good enough because I was drafted into a trio and played one of the three kings.

The first day of rehearsal, John came along to sing my part just in case I didn't work out. They told me to sing the melody. I had no idea which part was melody and which was harmony. Naturally, I began to sing the melody. They told me to sing little louder, so I did and I got the part. There were three services at Hope Church, and each was packed with around

700 per service. I prayed, "Lord, help me." Yes, I loved to sing, but I was totally out of my element.

It was almost the same feeling you get as a rookie sitting at your locker on Sunday morning dressed in your game uniform. You *know* this is not another practice. This is the real deal, and it counts. Some of the lessons I learned about life and success were not taught in a classroom; they were taught on a football field. There are so many parallels between football and life. The keys to conquering your fears, blocking out voices that scream, "You can't do it," I learned from playing football.

Beginning with my first year of high school football at Withrow to my freshman year in college at New Mexico State to my rookie season with the New York Jets, I was a starter at the defensive end. I had to overcome some serious fears. It wasn't only the fear of failure but the fear that I wasn't good enough.

For me, it always goes back to the question of my life's purpose. If you know that you have a purpose, then you know that there is a design and a designer. You don't get purpose from the lack of it. God has a plan. If I were to ask an atheist or an agnostic why he or she has hands, the first word you hear is *for* because the word *for* is a preposition meaning "in place of"—a rope for a belt. You don't replace a belt with a can of soup. It wouldn't work. Even in my darkest moments, I know that God has a plan. The difference between knowing and believing reduces your fears. When you know something, it's been tested. This turns into knowledge and is converted into a belief.

In that performance, the three kings marched into the sanctuary dressed like the magi bearing gifts. I looked like Melchior, the king from Persia. As we took each step, my confidence grew. I not only looked the part, I became the part. The song "We Three Kings" would be the beginning of a new chapter in the pursuit of a championship.

The next year Hope Church asked me to have a solo in the Christmas play on a song called "It's a Great Day" by contemporary Christian music pioneer Barry McGuire. Barry was formerly a member of the New Christy Minstrels. He also had a hit song in the '60s titled "The Eve of

Destruction." I met Barry at the Soul Liberation Festival in Minneapolis in 1982 when our band opened for him. McGuire was a real pro and gave me some tips in songwriting.

The following year, Faith Covenant Church asked me to sing "It's a Great Day" in their Christmas play. I thought, *Maybe I should do more singing and stop complaining that nobody wants to book me in December.* Sometimes we need to be reminded of the gifts we have. God's gifts and His call are irrevocable (Rom. 11:29).

When I made the transition from music ministry to evangelism, I realized that singing was a stepping stone that led me to preach the gospel. I was so excited that I was finally able to confidently say more than a few words without fear of stammering and mumbling over my words. I embraced this new revelation with the same passion I had as a defensive end with the New York Jets. Yet, God's gift was still there. I thank Him for rediscovery. Music is powerful. Good worship music enables me to enter into that place where even the spoken word cannot bring a heart to worship as a song of praise.

# Chapter 56: The Arizona Bowl

When it comes to rediscovery and praise, nothing defines this more than the New Mexico State University football team. After a 57-year drought, the longest gap between bowl game appearances, the New Mexico State Aggie football team accepted a bid to play in the 2017 Arizona Bowl in Tucson, Arizona. The last time NMSU had played in a bowl game was the 1960 Sun Bowl in El Paso, Texas when they played the Utah State Aggies.

In the 1960 season, New Mexico State was stocked with All Americans Pervis Atkins, Preacher Pilot, Bob Gaiters, and quarterback Charley Johnson. They beat the Utah State Aggies 20-13. Then 57 years later, these same two Aggie teams would meet in the Arizona Bowl. The Utah State Aggies boasted the quarterback talent of Jordan Love, future first-round draft choice of the Green Bay Packers. The NMSU Aggie defense would have to apply pressure, be alert, pursue, and tackle hard.

Would history repeat itself? Both teams finished the season 6-6. New Mexico State hadn't had a winning season in 15 years. In 118 seasons, their overall record was 417-606-30. NMSU needed a win. The Arizona Bowl drew a record crowd of over 40,000 fans, many of whom drove up from Las Cruces.

From the opening kickoff to the final overtime whistle, the stadium was electrifying. Both teams had back-to-back kickoff returns. NMSU fans were prisoners of a vision and a long dream that was on the brink of fulfillment. Could the drought that some call the curse of the old man Warren Woodson be broken?

Warren Woodson coached the Aggies in their last 1960 Sun Bowl victory. Woodson was a great coach with a career college football record of 202-94-14. He was a trendsetting coach who dominated the Border Conference. Some say Woodson wore out his welcome at NMSU and was forced out. His arrogance and personality caused friction with some of the board of regents. He was let go because New Mexico State determined that at the age of 65 it was time for him to retire. They booted him out in the spring of 1968, which was my freshman year. He was inducted into the College Football Hall of Fame in 1989.

The fifty-seven year drought ended December 29, 2017, with a thrilling overtime win against the Utah State Aggies, 26-20. Out of the forty bowls, our game was voted the eighth-best.

New Mexico State head coach Doug Martin was interviewed after the game. He said, "Yes, this is the end of a drought that began in 1960, but this is the beginning of something very special at New Mexico State University."

He and his wife, Vicki, felt a divine call, not only to rebuild this program to a competitive level but to also to build godly character into the lives of the young men and future leaders. Great job, Coach Martin! Hopefully, this win will lead to future success for New Mexico State. I don't think I'll be around for another 57-year drought.

When you're walking through a desert, everyone's laughing but you. Your favorite food no longer tastes good, life has lost its flavor, hope has dried up. Yet you keep fighting because you still believe. The Bible says that faith is the substance of things hoped for, the evidence of things not yet seen (Heb. 11:1, *my paraphrase*). There's such a big difference between "not seen" and "not yet seen." *Not yet seen* gives us hope worth fighting for. God promises to bring us out of whatever drought we're walking through, and we know He's going to make a way through the desert.

New Mexico State found a way through. They didn't allow the facts to circumvent their vision. They're not living the dream; they're living the promise of Hebrews 11:1.

# Chapter 57: Snoop Dogg

The tenth anniversary of the NFL Super Bowl Gospel Choir was celebrated in Minneapolis during the week of Super Bowl LVII. I was really excited about this concert because my music ministry began in Minnesota. Since 2008, the NFL Super Bowl Gospel Choir performed at a concert venue in the hosting city of the Super Bowl. This year's concert would be held at Bethel University in St. Paul.

The concert is usually held on Friday, two days prior to the big game; however, this year's concert would be held on Thursday. My flight was scheduled to land in Minneapolis on Thursday at 1:45, which didn't give me very much time to learn the music and rehearse.

When we landed in Minneapolis, the pilot announced that it was five degrees above zero. When I left Phoenix, it was seventy-five degrees. It's hard to believe that I lived here for eleven years and played outdoors with no dome, heaters, or gloves.

I was seated in an exit row in coach, so it took a few minutes before I deplaned. My mind was in a thousand places. Lots of great memories here, and I was trying recapture each one. I typically look around my seat for something I may have forgotten, but I was focused on getting to baggage claim and then to my rental car.

I retrieved my baggage and caught the tram to Alamo car rental. There was some concern on my part that I wouldn't be able to rent a car. I lost my driver's license on a flight from Scranton to Charlotte the previous week. The only license I had was a temporary paper one. I prayed, and they accepted the temporary license.

Later I realized that something was missing. I had left my Beats Studio wireless headphones on the plane. I was sure someone had turned them in and figured I would retrieve them after the concert. We rehearsed at Bethel, and it sounded pretty tight. Most of the football players either can sing or think they can. There are several players in the choir who have great voices and can sing. Hall of Famer Tim Brown showed up two minutes before we went on stage. Someone ran and found him a robe and gave him the songs we were singing, and he did okay.

The concert featured The Clark Sisters, Faith Evans, the Sounds of Blackness, Sheila E., Rance Allen, and Donnie McClurklin. Seattle quarterback Russell Wilson of the Seahawks received the Man of Faith award. His testimony was anointed and powerful. He talked about never giving up and trusting Christ in every situation.

There was word that Snoop Dogg would also perform, but I thought that was a joke. Snoop Dogg singing (rapping) gospel—you got to be kidding. Well, it turned out to be no joke. He actually performed with Rance Allen and Faith Evans. He has a new gospel album coming out. Who would ever think that Bethel University would host a concert that featured Snoop Dogg and NFL players' Super Bowl Gospel Choir? After the concert, I hurried to the airport to pick my headphones, but I was too late—someone had already stolen them. I wondered out loud why someone wouldn't turn them in.

The thought of stealing anything is so foreign in my life now. I have lost car keys, headphones, and iPods on planes and never had them returned. I wonder if this is the fruit of some of the seeds I had sown in my Madisonville days. My short-term memory could be the result of too many headshots.

The Super Bowl weekend not only featured the big game but also gave me the opportunity to preach at Eden Prairie Assembly of God church pastored by my good friend and brother, Jac Perrin.

Pastor Jac is a student of the Bible who challenges your vocabulary with Word integrity. His PhD thesis is entitled "Family 13 in Saint John's

Gospel." Yet in spite of his brilliance, Jac is very giving and has a great sense of humor.

Jac and I were having dinner at a local spot in Minneapolis. I told him that I lost my Beats on the plane. For a minute he thought that I was talking to him about beets, the veggie. He said, "No problem, we'll pick some up on the way to the hotel."

I said, "No, no Jac, I'm talking about my headphones. Forget it. They're around three hundred bucks."

The next morning Jac went to Best Buy and bought me a pair of Studio Beats by Dre headphones. He just said, "We want to bless you." I was speechless, humbled, and very thankful.

Jac also has an appetite to learn. At the men's breakfast we were talking about the Vikings' loss to the Eagles. I mentioned that Case had thrown a pick-six, which was a game-changer. Jac asked, "Hey Joe, what's a pick-six?"

I explained the meaning of the term *pick-six* then I asked him to explain his doctoral thesis, "Family 13 in Saint John."

I was able to connect with the members of my former band Refuge, including John Hiiva, Dave Peterson, Angie Johnson, and Chris Anderson. I believe the Lord planted these beautiful people in my life for a season and a reason. These dear friends came along at the precise moment as part of God's plan when I really needed them. They helped to shape my destiny, and even though some I hadn't seen in 34 years, it was so good.

# Chapter 58: Dan Quayle

I n 1996, I met Vice President Dan Quayle. America's 44th Vice President wrote a book entitled *The American Family: Discovering the Values That Make Us Strong*. He collaborated with psychologist Diane Medved and journeyed thousands of miles to interview a diverse mix of families to talk about what values gave them strength. Liberal, conservative, Christian, non-Christian, Black, white, and mixed race.

Pastor Craig Lauterbach of then Lambertville Assembly of God invited Vice President Quayle as a keynote speaker at a conference called Lambertvision. The conference always features speakers, singers, evangelists, or pastors. This was the first time a political leader would be a keynote speaker. I think the bar was too low regarding my expectations of what he would say.

His message was not a political amendment; it was conversational. He gave his personal testimony of his childhood and being raised in Indianapolis, Indiana. He talked about a new consensus on the importance of the traditional family. At the time, I was single and couldn't relate experientially; it was only from the knowledge addressed and what I previously had read. Now that I'm married, I learned that when you're in marital distress, don't use the D-word. If divorce is not an option, then you'll find a solution to your problem. My wife and I have never used that word.

We've faced struggles and have had various disagreements, but we know that divorce is never an option for us. We'll find an answer, and if we don't we'll still build a bridge and not allow a wedge to divide us.

This is what I took from Dan Quayle's book. I am truly convinced that the Lord loves us enough to keep us headed in the right direction. And when we do go off course, He gently guides us back on track. I hope and pray that America regains some of its moral values that made us a light to the world. But, of course, this will not happen through a political voice in government, mandates, or amendments.

We should pray for our leaders. Laws don't change hearts, they only change how people are governed. It's been 155 years since the Emancipation Proclamation, and we have come a long way from legalized slavery to a Black man being elected to the highest political office on earth. But 155 years is a long time. I don't have 155 years left. No one does.

Real change comes from a change of heart and a new mindset. Almost instantly, Saul of Tarsus was transformed by a vision. He became Paul, the apostle. Saul heard the voice of Jesus and was knocked on his hindquarters. In a mere three days, he went from pursuing Christians for persecution and execution to falling in love with Jesus. The scales were removed from his eyes. That's the miracle of regeneration. And that's what will make the American family strong!

# Chapter 59: I'm a Packer Fan

The first time met Bill Fyfe was in 2005. Our new Toll Brothers home was in the final stages of completion. In less than a month, I would be married and move into a brand new home. I would drive 46 miles from Central Phoenix to Gold Canyon for a progress report almost every week.

This was a very exciting time for Terill and me. Neither of us had ever married or owned a brand new home. We could hardly wait. As I walked in the backyard (if you could call it a yard—in reality, it was nothing but a home for tumbleweed, cacti, rocks, scorpions, rattlesnakes, bobcats, and lizards), in my mind it was transformed to an beautiful oasis with a barbecue grill, nine-foot-deep swimming pool outlined with pavers, a lemon tree, and a putting green.

What I didn't imagine was to be rudely greeted with the words, "Hey, neighbor, I'm a Packers fan."

When I heard that, I thought of asking for my down payment back. That was my introduction to my new neighbor, Bill Fyfe, which was incidentally the last time I referred to him as Bill. In sixteen years, I've never called him Bill. He is forever Fyfe.

Fyfe and Angie Fyfe lived across the street in a beautiful two-story semi-custom Toll Brothers home. He was aware that I played with the Vikings, and that was his good-natured welcome to the neighborhood. Fyfe grew up in Cozad, Nebraska. He played defensive end for the Nebraska Cornhuskers under legendary coach Tom Osborne.

If you ever wanted to know the dictionary's definition of a neighbor, you would find Bill Fyfe's picture and name. For Fyfe, the expression of going the extra mile is no more than the distance from his house to mine.

I later learned that Fyfe had three brain surgeries, the result of which cost him his career with Carlson Companies. He's not sure if it was one too many concussions while playing football or if it was hereditary. He's grateful to be alive and never complains.

It was December 2005. Christmas would soon be here. Terill and I were coming home from a Wednesday night church service. As we turned into our subdivision, we noticed that our home was strung with Christmas lights. I thought Terill hired someone to decorate the house to surprise me. She thought the same for me. It was Fyfe; he completely surprised us and decorated our house, front and back! He gave us the Christmas lights and other decorations. Another time I sold a car to someone who lived in Benson, Arizona. Unfortunately, I had to drive to Benson where the potential buyer lived. It was worth it; I sold the car, but had no way back to Gold Canyon, which was about 120 miles away.

Fyfe called about something. I told him I was in Benson and had sold my car. He asked, "How you getting back?"

I said, "I'm not sure."

He said, "I'll pick you up in the morning."

I offered to pay him, but he said, "Buy me a taco, and we're even."

In 2010 I was driving my mom's car from Cincinnati to Phoenix. I felt tired, so I pulled over at a convenience store. Most likely, I got out for a stretch and ended up wandering the streets of Albuquerque, New Mexico, confused and disoriented, with no memory that I just drove twelve hundred miles in a car not much bigger than me.

I flagged down a cop and said, "Officer, I know this sounds crazy, and I'm not drunk or on drugs, but I have no idea how I got to Albuquerque."

He called an EMT. They determined that I had some kind of memory lapse, maybe a seizure. They asked if I was married and was there someone I could contact. Bingo, that was it. A light came on. I remembered that I was married and I called Terill. Concerned, she calmly reminded me that I had visited my mom in Cincinnati. I had purchased her car and was driving it back to Phoenix to give it to Olivia.

The EMTs highly recommended that I go to the hospital, but I refused and walked back to my car. To my surprise, my keys were still in the ignition, my wallet on the seat, Super Bowl ring in the unlocked glove box.

Thank the Lord nothing was taken. It's hard to admit, but I most likely had a seizure. My wife contacted Dana and Sandy McQuinn in Las Cruces and asked if they knew anyone I could stay with in Albuquerque until I was able to travel. They said, "Our daughter Marce lives in Albuquerque."

When I was a student at New Mexico State, I would drive Marce and her baby sister, Holly, to Baskin-Robbins. The two little girls would sit in the front seat of my '64 Corvair with no seatbelts on, saying, "Jo Jo, let's get some keem. Let's get some keem." They couldn't say "ice cream." I stayed with Marce and her family for a few days.

Terill suggested that I fly home and said under no circumstances was I to drive to Phoenix. She called Fyfe, and he said, "Stay where you are; I'll come get you."

After much debate, I convinced him that I was able to fly. My brother-in-law Mr. Steve Jerry who works for Delta Airlines gave me a buddy pass to bring me home.

On another occasion, Fyfe rallied the troops and said, "Let's throw a party for Steve." Our neighbor Steve was fighting a losing battle with ALS. He was in a wheelchair and soon would be on a feeding tube. Fyfe opened up his home and catered all the food, and even helped out with transportation for out-of-town family members. This would be Steve's last party. He died several weeks later. I officiated his going home celebration. I cannot list all the acts of kindness Fyfe has done for my family and others in our neighborhood.

In 2010 the Minnesota Vikings' alumni weekend would match the Vikings against the Chicago Bears. The Vikings played their home games at the Metrodome. However, because of heavy snowfall, the Metrodome roof caved in. The game was moved to the Minnesota Gophers' outdoor stadium. Man, it was cold!

For the alumni weekends, the Vikings will cover two nights at the Downtown Hilton, meals, and tickets to the game. I would normally bring Terill with me. She's not a football fan, but she loves this event. I love it too. It's like she's experiencing what it would have been like to be a player's wife when I was playing. This particular weekend she couldn't come with me, so I brought Fyfe along.

It was a Monday night game. I was able to preach that Sunday morning in a small Assemblies of God church on the south side of Minneapolis. It wasn't in the greatest neighborhood. The pastor told us that someone was killed on the church doorstep the previous week. What a great place to reach the lost sheep! The people were very friendly and glad that we came. Just before I was introduced to preach, the pastor asked Fyfe if he would open in prayer.

I didn't know what to expect from Fyfe, but he prayed like a seasoned deacon. We stayed afterward for the church's potluck, which Fyfe greatly enjoyed. On game day, Fyfe and I went to the Vikings' chapel and pre-game meal. It was a great weekend. How do you top that? Not only was it the alumni weekend, but it was also the Vikings' 50th anniversary. Many of my teammates, including Vikings' greats, were honored as *all-time* greatest Vikings.

The Vikings made a coaching change in the middle of the season. My friend Leslie Frazier was named the Vikings' new head coach. It was certainly a wonderful moment. We were treated like royalty. Fyfe talked about our experience as if it happened last week.

That was a great weekend. It was great to do something special for Fyfe. I know thousands of people, but outside of my family I only have a handful of true friends—and Fyfe is certainly in that circle.

# Chapter 59: I'm a Packer Fan

I guess you're important when the five motor coaches carrying the Vikings alumni and family members travel north in the southbound lane escorted by a police escort to arrive on time for the kickoff. I suppose the only thing missing was a Vikings win. The Bears knocked Brett Favre out of the game in the second quarter. The Vikings lost, and Brett would never play again in the NFL.

# Chapter 60: Superstition Mountains—Majestic and Deadly

I had just finished working out when I noticed a message on my cell. Fyfe called and left me a voicemail. He asked if I had heard of the helicopter crash and asked if Chad was okay. Our neighbor Chad was a flight nurse attendant on Native Air 5, a helicopter air ambulance. I told Fyfe I hadn't heard any news. Surely Chad wasn't involved in any crash. It couldn't be Chad! He's only 38 with a wife and young daughter. I had buried his father, Steve, who suffered from ALS. No way! I further checked some sources, and to my complete horror and disbelief, it was Chad.

He and the pilot were killed. For some unknown reason, Chad's aircraft crashed into the Superstition Mountain range. There were two fatalities. It was revealed that Chad survived the initial crash, but because of a delay in rescue he tragically died on the mountain. Terill and I reached out to his mother and sister, Lark and Tiff.

Chad was one of the first to welcome our family into the neighborhood. I will never forget that day. Our doorbell rang, and there was Chad. He brought a bottle of wine and, with a big smile, said, "Welcome to the neighborhood, we're glad you're here!" That meant a lot. Even in 2005, you didn't know what kind of neighborhood you're moving into.

Growing up in Cincinnati, there were Black neighborhoods and white neighborhoods. There were certain areas in Cincy like Mariemont where Blacks couldn't live. It meant so much to be welcomed as part of the Los Colinas (our subdivision) family. Even though my wife and I don't drink, we were very appreciative of his gift and still have it.

Chad said, "You need to come over and meet my dad; he loves football." At that time, Steve was mobile but used a cane. Terill and I went over to meet Steve, Lark, and their daughter, Tiff. We became good friends.

My heart broke for Lark. First, she lost her husband, Steve, now her only son, Chad, had been killed. There was a private service for family and friends, then a military service to honor Chad. I officiated the private service. Both were packed.

I'm not sure Lark ever recovered after losing Chad. She eventually sold the house and moved. Our street was changing overnight. Even Fyfe and Angie moved. Terill and I were one of the only original owners left. I had no doubt the Lord brought us to Gold Canyon. I thought it was for the sole purpose of living in a nice home and neighborhood and to build a family and some equity—but it was much more.

It was to sow into the lives of the people the Lord brought to us. It was to be there for Lark and Tiff as they mourned the loss of Steve and Chad; for Terill to pray and lay hands on a dying lady thrown from a Harley just a few yards from our house. That's what *Championship Sunday* is all about—being prepared to put your faith in action in season and off-season.

# Chapter 61: New Season

Our season ended in Gold Canyon. In football, one season ends, and another soon begins. You add some new players and coaches. You make adjustments to put yourself in the best position for success. The names on the jerseys may change, but the goals remain the same. You're always trying to catch up to your potential, never satisfied with yesterday's victories.

Our destiny continues to unfold. The Bible says old things have passed away, behold the glorious new has come (2 Cor. 5:17). We moved on. We lost the house but not our faith, and not the war. It's not about why; it's about what we will learn going forward. Good teams never rebuild—they tweak, they reload.

You find a system that works, then you find the players to execute, or you find great players and build your system around them. We're excited about our new neighborhood and who the Lord will bring our way.

We've already met Sandy, who wears a big smile and has a heart for the homeless. She stopped by our house after noticing our Christmas snowman wearing a Minnesota Vikings beanie. Sandy not only has a heart for the homeless, she's hands-on. Many times you'll find her under a bridge or cardboard home just being a friend to someone who landed on the Jericho Road. After being nominated by her daughters, Sandy appeared on *The Ellen Show* for being a servant to those in need.

Over the years, Larry and I have walked with Olympic gold medalists, NFL Hall of Famers, NBA legends, Super Bowl MVPs, MLB World Series champs, CFL heroes, heavyweight boxing champions, NHL greats, and Heisman Trophy winners. They all shared one common thread—the willingness to pay the price for greatness, to make difficult choices because they were prisoners of a dream. They realized that talent and gifts are only potential if not utilized.

They all possessed potential, but potential never scored a touchdown, preached a sermon, ran for office, saved anyone in a courtroom or operating room, or taught a subject in a classroom. Some of the greatest athletes in my neighborhood never even made it to the minor leagues of life—not because of a lack of talent, but because of poor choices. I'll say it again—you're free to choose, but once you make a choice, the choice will always choose the consequence. That's why it's imperative to make good choices, to make godly choices—especially in this millennial age.

This generation must guard its minds. The Bible tells us to take every thought captive to the obedience of Christ (2 Cor. 10:5). But you certainly can't make a godly choice if you don't know truth. This generation needs to know that something that sounds true-ish is not necessarily truth. Our culture today seeks to erode truth with something called relativism and subjectivism.

Relativism is the assumption that there is no such thing as absolute truth; anything goes. Subjectivism says that I, the subject, have the right to determine what is right and wrong without submitting my judgment to any authority outside of myself. When I was in college, it was considered wrong—illegal—to smoke or use marijuana. You could be arrested, kicked off the team, or expelled from school. Today it's legal in sixteen states plus Washington DC.

What made it wrong in the '70s is no longer true today. Absolutes aren't being taught today. Where there's no moral ground, then there's no foundation.

It was a blessing to hear testimony from Philadelphia Eagles head coach Doug Peterson and Super Bowl MVP quarterback Nick Foles. Sure, they were underdogs and not favored to win, and they won Super Bowl LII. I'd be shouting, "Praise Jesus" too. But it was more than a big win, more than thanks to the Big Man Upstairs. It was gratitude and thanks to the Lord and Savior Jesus Christ. He made it all happen.

Outside of the church, there's no voice louder or clearer with the gospel message than the voice of athletes. You won't hear much from entertainers, politicians, actors, or even educators. Sports is real. Competition is real—nothing superficial. There's no quiet on the set, take two. The blood is real, the pain is real, the goal is real, and the loss is real. The testimony is real.

And a lot of it is coming from football players. Are they the only thankful souls on the planet? No, of course not! Football is a violent game, and we are grateful every time we're able to walk off the field rather than to be carried off on a stretcher. This may sound crazy, but I really do believe that God cares who wins. No, I don't believe that the Dallas Cowboys are His favorite team (the Vikings are, of course), but He has a purpose in all that we do. Who knows how many people came to Christ or rededicated their life back to God after hearing the testimony from Case Keenum, Nick Foles, Doug Peterson, and others?

These superstar athletes realize that their talents and gifts are from God, that God has a divine purpose for our lives. And win, lose, or draw, I'm giving Him praise. Over twelve thousand athletes and coaches have attended the AIM conference. They have discovered that their powerful platform can give them more than a following on social media; it can be used as a place to lift their voice for Christian reform and lead our youth in the right direction.

## Either Way, God's Gonna Heal My Knees

I know it's only a matter of time before I have to have my knees replaced, unless God does a miracle. If and when I do have surgery, I'd like to have them replaced at the same time. There are some mornings when I can barely walk, not to mention the pain and stiffness. When I go to the pulpit to preach, I cue the pastor to extend his hand as if he were shaking mine to pull me up. Someone once said that you know your knees are bad when it's more difficult going down the stairs than up.

Until 2013, I was able to run. My last 10K race was in 2009. I know I don't look like a runner, but running was my passion. I'd run five or six miles daily, and if I didn't run I would do cardio on my step machine.

I miss running. Now all I can do is the elliptical. Pretty soon, it'll be the stationary bike, then maybe swimming, then I guess someone will have to push me around in a wheelchair. All of my friends and teammates who have had their knees replaced say it's something they should have done years before. Maybe I'll say that too, but for now I'm trying to keep what God gave me.

Like many people, I'm finding the older you get, the easier it is to gain weight. My weight had always been around 257. After every five-mile run I would go to the bakery and buy three apple fritters and a large diet Pepsi. I wouldn't gain a pound. The most I ever weighed in the NFL was around 265. Today I can't get under 270.

I'm still lifting weights pretty heavily. Thank God, I have no back or shoulder issues. I usually spend about an hour working biceps and triceps, then another half hour on shoulders and chest. After that, I do fifty-five minutes of cardio. I normally do weights three times a week and cardio every day. It's hard to believe that when I was with the New York Jets and Minnesota Vikings, they had no serious weight program. The only equipment they had was a universal gym. They never gave you an off-season workout program.

Of course, the off-season was a real off-season. You wouldn't hear from the team for six months. No mini-camps, no organized team activities. Not even a phone call. I would just train with the NMSU football team. They had more weights than the Vikings and Jets put together. Of course, the Jets and Vikings now have state-of-the-art training facilities and equipment.

Since 1990, I've trained at LA Fitness. They have hundreds of locations across the country. Because I travel every week, LA Fitness is my workout gym club on the road. Usually, the hotels where I stay may have a fitness room. Sometimes their equipment is more residential than commercial, unlike a local gym. It's something you'd find in a home or office.

I know that football was a major contributor to my bad knees, head issues, and seizures. Of course, my quality of life could be better, but

I'm glad I had the experience to live out my dream and, of course, I'd do it again.

## I'm Grateful, God. Thank You!

Most of my experiences on the road have been great. I am grateful for my calling as an evangelist. During my travels, the Lord has led me throughout the United States and the world. God has an amazing family.

I am convinced that His sons and daughters don't match. We don't all look the same, walk the same, talk the same, but because of faith in the Lord Jesus Christ we're family.

The Lord's faithfulness continues and will always amaze me. I have been given cars, clothing, and much love. I cannot say thank you enough for the love, kindness, and generosity I have received since I began this journey in 1981.

There have been so many friends who have encouraged me not to give up when it seems that the bottom has dropped out. When I needed a miracle or a breakthrough, God always came through. Someone will send an email; I'll receive a text, phone call, or maybe a check in the mail just at the perfect time. There's a saying that I learned as a boy at Trinity Baptist Church. Reverend Mosely would testify that "God might not come when you call Him, but He's always on time." God's sovereign will is always right on time. He sees eternity; we see now. We can see to the corner, but God sees around the corner.

I think of the many times I've asked God for something because I was absolutely certain that this was His will, only to look back and say, "Thank you, Lord, for *Thy* will be done." When was I was left at the altar twice within two months by the same woman, I agonized in my closet, in my spirit with deep supplication. "Lord, why? Lord, please change her heart. Let her call and tell me she still loves me and that she made a mistake."

The Lord was graciously saving me from a big mistake. At the time, I couldn't see it—I didn't want to see it. When I look back at that trial, I remember Isaiah 55:9 (NKJV): "For as the heavens are higher than the earth, so are My ways higher than your ways, and My thoughts than your thoughts."

When you're praying, you're asking God for something. When I was a kid, I asked my parents for a new go-cart I thought I just had to have. Their answer was, "No, you can't have that; we can't afford it." Even though I didn't receive what I asked, my request was answered. No is still an answer too.

God, who loves you and who knows the beginning from the end, also knows what your needs are. He also knows your wants. He promises to meet every need according to His riches and glory in Christ Jesus our Lord (Phil. 4:19). The Bible says, "The effective, fervent prayer of a righteous man avails much" (James 5:16 NKJV).

There are some things in life that are hard to understand. On this side, you may never understand why. We are aware of the heartbreaking and tragic life-changing stories that are all too common today. Whether it's a mass shooting in a school, terrorist attack, natural disaster, a crash on Wall Street, or loss of a loved one, some things can't be explained. What I do know is that we walk by faith.

Romans 8:28 (NKJV) says, "And we know that all things work together for good to those who love God, to those who are the called according to His purpose." How many things? Some things, most things, many things? No, He says *all things*, even that thing. That's a promise from God who never lies. The Bible also says that, "It doth not yet appear what we shall be: but we know that, when he shall appear, we shall be like him; for we shall see him as he is" (1 John 3:2 KJV). We'll have complete understanding one day; explanations will no longer be needed, no questions asked. We'll have divine revelation. Until then, we still walk by faith and not by sight.

# Chapter 62: Joe, Say It Ain't So

After 47 great years, the Joe Namath football camp ended. New York Jets teammates Joe Namath and John Dockery began the camp in 1971. It was one of the longest-running football camps in America. Usually when an NFL player retires, the camp also retires, but Joe, Doc, and John Schneider kept it going. Thousands of campers received expert coaching from NFL greats and college coaches.

They were taught football and, more importantly, they were taught invaluable life skills that they would need once their playing days have ended. This camp was like a family reunion with teammates and friends made over the years. There were no attitudes or egos. We genuinely cared for each other. There's a bond, a kindred spirit when you battle as a team, win, lose, or draw. It was something very special that only a few find success in doing. Many are called, but few are chosen (Matt. 22:14).

The Joe Namath football camp also had a special connection with the community as well. It received positive press from the media. Joe Namath has star power. His charismatic personality and legendary place in NFL history made the camp almost a destination spot. I will personally miss hanging out with my teammates Joe Willy, Doc, and Earl Christy. We lost one of our bookends, Winston Hill.

The camp wasn't the same without Winston, who passed in 2016. Also, Stack (Dave Herman) was no longer able to attend because of illness. Maybe it was time to blow the final whistle. We had a great run, 47 years. It's sad that it's ended, but the memories will always live on in our hearts and minds.

# Chapter 63: First the Car Keys, Then the House Keys

After my father died in 1973, my mother never remarried. She had a couple of long relationships, but no marriage. Eventually she moved into the house of my ailing grandmother, who loved her as if she was her own daughter. She continued to work as a dental assistant and managed rental property.

Mom loved to play scrabble. Each week her girlfriends would meet at a different home for food and scrabble. One of her girlfriends was Shirley Larkin, Cincinnati Reds shortstop Barry Larkin's mother.

She was just one of the girls, sweet as she could be. Barry Larkin was a high school legend. He attended the famed Cincinnati Moeller High School where he played baseball, football, and basketball.

Unfortunately, Mom had to give up her scrabble, her car, and her house. Dementia and Alzheimer's rocked our world. Freedom and independence were replaced by 24-hour care. For two years, she lived with my brother Mike and his wife, Jill. Her condition worsened as she would just take off walking and find herself sitting on the front porch of a neighbor's home.

We debated whether or not to put her into an assisted living facility. Jill's cousin, Bessie, who was one hundred years old, also lived with them. I felt guilty for not being there. It was wearing Mike and Jill down too much, and they needed help. We made the decision to place Mom into a facility not too far from Mike.

She lived there for a couple of years. They gave her great care, but it was very expensive. We needed to find a place just as nice but more reasonable. My sisters Mary and Barb lived in Atlanta. Maybe she could live with one of my sisters and be close to family? It sounded like a good idea, but they both worked and couldn't give Mom the extended care she needed. They looked at a facility in a home that was deplorable. The patients were left alone, just waiting to die. It was disgusting. We prayed that God would lead us to the right place.

We found a great facility named Autumn Leaves. So Mom moved back to Georgia, where my sisters and nieces and other family members lived. Sadly, she doesn't know me at all. She has good days and challenging ones. It breaks your heart to see someone you love who was so full of life, funny, youthful, independent, and mentally sharp suffer from this dreadful disease. She's still Mom, and even though she doesn't know us, we know her. We share those special moments and treasure the times when something connects, and she smiles.

It might be a gospel song, the mention of an old friend, or something that briefly turns the light on and clearly reveals the path once traveled.

At this writing, mom is 99 years old. In spite of her cognitive struggles, her body is free of cancer, and her other organs are in great shape. We're thankful that she's still here and God's not finished yet. On November 23, 2018, she checked into her new heavenly home.

# Chapter 64: Withrow's '68
# Class Reunion

I was talking to an old friend I hadn't spoken to since graduating from high school. She was on the committee to contact class members for our fiftieth high school reunion, which means that we've all got to be well into our sixties.

How can that be? It seems impossible. My memories are so vivid and full of color of long summer days at Stewart Park, picnics, the tasty smell of my dad cooking ribs, daily vacation Bible school, and the melody of Mr. Softee's ice cream truck. When a day seemed like a month, a month a year, a year a lifetime, now it's the exact opposite. The decades pass so quickly, and the only way I know to slow time down is to pump some iron at the gym and do 55 minutes of cardio. It seems like it takes forever.

My friend asked if I knew of any names to contact for the class reunion. Our senior class had 864 students. I was sure she wouldn't have a problem locating at least half that number. I was surprised by how many fellow students had died. This girl overdosed, that student went to the gas chamber, another one died in a firefight on the street corner, this one was killed in Vietnam, that one was killed arguing over a slice of cherry pie. I'm certain that if I had not found a new path, I would have probably been listed in one of those categories. God's mercies are new every morning (Lam. 3:23).

Music and sports were my two primary influences, along with good singers. I learned to sing by listening to music I heard on the radio. We formed a group and started singing on the corner. My house was located on the corner of Chandler Street and Ravenna. At night we would sing on the street corner underneath the street light. In the daytime, you'd find us playing football on those same streets.

Hands down, my older brother Jerry was the real musician. He studied at the conservatory of music in Cincinnati where he produced, arranged, wrote, and played several instruments. I'm just a football player who loves music, loves to sing, and bought a whole lot of records as a kid. One day I'll have to find the courage to get rid of 45s and LPs just sitting in boxes collecting dust. I can't read a note. The only songs I can play are the same three or four songs I learned on piano and guitar at thirteen years old.

My brother's band, the Sidewinders, toured with every major R&B artist, including the Commodores, Fat Back Band, and even played with musical royalty the great Duke Ellington. Jerry was musical director for the R&B vocal group The Persuaders. Music and sports were always in our home.

## Branson

I first visited Branson, Missouri in 1991. I had heard about this small Ozark town where country legends could find an audience and eventually a residency in their own theater, much like Las Vegas. On the Branson '76 Boulevard, you could find anyone from Jim Stafford to Andy Williams. These artists still have a following and their own theater. Who would ever think that this destination that was once the home of someone called the Baldknobbers would grow into a combination of Nashville and Las Vegas?

Today you'll find a variety of entertainment from various musical styles in Branson. No longer purely country and bluegrass entertainment, Branson offers a diverse menu of music performers. I remember once going to a dinner theater and saw The Drifters and The Coasters perform.

Whenever I'd visit Branson, Pastor Howard and Kathy Boyd would arrange for me to see a show. They pastored at Branson Hills Assembly of God. Their church was the home of many musicians and artists who gave them free tickets to their shows. Branson was a great destination for the family without the casinos and Vegas attitude. Some of my favorite restaurants are in Branson, especially Lamberts. It was Branson where I reunited with Glenn Campbell. Pastor Howard's son Isaac was a star running back on the Branson High School football team. Before the kickoff, Glenn Campbell sang the National Anthem, and I opened in prayer. Wow, that's got to be a first!

Branson was a great landing spot for artists who can still perform but perhaps no longer have the drawing power to pack out an arena or outdoor stadium. If you enjoy the champagne music of Lawrence Welk, country music of Moe Bandy or Wayne Newton, R&B classics like The Platters, the comedy of Yakov Smirnoff or Silver Dollar City, great gospel music, and much, much more, Branson, Missouri should be on your bucket list.

One of my all-time favorites is Jimmie Rodgers. He had his own theater, the Honeycomb Theater. As a kid, I liked the friendly tone of his voice and the melodies of his music. Howard, Kathy, and I went to the Honeycomb Theater one night to see his show. There were just a handful of us in the theater. Jimmie sang all of his hits, like "Honeycomb," "Kisses Sweeter Than Wine," "Secretly," "Oh, Oh I'm Falling in Love Again," and "Tucumcari."

I was impressed with his testimony for the Lord. We met after his concert. He said, "Joe, if I knew you were here, I would have introduced you."

Though the crowd was small, he believed the Lord opened the door for this opportunity to perform. No matter how many people showed up, he's going to sing until God closes the door. On January 18, 2021, God closed the door to his earthly home and welcomed him into eternity.

In college, I loved the song "Knock Three Times" by Tony Orlando and Dawn. His drummer was a member of Pastor Howard's church. He arranged for us to attend Tony's show at the Yellow Ribbon Music Theater. It was a great night. Tony sang all of my favorites. After the concert we met Tony Orlando, his family, and Little Mickey Carroll of *The Wizard of Oz*. Lots of fun, pictures, conversation, and a great memory. Like Jimmie Rogers, Tony said, "Joe, if I knew you were here I would have introduced you." It made my night!

Eventually I brought Terill and Olivia to Branson for *Christmas in Branson*. We enjoyed a dinner theater on the Branson Belle and almost everything that makes Branson so special.

Many of these experiences would not have been possible had I not stayed at New Mexico State. Yes, I hated the place. I was determined to transfer after my first semester. But God brought people into my life like Yolanda, who I dated in my freshman year. Yeah, that's right, the same Yolanda who dumped me in January of 1970. She was the perfect person the Lord used to change my negative attitude about Las Cruces. After we began dating, gradually this desert wasteland that I was convinced was uninhabitable transformed into the Land of Enchantment.

I love Las Cruces and would probably move back there if my wife was on board. Yolanda stayed in my life just long enough to keep me in Las Cruces until it was too late to transfer to another school. After a year of dating, she dropped me like a used Kleenex. In each relationship that didn't work out, it worked out perfectly as a tool in the Carpenter's hand. I can look at every heartache and heartbreak and say, "Lord, Your hands are on my life, thank You for saving me for Terill."

In 1984 I recorded my first album, *Special Way*, in Nashville. This was produced by Jim Murray of The Imperials. Jim's a great friend, and I appreciated his help. Things were moving fast, maybe too fast. The Imperials' backup band laid the tracks. Most of the songs were original. My intention in recording an album was probably for all the wrong reasons. Foremost I thought this would advance my career as an artist and not the kingdom of God.

We shipped the project to all the major Christian labels with no takers. I was approached by Morada Records for manufacturing and distribution. Without hesitation or prayer, I said yes. The album was distributed nationally to every major Christian bookstore and radio station. In Minneapolis, I received heavy rotation on the local Christian radio station. I must admit that it was exciting to hear my music on the radio for the first time. The only money I ever saw was when I sold the product at my concerts, and that wasn't very much.

I reached out to Morada Records for an explanation regarding royalties. They said, "We manufactured your product and gave you national distribution; what else do you want? To sue us?" I naïvely fooled myself into thinking that I could trust people only because they said they were Christians and thought a record deal would put me on the map, that I would be a legitimate artist, on the way to a Grammy.

I contacted Alan Page for help. He asked, "Do you have any signed documents regarding royalties?"

I said no.

He said, "Sorry, I wish I could help, but there's nothing I can do."

Decisions made without prayer can lead to destruction. Jonah found himself in the belly of a fish and almost got killed because he made a decision without prayer. I learned my lesson and moved on.

# Chapter 65: Walking
# among Giants

I met Michael Jordan in 1991 at the Biltmore Country Golf Club. This charity golf tournament was mostly comprised of basketball players. At six feet five inches, I was one of the shorter golfers. I introduced myself to Michael as Joe Jackson. He said, "I think I'm gonna call you J.J." He reached in his pocket to grab a tee and pulled out a roll of one hundred dollar bills.

I said, "J.J. is fine with me."

Michael Jordan's mother was a member of our church, Phoenix First Assembly of God. Mrs. Jordan was involved with women's ministry. Through the trials, including the senseless murder of her husband, her faith never wavered. Her testimony was an encouragement to many who experienced some loss in life.

Mrs. Jordan shared her story during a Wednesday night church service. It was powerful and from the heart. Whenever she mentioned her late husband, she consistently referred to him as Mr. Jordan. Her respect and love for her husband were real. Her commitment was real. She was an example of how to overcome after a tragic loss. I'm sure it wasn't easy, but through God's grace and her faith, she persevered. Recovering from a fall is part of the DNA of a champion.

On February 11, 1990, Buster Douglas was a 42-1 underdog against heavily favored world champion, Iron Mike Tyson. Tyson had never lost a fight or been knocked down, 37-0. In the eighth round, a right uppercut from Tyson sent Douglas to the canvas. Everyone thought, *The fight's over; surely Tyson will knock him out in the ninth.* But no one told that to the Columbus, Ohio native. Douglas got up, dominated the ninth round, and eventually knocked out Mike Tyson in the tenth. He overcame a knockdown and won the heavyweight title. Like Coach Tom Landry said, years before, you can recover from a fall if you don't quit.

There were many NBA guys, including one of my favorite players, Dr. J (Julius Erving), playing in the golf tournament. Dr. J and I met years earlier at the Jets' training camp at Hofstra University. He was rehabbing a knee injury. After the golf tournament, we shared lunch together and realized that we shared something else too.

We once dated the same girl, Lisa. I remember the word got around the Jets' locker room that Julius Erving and I had dated the same girl. My Coach, Buddy Ryan, would tease me in front of the other players by saying, "Hey, did you hear that Joe Jackson snaked Dr. J?" It was all harmless fun, but in no way did I take Lisa from Dr. J. They had broken up two years before I came along.

Lisa and I were later engaged and planned to get married in the off-season. My off-seasons were spent in Las Cruces. She lived in New York City. Don't be fooled—long-distance relationships are difficult, especially if you're immature. I was at twenty-three. She was a flight attendant with Pan Am, so we tried to see each other twice a month.

I wasn't ready for marriage. I kept putting the wedding off, making excuses while I was dating other girls. We finally called it off in the fall of 1975 after she called my apartment and a girlfriend answered the phone.

I felt bad about my lack of commitment. This time, it was me who caused the hurt, but it just wasn't meant to be. Lisa eventually married and moved on. Again, everything works out for good to those who love God, who are called according to His purpose (Rom. 8:28).

# Chapter 66: Intent and Content

That's one thing I appreciate about traveling to different parts of the country—nothing is the same, yet people are so alike. The four Gospels of Matthew, Mark, Luke, and John are different in style, but the intent is right on. Content can be different, yet intent remains the same.

Remember the parable that Jesus used when He talked about not giving up in Luke 18? The subject or the content was the widow. The intent has the same goal, the result—breakthrough. The parable is about perseverance, not quitting.

There are many analogies in life to show content and intent. Content changes; intent doesn't. Remember Chris Hogan of the Patriots? He was cut by three different teams, an undrafted free agent, played one year of college football at tiny Monmouth in West Long Branch, New Jersey.

In the pursuit of a championship, the Lord will bring the right people at the right time who will impact your life in ways you may not immediately see. There are seeds planted inside of me that would have never yielded any fruit had I stayed in Cincinnati. Maybe God would have opened other doors that would have gone unopened in Las Cruces. I think I could have done what I've done in other places, but the circumstances would have been different. There's something that clicks with your soul and spirit when you know you're on the right path.

If God called me to be an evangelist, He could have ordained another set of circumstances and people in my life to accomplish His purpose. I learned years ago that the method is not sacred, only the message. The age of social media and the Internet has changed how we approach ministry.

The way my grandfather built a ministry or even a church is very different than how it's done today.

When I started my full-time ministry in 1985, I didn't own a type-writer, I couldn't type, and I was scared of computers. A *mail merge* was a term that you'd hear my dad talk about at the post office. Network marketing meant one of the big three television networks. Today you can download my entire portfolio, promotional packet, and bio from my Facebook page or website. It just takes a minute to copy and paste. I have posters and brochures that I haven't mailed out in months. Who needs a Bible concordance when you have Google? I remember when Zoom was a song by The Commodores, not video conferencing.

Today we use this new technology as an effective tool to help fulfill the great commission in taking the gospel to all the world. When I think of the use of modern technology in taking the gospel throughout the world, I think of the Reverend Billy Graham. He was a pioneer for using radio, television, and movies. They say football, and particularly the NFL, was made for television; a game played on a rectangular field shown on a rectangular screen.

Graham's preaching style, tonation, passion, looks, and love for his Lord was transported to hundreds of millions through radio and television. With the homecoming of Billy Graham, I couldn't help but wonder what direction my life would have taken had I accepted the job as crusade coordinator with the Billy Graham team in 1984. At the time, I felt a strong calling to pursue music ministry.

The Lord had opened doors and given me confirmation that I was on the right path. Had this offer come along a couple of years prior, maybe I would have made a different decision. Although I have no regrets, I can't help but wonder what direction my life would have taken had I accepted the opportunity as crusade coordinator for the Billy Graham Association.

The possibility of a salaried position with health insurance and retirement plus serving in ministry looms large. I am self-employed. There are positive and negative sides to both. Financially, there's no ceiling;

however, there are also no guarantees. The only regret I have is I never met Billy Graham on this side of heaven.

Billy Graham operated in integrity and honor. His message was simple yet very powerful and effective. He was loved and admired by millions. As a young boy, he grew up on a farm in North Carolina and dreamed of one day playing professional baseball when he heard from God. The Lord directed him to a new field. His life was a testimony of one who stayed true to his calling as a servant. Jesus says, "For even the Son of Man did not come to be served, but to serve, and to give his life as a ransom for many" (Mark 10:45 NIV). Well done, thou good and faithful servant. Come on in, Billy!

# Chapter 67: Lost at Sea

Marquis Cooper played college football at the University of Washington. He was drafted by the Tampa Bay Buccaneers in the third round. He also played for the Vikings and Raiders. But more than a football player, he is the beloved son of Bruce and Donna Cooper.

I first met Bruce Cooper in February of 2009 at the St. Vincent de Paul center in Phoenix. Jimmy Walker scheduled me to speak to some of the men and women in transition who needed a word of encouragement. It was a great morning. After the service, we had some prayer, ate breakfast, and had good fellowship.

As I left St. Vincent de Paul, I met Bruce Cooper, who had just arrived. Everybody in Phoenix knows Coop. Bruce is the beloved sports anchor at NBC affiliate Channel 12. This was the first time I met Bruce, and without hesitation we hugged each other and chatted briefly. I had a good feeling about Bruce. I hoped to connect with him in the future and invite him to our athletes' conference. I had no idea he had a 26-year-old son playing in the NFL. He or his wife didn't look old enough.

On March 1, 2009, Marquis Cooper and three other football players went fishing in a 21-foot boat near Clearwater, Florida. Their boat capsized in rough water, and the four went missing. After several days, search parties discovered that one player had survived, Nick Schuyler. Details were very sketchy as to the whereabouts of the other players and how Schuyler managed to survive. After the rescue mission turned into recovery, the Coast Guard determined that Marquis Cooper, Detroit Lion Corey Smith, and Will Bleakly were lost at sea.

My heart ached for Bruce and his family. I emailed him a week or two after the search was called off. Bruce gave no interviews, including a request from CNN's Larry King. I just wanted him to know we're praying and that if he needed a friend, someone cared. He answered my email, and we met for lunch.

I could see that Bruce was hurting and needed time to heal. They still have no closure. There are no words you can say. Bruce and Donna have become good friends. I invited them to attend our athletes' conference. We honored Marquis as NFL Man of the Year at our awards banquet. Bruce and I meet probably four or five times a year. His schedule has him hopping all over the country and destinations in between. They've moved on the best way they can. Their faith is strong, and they're trying to walk in God's peace every day.

In the natural order of things, parents are not meant to bury their children. I've heard parents say that the loss of a mother, twin, father, or other relative doesn't compare to the loss of a child. Parents expect to sit back and enjoy their children's lives and the lives of their grandchildren. The death of a child shatters the thought about how life is to unfold. Even after twelve years, the loss is still very raw.

They're still grieving, hoping, and probably always will. Bruce kept the dream alive that maybe Marquis is somewhere and unable to make any contact. Or he's alive and has amnesia. They think, *Pretty soon, I know he will walk through that door.* This scenario plays out every day and every night. And then another year passes, and you slowly begin to accept the reality that he's probably not walking through any door. Yet you still hope for a miracle. The what-ifs, whys, and stress build up inside your chest, and then one day—boom.

Bruce Cooper flat-lined twice before he arrived at the hospital. Doctors saved his life, but it was close. He's fully recovered—that is, his body. A champion lives to fight for another Sunday. His heart's still broken, though his spirit is strong and resilient.

# Chapter 68: Along My Path

In 2012 I flew to New York City for ministry in Connecticut. Because of my status with American Airlines, I'm usually bumped up to first class. I was a late arrival at the airport and had to hustle through security. By the time I got to the gate, all the first-class seats were taken except in the bulkhead.

As I took my seat, I passed in front of the gentleman seated in 1D. His name was Scott Sandler. He lived in Scottsdale. Scott looked like he'd played some ball back in the day. He had the build of an NFL offensive guard. Scott was about six feet three inches and weighed 350 pounds. That weekend the Super Bowl Gospel Choir would be doing a concert in New York City, so I initially thought, *Maybe he's part of the choir?*

I was only partly correct; he did play some ball but only in high school. Big Scott was not in the choir but seemed to know everyone in the entertainment business, from Bruce Springsteen to actor James Woods. We had a great conversation and exchanged numbers.

One of the reasons I wear my ring is because it starts a conversation. Scott asked, "What are you doing in New York this weekend?"

I told him, "I'm preaching in Danbury, Connecticut and doing a concert with the NFL Gospel Choir at the Waldorf Astoria on December 10."

Scott said he was in New York for business but may come to the concert. Danbury is only eleven miles from Newton, Connecticut, where three days later, on December 14, the deadliest shooting in an elementary school in American history would occur. For years I had survivors' guilt. I was so close to Sandy Hook. Maybe if I had been doing one of my school assemblies there, I could have done something. I gradually realized that humans make hideous, heinous, and horrid choices. Like the grieving family members, I had to move on. Scott and I became close friends. He's very successful and generous. I brought him to a couple of games and introduced him to many of my New York Jets and Viking teammates.

Scott came to one of the churches when I preached in Phoenix. He also attended our athletes' banquet and rededicated his heart to the Lord. Evangelism is about sowing seeds along the path. In Matthew 13, Jesus talks about the parable of the sower. A farmer sows seeds indiscriminately. Jesus said some fell on the path, and the birds came and ate it up. Others fell on the rocky places; it grew for a minute but withered because it wasn't rooted. Some seed fell among the thorns and thickets, which grew up and choked the plants; others fell on good ground and produced a good crop of a hundredfold. Scott was good ground. He heard the Word and understood it. He came along just at the right moment. Big Scotty passed away on January 10, 2021, and we miss him greatly.

*Championship Sunday* has been a journey marked with victory, defeat, failure, deep hurt, betrayal, death, loss, redemption, completeness, hope, faith, peace, rejection, triumph, and Terill. There are lessons taught and lessons caught. For a kid who grew up in the Cincinnati suburb of Madisonville and wanted acceptance at almost any price, I discovered that acceptance begins with knowing that my life counts. I have intrinsic value; I am destined for greatness regardless of pants size—husky, slim, or regular. Our uniqueness does not translate to weirdness, the unpicked flower, or the kid that nobody wants when choosing sides.

The road of a champion narrows and widens. There are valleys and plateaus. The road most traveled, the easiest, or the path clearly marked is not always the one that leads us home. Sometimes the map doesn't reveal every step and turn.

I discovered that *Championship Sunday* is a faith journey, not always of sight and sound but a journey from the heart and soul. Championship Sunday was a journey that began in Madisonville and continues. There have been goals met along the way to destinations never dreamed of. Being inducted to the Withrow High School Hall of Fame, New Mexico

State University Athletic Hall of Fame, and Global University Hall of Fame are destinations that were not on my radar.

When Larry Kerychuk invited me to minister at Phoenix First Assembly of God in 1987, a spark was ignited that became my vision. Because of the leadership and light of Pastor Tommy Barnett, I saw the reality of Acts 2:17. The Bible says that the young will begin to have a clarity of vision; I realized that I could have God's vision for my life, and that my past decisions and choices, though many were regrettable, were not just discounted artifacts of a chaotic and confusing world. God has a master plan for my life.

For over 30 years I served as a church evangelist for one of the greatest servant leaders and churches in the world—Tommy Barnett and Phoenix First Assembly of God. There was never a thought of finding another church home or pastor. But seasons change, and dynasties and kingdoms are replaced. After serving as a senior pastor for over 50 years, Pastor Tommy felt it was time for a change. With much prayer and fasting, he passed the baton to the very capable hands of his son Luke. The church no longer has the iconic name of PFA. It's now called Dream City Church, with locations throughout Phoenix and beyond. Although the name is different, the vision is the same—reaching the lost.

Like my move from Minnesota to Phoenix in 1988, I felt in my spirit that it was time for another transition. Terill and I visited several churches, looking and praying for the right *House*. We knew that it would be impossible to replace Phoenix First Assembly, but we also knew that the Lord would lead us home.

Our friend James Brown served as lead pastor at Apache Junction First Assembly of God. James is a great communicator and has a love for biblical history. James had moved on to another church and was now senior associate pastor at Chandler First Assembly of God. He invited me to check it out. After one visit, we knew that this would be our new home. Terill and I are members of Chandler First Assembly of God under the leadership and vision of another Tommy; this time, it was Tom Rakoczy. Pastor Tom Rakoczy is from Pennsylvania, where he starred as a high school quarterback and a long-distance runner on the track team. He dated and married his high school sweetheart and varsity cheerleader, Arlene. Tom has been the senior pastor at Chandler First for 21 years and has been in ministry for over 50 years. Pastor Tom is a soul winner with a strong passion for God's Word and God's people. We bonded immediately. I now serve as a church evangelist at Chandler First Assembly of God Church.

# Chapter 69: New Knees, New Miracle

L iving with knee pain for over 30 years caused me to walk and jog with a noticeable limp. I knew because of past surgeries my knees weren't the greatest, but I figured, what the heck, I can live with the pain. I ran almost every day.

As an athlete, speed was my greatest asset. Running was my gift and passion; I loved it. But sometimes your gift doesn't love you back, especially after a thousand of traumatic hits in college and the NFL, not to mention pounding your joints while running on concrete and asphalt streets.

Later in life, the body will remind you of the cost you paid for living your dream—a price I would pay again if I could have a do-over. In professional sports, you have a window; once it closes, it can never be reopened. No matter how strong my love for the game, I'll never play again. I have the same passion for the game I played, but I no longer have the opportunity to fulfill those desires. That's why an athlete's career is different from almost any other profession. The average NFL career is around two and half years. My friend and teammate Jim Marshall had an amazing career. Jim played defensive end in the NFL for 20 years and never missed a game. I suppose in the days of Methuselah and Jared, I could easily have a four- or five-hundred-year career, but not today.

I noticed that my knees were starting to bow. My heels and soles were always worn on the outside of all my shoes. Over time I developed knee osteoarthritis, a chronic condition due to degeneration of the cartilage. My cartilage was gone, forcing the knees to bow. Severe bowing will require knee replacement surgery to restore the alignment and length. My height shrunk to barely six feet four inches. I was almost shorter than my younger brother. I couldn't live with that.

I needed to find an orthopedic surgeon. I spoke with several doctors regarding my knees, and it was the same story, "Your knees are gone and need to be replaced." The knee joint is the largest joint in the body. The operation would be invasive. My imagination ran wild with images of removing my kneecap to sawing my legs off. Most of my friends who have had knee replacements told me that they should have done it years ago. Only my brother-in-law Doug said that he should've never had the surgery done.

It was time. I couldn't walk 30 feet without stopping to find a place to sit down. I couldn't climb two steps to the pulpit. I had to hold on to the pulpit while preaching. The pain was crippling.

A dear friend named Jim Golba reached out to me. He told me that he had knee replacement surgery, and it gave him a new lease on life. I drilled Jim with questions and excuses as to why I couldn't schedule knee surgery now. My reasons were legit. I would have no income for around three months.

Even though I had health insurance, how would I pay my bills? A few pastor friends suggested establishing a GoFundMe account. I prayed and thought about it, but decided it wasn't for me. Jim recommended that I at least make an appointment with Dr. Sherwood Duhon, who performed his surgery. I said sure, but I really didn't have any intention of calling Dr. Duhon. I think Jim realized that, so he made an appointment for me.

Jim made sure that I kept it by picking me up and taking me to Dr. Duhon's office. This was a big step for me. I carried a lot of apprehension and fear on my way to the office. After checking in, finally they called my name. Jim came with me to Dr. Duhon's office.

We waited for several agonizing minutes before Dr. Duhon knocked on the door. As soon as he walked into the room, he greeted me with a big smile, and almost instantly my fears were replaced with peace and confidence. I asked if we could do a partial knee replacement or injections.

He said, "No, I looked at your x-rays, and that horse left the barn twenty years ago." Dr. Duhon would be the orthopedic who would replace my knees.

Even though he's done thousands of knee, shoulder, and hip replacements, Dr. Duhon is a man of strong Christian faith and prays before every surgery. Both times, just before the anesthesia was administered, he grabbed my hand, and we prayed.

On May 1, 2019, I had my right knee replaced. On July 2, 2019, I had my left replaced. I wish that I would have done it years ago! For the first time in decades, I have no knee pain, straight legs, and can walk forever. It's a modern-day miracle!

# Chapter 70:
## Championship Sunday

On Championship Sunday, the winner of the National Football Conference and American Football Conference games will compete in the Super Bowl. It is estimated that 190 million viewers in the US will watch several portions of the Super Bowl 2020 broadcast.

When we played the Dallas Cowboys on Championship on Sunday, January 1, 1978, a lot was on the line. The Vikings were the only team to compete in four Super Bowls in the '70s—yes, and lose four. If we had beaten Dallas, it would've been our fifth trip to the Super Bowl in nine years. With our Hall of Fame quarterback Fran Tarkenton injured, the odds were against us. We lost the championship game and a bid for a Super Bowl title—Cowboys 23, Vikings 6.

For many, Sunday is just another day in the week. We may go to church, play golf, go to the gym, or go shopping at the mall. Championship Sunday is understanding and knowing who we are in Jesus Christ. It's about celebrating the victories of a transformed life, the renewing of your mind, and therefore proving as a living testimony the good, acceptable, and perfect will of God (Rom. 12:1-2).

In 1977, major league slugger Andre Thornton and his son were injured in a tragic automobile accident that claimed the life of his wife and three-year-old daughter. An icy road caused his vehicle to lose control and overturn. Andre was invited to share his testimony at a pro athletes outreach conference I attended in 1978. He talked about the darkest moment in his life. Though hurt, lonely, and broken, Andre shared that only his faith in God could lead him to triumph. He gave an inspiring and encouraging testimony. There wasn't a dry eye in the room as raw emotion flooded from his eyes and heart. His faith was unwavering as he reconfirmed his deep love and commitment to his Savior, Jesus Christ.

In 1983 Andre's book *Triumph Born of Tragedy* inspired thousands that in spite of loss, divorce, death, foreclosure, or bankruptcy, God will not break a bruised reed or quench smoldering wick. In faithfulness, He will bring you through.

You don't have to be an athlete to be a champion. It's not about a celebrated victory on a certain day. It's my daily walk, not my Sunday walk. It's the attitude and character of the apostle Paul (Phil. 3:8).

As the world looks for a new normal after a pandemic that resulted in the deaths of nearly 600,000 Americans, many are frightened and bewildered by an uncertain future. Scientists and our leaders tell us to be patient; things will change. Economists say things could worsen. Some preachers and teachers don't know what to say.

Among all the noise, what is the Lord saying, and who's listening? God's voice never changes. His words are clear:

> Before I formed you in the womb I knew you; before
> you were born I sanctified you; I ordained you a
> prophet to the nations (Jeremiah 1:5 NKJV).

> "For I know the plans I have for you," declares the
> Lord, "plans to prosper you and not to harm you, plans
> to give you hope and a future" (Jeremiah 29:11 NIV).

Philosophers say we're all in the same boat; wherever the current takes us, that's where we'll sail. We may be in the same storm, but we're not in the same boat. In the storms of life, who's in your boat?

Maybe you've been left for dead on the Jericho Road, robbed, beaten, broken, and bruised. That 17-mile road from Jerusalem to Jericho can be a treacherous, dark, dangerous, and lonely walk as no one stops to help, not even the church. You expect to be mistreated by robbers, but now the church doesn't seem to care as Christians walk on by.

Just when all hope is lost, a Good Samaritan comes to your aid and bandages your wounds. Jesus promises to never leave or forsake us. He's that Samaritan who paid the price for your redemption by His wounds. God loves you; He'll find you on the Jericho Road or wherever you are. All that's required is for you to ask Him to come into your life by faith. The prayer of faith comes from the heart. You can say it in your own words or something like this: "Lord, come into my life, I'm a sinner, forgive me, I need You. Amen."

It's been an incredible, unbelievable, and amazing journey. I'm not certain what lies ahead; my certainty is that the steps of a righteous man are ordered by the Lord. In 1969 Ken Johnson told me that God loved me and had a plan for my life. I've learned that regardless of the next chapter or where the next open door leads, the words of Psalm 119:105 (KJV), "Thy word is a lamp unto my feet, and a light unto my path"—will one day guide me to Championship Sunday. I'm gonna keep walking. Walk with me!

Update: My walking pace has quickened. Dr. Duhon says I now have the knees of a *nineteen*-year-old college freshman. No more pain. Maybe I'll get my old job back!

# About the Author

Joe Jackson is an evangelist, former NFL football player, English teacher, graduate of New Mexico State University, and college and high school football coach. His story began in Cincinnati, Ohio, with a dream that motivated him to rise above the Jim Crow laws, separate but unequal, and the racial injustice of the early sixties.

Joe's unique experiences along his journey are what Hollywood movies are made of. He transcribes a difficult past of low self-esteem and poor choices that nearly cost him his dream to play in the National Football League. His story is not only one of triumphantly entering the NFL; Joe's story resonates with anyone who has a dream. His sensitivity allows him to easily relate fundamental principles necessary for living the dream and living the promise. Joe knows what it's like to overcome a giant larger than any offensive lineman he ever faced in the NFL—fear. Fear is the biggest dream-killer known to man. In his unique way, Joe shares his amazing story to give hope to those crippled and hamstrung by fear.

Joe earned a four-year scholarship to New Mexico State University. In college he studied English Literature under award-winning playwright Mark Medoff. Joe and his wife, Terill, reside in Gilbert, Arizona. He has been an evangelist since 1986.

Joe can be contacted at:

Joe Jackson Ministries
Post Office Box 3881
Gilbert, Arizona 85299
(480) 656-5952
jojk86@aol.com
JoeJacksonMinistries.org

CPSIA information can be obtained
at www.ICGtesting.com
Printed in the USA
BVHW080744041121
620689BV00003B/9